Beyond the Red Notebook

Penn Studies in Contemporary American Fiction
A Series Edited by Emory Elliott, University of California at Riverside

A complete list of books in this series appears at the back of this volume.

Beyond the Red Notebook

Essays on Paul Auster

Edited by Dennis Barone

University of Pennsylvania Press

Philadelphia

Permission is acknowledged to reprint material from published works. A complete listing can be found following the index in this volume.

Library of Congress Cataloging-in-Publication Data
Beyond the red notebook : essays on Paul Auster / edited by Dennis Barone.
    p.   cm. — (Penn studies in contemporary American fiction)
  Includes bibliographical references and index.
  ISBN 0-8122-3317-4 (cloth : alk. paper). — ISBN 0-8122-1556-7 (paper)
  1. Auster, Paul, 1947–   — Criticism and interpretation.
I. Barone, Dennis.   II. Series.
PS3551.U77Z463   1995   95-13881
813'.54 — dc20   CIP

Contents

Introduction: Paul Auster and the Postmodern American Novel

Dennis Barone

Before the publication of *The New York Trilogy,* Paul Auster was known primarily for having edited the Random House anthology of twentieth-century French poetry and for having written several insightful literary essays. In the short time since the publication of the *Trilogy* (1985–1986) he has become one of America's most praised contemporary novelists. He has frequently been compared to authors ranging from Nathaniel Hawthorne to Alain Robbe-Grillet. Yet, perhaps because of the speed at which his novels have appeared and his reputation has grown, there is little scholarship available on his work. One has the sense, however, that just as he burst on the world scene in the late 1980s, Auster scholarship will witness an exponential growth in the late 1990s. This volume may be the catalyst for such growth.

Paul Auster is the author of *Mr. Vertigo, Leviathan, The Music of Chance, Moon Palace, In the Country of Last Things,* and the three novels known as *The New York Trilogy: City of Glass, Ghosts,* and *The Locked Room.* His other books include *The Invention of Solitude,* a memoir; *The Art of Hunger,* a collection of essays; and *Disappearances,* a volume of selected poems. He has written screenplays for the directors Wayne Wang and Wim Wenders. (He had a brief cameo appearance at the conclusion of Philip Haas's film adaptation of *The Music of Chance.*) He has been awarded literary fellowships from the National Endowment for the Arts in both poetry and prose, and in 1990 he received the Morton Dauwen Award from the American Academy and Institute of Arts and Letters. His work has been translated into more than fifteen languages. He accomplished all of this in little more than a decade.

Auster's fiction often draws on autobiographical material, but—as many of the essays in this volume explain—it does so in a very complex way. One reads Auster's fiction and the general outline of his life becomes clear. Born in 1947 in Newark, New Jersey, he attended Columbia University in New York, traveled and lived in France, and married writer Lydia Davis, whom he later divorced. He received an inheritance after the death of his father and married writer Siri Hustvedt, events that he credits with having in some sense rescued him. Herman Melville said that the bones of the whale tell us little of what the whale looks like in all its flesh (568). These facts of Auster's life are but autobiographical bones; the author in some sense remains an enigmatic leviathan for the reader. Yet, the reader also feels at the same time a bit like the narrator of *The Locked Room* who, after reading his old friend Fanshawe's red notebook, concludes that even though words, sentences, paragraphs canceled and erased one another, a feeling "of great lucidity" (179) survives from the reading.

The autobiographical bones on which — perhaps — Auster's art hangs become immediately visible to readers, even if they remain enigmatic. So, too, do many of his themes. The titles of his books state these themes most explicitly: hunger, chance, disappearance, solitude. This transparency is evident, but tricky. What does he mean by his themes and concepts that may strike some readers as too obvious to need deep explication? The number and variety of readings offered in this collection indicate that Auster's themes do encourage repeated analysis.

Consider "the red notebook," that phrase from which this volume takes its title. It is obvious: the red notebook belongs to Quinn in the first novel of the trilogy, *City of Glass,* and it belongs to Fanshawe in the trilogy's final installment, *The Locked Room.* But then one looks again, considers that Auster, too, writes in such a spiral bound notebook, that Black in the second book of the trilogy, *Ghosts,* writes in a notebook of unspecified color with a red fountain pen (11). One reads Auster's subsequent novel to the trilogy, *In the Country of Last Things,* and notes a quickly passing detail: the main character here, Anna Blume, writes in a blue notebook. So what do these colors, these notebooks, these intertextual relationships mean? Trying to pin the red notebook down is even more difficult than claiming once and for all that Hawthorne's scarlet letter "A" is this or that. The "A" after all is but a single letter whereas these notebooks potentially have pages and pages for many letters. Nonetheless, the essays in this collection offer some possible explanations for the many questions Auster's books raise. These essays don't try to decide them once and for all, but invite further discussion, a discussion rooted in the work itself. These essays take us beyond the red notebook, but do not and cannot replace it.

There is much pleasure in this journey, too. To speak of "enigmas" is to sound awfully serious. Seriousness of purpose is not to be slighted and is not without its pleasures, but if Auster is one of the two or three major American authors of the post-1970s era, one reason for his phenomenal rise in popularity over the past decade may be simply that his books are fun. He is a writer willing and daring enough to probe the depths of a horrible despair one moment and tell a joke — perhaps at his own expense — the next. When Quinn purchases his red notebook he feels an urge to do so, as the author puts it, "for reasons that were never made clear to him" (*City of Glass* 63). (The author never gave the character any!) Quinn puts his initials in the front of the notebook and considers that it is the first time in years he has done so since he writes mystery novels under the pseudonym William Wilson, a name that is the title of a short story about doubles by Edgar Allan Poe. Quinn has now accepted a real detective case under the assumed name "Paul Auster," a character in the novel whom Quinn will later meet. Quinn begins to write his first entry in his new notebook. He concludes this entry: "And then, most important of all: to remember who I am. . . . My name is Paul Auster. This is not my real name" (66). Talk about postmodern shifting subjectivities if you want (I will later), but don't forget how much fun all this is too.

Auster's recent essay entitled "The Red Notebook" is about living "permanently on the brink of catastrophe" (236), about fortuitous chance and odd, barely credible coincidence. It ends with a humorous reference to Quinn and *City of Glass*. Auster tells the story of his first novel's genesis. Then he says that ten years after he finished it he received a phone call from a man who asked to speak to Mr. Quinn. "For a moment I thought it might be one of my friends trying to pull my leg," Auster recalls. But the caller assured him "it wasn't a joke." After an apology from the caller, they both hang up. Then Auster concludes "The Red Notebook": "This really happened. Like everything else I have set down in this red notebook, it is a true story" (253). "A true story" — has the author pulled the reader's leg here? Has this anecdote that "wasn't a joke" become a joke on the reader? How can a "story" be "true"? Epistemological underpinnings have been shaken and this leaves the reader wondering.

There are some questions that can be answered in this introduction; a strong foundation for reading the essays that follow can be built. The purpose of this introduction therefore is to provide the cultural, historical, and theoretical contexts for the reading of Auster's fiction, to provide compelling reasons for regarding Auster as a major writer, and to introduce the contents of this book.

*   *   *

On 25 December 1990 Paul Auster published a Christmas story in the *New York Times*. Though it bears the author's byline, it is "Auggie Wren's

Christmas Story," a story in which "Paul" is a character. "Paul" is an author who has received a request from the *New York Times* to write a story for the Christmas morning edition of the paper. He gets nowhere with it until he mentions his problem to Auggie Wren. Wren promises to tell Paul "the best Christmas story" he's ever heard, if he buys him lunch. Auggie and the author have known each other for more than a decade. Wren works at a cigar store where Paul buys the little Dutch cigars he likes to smoke. Wren is also a photographer. His project has been to photograph the same corner at the same moment every morning for twelve years. The story Auggie tells Paul reveals how he began his career as an artist.

In the summer of 1972, Wren tells Paul, a young man entered the store and proceeded to steal some paperback books. Auggie chased him and right before he gave up the chase, the young thief's wallet fell out of his pocket. Wren held on to the wallet. On Christmas day he decided to return it in person. He goes to the address in Robert Goodwin's wallet, rings the bell, and an elderly blind woman greets him and hugs him. She says that she knew he wouldn't forget his grandmother on Christmas. In a flash of an instant he decides to play along. He even goes out and buys food for a Christmas dinner. When he goes to the bathroom things take "yet another turn." He sees a number of boxes containing brand new (most likely stolen) thirty-five millimeter cameras and he takes one. Granny has fallen asleep. Auggie does the dishes, puts the wallet on a table, picks up the camera, and leaves. A few months later he goes back to the apartment because he feels bad about having stolen the camera, but Ethel is gone and someone else lives there now. Paul says that Auggie did a good deed, he made Ethel happy. Auggie says that he lied to her and stole from her. Auggie then grins as if to say he fabricated the whole story, and Paul returns Auggie's smile with a wicked grin of his own.

This brief story presents in miniature many of the methods that Auster uses in his longer fictions. This is a story by Paul Auster told by a character named Paul who listens to a story told by a man named Auggie Wren who in the course of telling his story assumes the identity of Robert Goodwin and at the story's conclusion the ontological grounding of all destabilizes in a blink of the eye. This story of responsibility and culpability also self-consciously comments on art in general and storytelling in particular. As Paul looks at Auggie's photographs, Auggie tells him to slow down. "He was right, of course," the narrator states. "If you don't take the time to look, you'll never manage to see anything. I picked up another album and forced myself to go more deliberately." When Paul looks once again at Auggie's project he is "able to detect subtle differences in the traffic flow, to anticipate the rhythm of different days."

Auster's work always contains aspects of the author's own life, references to other literature, and descriptions of actual historic figures and events. This is historiographic metafiction as Linda Hutcheon defines it (*A Poetics* 52). Auster's work investigates subjectivity and representation, but not in the overt political manner of a postmodernist such as Ishmael Reed in whose work, according to Hutcheon, "political satire and parody meet to attack Euro-centered ideologies of domination" (130). Auster's postmodern ironies are more philosophical than overtly political. Hence at the end of "Auggie Wren's Christmas Story" the narrator realizes that he "had been tricked into believing him, and that was the only thing that mattered. As long as there's one person to believe it, there's no story that can't be true." The author here has commented on the nature of truth and the nature of belief, and on the relation between truth and belief and action and responsibility. In doing so, Auster has commented in a profound way on *the* Christmas story.

Jorge Luis Borges, the Argentinean modernist who anticipated so many of the techniques and themes of postmodern writing, asked in one essay, "Why does it disturb us that the map be included in the map and the thousand and one nights in the book of the *Thousand and One Nights?* Why does it disturb us that Don Quixote be a reader of the *Quixote* and Hamlet a spectator of *Hamlet?*" Why, I might add, does it disturb readers that "Paul" is a character in, is the narrator of, Paul's own fiction? Borges answered: "I have found the reason: these inversions suggest that if the characters of a fictional work can be readers or spectators, we, its readers or spectators, can be fictitious" ("Partial Magic in the *Quixote*" 196). And if fictitious then like Marco Stanley Fogg, the protagonist of Auster's *Moon Palace*, free to fashion our own life-as-work-of-art. Fogg delights that his initials stand for manuscript and his Uncle Victor tells him that "Every man is the author of his own life. . . . The book you are writing is not yet finished. Therefore, it's a manuscript" (7).

Auster's postmodern self-fashioning does not end in aimless purposelessness or in a do-your-own-thing individualism. While he does not refuse to forsake the premodern notion of the individual so that a vestige of renaissance humanism can remain, he does examine in all of his fiction the consequences of actions taken in one's self-fashioning. Marco Stanley Fogg — MS — may be a life as work-in-progress, but his actions have impact on others, nonetheless. Auggie Wren instantaneously decides to be Ethel's grandson. "Don't ask me why I did it. I don't have any idea," he says. But once he takes an action, certain consequences follow. "Anything can happen": this phrase occurs in all of Auster's books and these books are examinations of struggles to find one's way, to make sense of this fact. This is why Auster is a major novelist: he has synthesized interrogations of postmodern subjectivities, explications of premodern moral causality, and a sufficient realism.

*   *   *

While this may be obvious, it is important to point out that postmodernism has been defined in many different ways. Consider just this one startling difference in definitions: whereas Fredric Jameson defines pastiche (a central component in his sense of postmodernism) as parody without a purpose (16), Linda Hutcheon defines parody (a central component in her sense of postmodernism) as "repetition with critical distance" (*A Theory* 6). The theory, which in many of its guises holds that there are no monolithic unities, paradoxically attempts to provide stable, overarching definitions for itself. Inevitably, critics read Auster through the screen of one or another of these definitions. But to read his fiction merely as illustration for a particular definition of the postmodern is to severely limit it, and which definition one begins with will make all the difference in how one reads his work.

While some readers have described Auster as the epitome of the postmodern others have described him as virtually premodern, while still others have criticized him for not developing full characters. For example, William Lavender finds that Auster's "biographical projections" "are kernels of reality buried in a text that everywhere seeks an effect of unreality." The result is a parody "not of realism, but of irrealism. To the postmodern statement that fiction is not truth, it opposes a new paradox: fiction cannot lie" (236). Yet, William McPheron finds that the style of *The New York Trilogy* "is dominated by mesmerizing felicity and fluid readability. Plot and characterization—though shorn of the pleasures of illusion—remain sufficiently coherent to satisfy conventional expectations" (142). If McPheron considers Auster's work to preserve "the traditional notion of referentiality," Birkerts and Bawer criticize it for not being referential enough. Birkerts has said that in *In the Country of Last Things* Auster "reasserted the traditional rights of the genre. . . . It is almost as if the author needed to put himself through a winnowing process . . . before he could find a way to begin writing" (341–342). *Moon Palace,* according to Birkerts, is that beginning. "Gone is the studious bricklaying, the sense of mind controlling hand" (343). In other words, gone are the metafictional devices of *The New York Trilogy.* (Birkerts is incorrect because as Weisenburger shows in his contribution to this volume, "Fogg's degenerative descents are . . . always checked and redirected by moments of coincidence, by glitches demonstrated in the text of the novel through characters' recognitions of the errant potentials in representational texts themselves.") Similarly, Bruce Bawer in his essay on *Moon Palace* has said that this novel demonstrates Auster's maturity as a writer. "Auster has grown more adept at translating his preoccupations into the language of action and form, *Moon Palace* feels more assured than its predecessors, and has a satisfying sense of closure that they lack. . . . It is certainly more realistic than *The New York Trilogy*" (69).

Whether a reader finds Auster too traditional, as McPheron does, or not traditional enough, as Bawer does, a reader has much to consider in Auster. This is a reason for his popularity. He does use the metafictional devices of his predecessors (in *Moon Palace* as well as elsewhere), but he does not use them to frustrate or disrupt the reading process. Whereas earlier metafictions problematized narrative with lists or collages of diverse elements, Auster's methods are less disjunctive but no less surprising. In *The Music of Chance,* for example, the constant repetition of the number seven (Nashe and Pozzi stay in a room on the seventh floor of a hotel, Flower and Stone won their money seven years ago, Flower's museum and Stone's City of the World are behind the seventh door) points to the work's fictionality and undermines its feigned verisimilitude. Auster does not turn typography on its head as William Gass did in *Willie Masters' Lonesome Wife* (1968), but rather he embeds philosophical investigations on the nature of fiction within a narrative that never takes itself to be the real itself.

Auster limits readers' reactions by the inclusion of authorial intrusions that seem to explain the work. Even if that *seem to* is accentuated in the work, such writing differs vastly from the sort of texts contemporary L=A=N=G=U=A=G=E writers produce. Auster does not use what Marjorie Perloff calls radical artifice.[1] Instead, one might say that Auster has created a conservative artifice. This, too, might be a means to meet the audience halfway, and an explanation for his popularity. Though Auster explores the relation between signifier and signified, he attempts to return thing and thing named to a state of tenuous stability. This approach to reference is part of his synthesis of postmodern themes and premodern moral questions.

In *In the Country of Last Things,* a novel that charts a woman's attempt to find her missing brother and to survive in a sort of postapocalyptic urban environment, the protagonist, Anna Blume, describes the disintegration of language. She decides to try to escape from the city, but all sea and land routes have been closed or are carefully guarded. She asks someone about the possibility of an escape by air. "What's an airplane?" he replies to Anna "in a puzzled sort of way" (87). "Words tend to last a bit longer than things," Anna says, "but eventually they fade too, along with the pictures they once evoked" (89). Because of this "process of erasure," "each person is speaking his own private language, and as the instances of shared understanding diminish, it becomes increasingly difficult to communicate with anyone" (89).

Yet, Anna does succeed, her message does get through. We know that it has because the novel is actually told in a third-person narration. Someone has received Anna's story-as-letter, had read it, and, in turn, is now telling Anna's story to us. This is a story of triumph, not of disintegration. It is difficult, lonely, and painful, but "still," Anna says, "there are those of us who manage to live" (13). The life Anna lives in this walled, post-apocalyptic city may be one of horror, but it is also one of more than mere survival. Though everything runs out, even words themselves, Anna is able to make distinctions. Anna refuses "to speak the language of ghosts" (10); she draws limits for herself, limits she will not go beyond. "Touching the dead, for example," even though "stripping corpses is one of the most profitable aspects of scavenging" in this city (36). While out scavenging Anna saves the life of an elderly woman, Isabel. Yet, Isabel "saved my life just as surely as I had saved hers," Anna writes, because "for the first time in my life there were people who depended on me, and I did not let them down" (58).

One of the central tenets often espoused about the postmodern world is that through the blurring of boundaries—whether political or artistic—important distinctions are trivialized. The Replacements sing a song called "I'll Be You." The band is a stand-in for an absent original; its members will exchange their identities with anyone willing to sing along. There is no essential self in such conceptions of the postmodern world, nor is there any meaningful politics. I remember an advertisement for a local clothing store. The ad includes a photograph of demonstrators atop the Berlin wall tearing it apart. At the top of the page the ad says, "The Close of the Old Era." At the bottom it says, "The Clothes of the New Era" and the name of the store. Instead of blurred boundaries and trivialized distinctions, I would rather believe that in the postmodern world new connections are established, much like the bond between Anna and Isabel in Auster's *In the Country of Last Things*.

*   *   *

The French sociologist Jean Baudrillard is the champion of a nihilistic view of the postmodern. Here is an example of Baudrillard's key notions of "simulation" and "hyperreality." One day in August 1992, the *New York Times* ran a brief editorial entitled "Reverse English." The editorial reported that "two or three years ago, Americans were buying Italian sports clothes that were made to look American. Now the spiral has turned another full twist as Americans buy American clothes made to look like

Italian clothes made to look American." For Baudrillard the simulation is a closed system in which signs no longer reflect a definite reality but are self-reflexive signifiers. Hyperreality, according to Baudrillard, is more real than reality itself, it is a manufactured, intensified version of reality with which the original cannot compete because representation has subsumed the original. Baudrillard believes we react to such "circulation" always ecstatically and never critically. Clearly, the infinite regression, the hyperreality of the Italian shirts that look American exemplifies Baudrillard's principle of circulation, and the demand for these clothes would seem to indicate our ecstatic response.

Many of Auster's books could be used to illustrate Baudrillard's ideas, yet Auster is not an ecstatic purchaser of these ideas; instead, he critically reveals the way in which simulation, hyperreality, and circulation can curtail communication by questioning, as Linda Hutcheon wrote at the end of *A Poetics of Postmodernism*, "what 'real' can mean and how we can know it" (223).

Baudrillard presents an at times amusing, at times exasperating view of America in his recent book about this country: "it is Disneyland that is authentic here! The cinema and TV are America's reality! The freeways, the Safeways, the skylines, speed, and deserts — these are America" (104). Whereas Baudrillard describes America as having "*shown genius in its irrepressible development of equality, banality, and indifference*" (89; italics in the original), Anna Blume moves from caring for the once known one (her brother William) to caring for the anonymous many at Woburn House. Auster presents a city that resembles present-day New York not so much as a simulacrum but as a way to question the processes that have allowed this recognizable world to become, as Baudrillard himself has put it, "the tragedy of a utopian dream made reality" (30). Anna describes homeless people who go to rental agencies even though they know there are no vacancies "just to be able to sit with an agent for ten minutes and look at photographs of buildings on tree-lined streets" (8) and hungry people who have conversations about food in which, Anna writes, "you will be able to forget your present hunger and enter what people call the 'arena of the sustaining nimbus.' There are those who say there is nutritional value in these food talks" (9–10). Anna describes a sect known as the Smilers whose "solution is to maintain a steadfast cheerfulness, no matter how dismal the conditions around them" (26). Baudrillard describes the American smile as "the equivalent of the primal scream of the man alone in the world" (33). "Americans have no identity," Baudrillard states, "but they do have wonderful teeth" (34). One can use *In the Country of Last Things* to illustrate the Baudrillardian postmodern or one can demonstrate that this novel calls that conception of the postmodern into question.

The experience in reading Auster's *In the Country of Last Things* is somewhat like being the king to whom Shehrzad tells her story. In *The Invention of Solitude* Auster says that "the function of the story" is "to make a man see the thing before his eyes by holding up another thing to view . . . and in so doing delight him . . . into a new feeling for life" (151). *In the Country of Last Things* never names present-day New York as its setting, yet in an interview Auster has said that "the country Anna goes to might not be immediately recognizable, but I feel that this is where we live. It could be that we've become so accustomed to it that we no longer see it" (*Art of Hunger* 267). Auster's "adversarial postmodernism," to use Paul Maltby's phrase, enables us to see it. As Linda Hutcheon has argued, "postmodern art works to contest the 'simulacrization' process of mass culture — not by denying it or lamenting it — but by problematizing the entire notion of the representation of reality, and by therein suggesting the potentially reductive quality of the view upon which Baudrillard's laments are based" (*A Poetics* 223).

Certainly Don DeLillo's *White Noise* contests "the 'simulacrization' process." There are many similarities between Paul Auster and his close friend, Don DeLillo, to whom he dedicated *Leviathan*. Indeed, both De-Lillo's *Mao II* (1991) and Auster's *Leviathan* (1992) can be read as responses to terrorism and contemporary politics and as studies of the role of the author in life as we know it today. Bill Gray (*Mao II*) mourns the declining significance of the author and Benjamin Sachs (*Leviathan*), who wrote his first novel in prison when he refused to serve in the army during the Vietnam War, stops writing so that he can engage in what he sees as meaningful action. Some of DeLillo's observations of urban America sound similar to Auster's. Consider how the following passage matches one of Anna Blume's descriptions of the breakdown of life in the city and the relation of that breakdown to the words we speak.

> People with supermarket carts. When did these things come out of the stores and into the streets? She saw these things everywhere, pushed, dragged, lived in, fought over, unwheeled, bent, rolling haywire, filled with living trivia, the holistic dregs of everything if that is correctly put. She talked to the woman in the plastic bag. . . . The woman spoke out at her from inside the bag, spoke in raven song, a throttled squawk that Karen tried to understand. She realized she understood almost no one here, no one spoke in ways she'd ever heard before. . . . It was a different language completely, unwritable and interior, the rag-speak of shopping carts and plastic bags, the language of soot, and Karen had to listen carefully to the way the woman dragged a line of words out of her throat like hankies tied together and then she tried to go back and reconstruct. (*Mao II* 180)

In Auster's novel Anna's very survival depends upon obtaining and keeping one of these shopping carts and on being able "to read the signs" (6), being able "to fuse again" "pieces of this and pieces of that" (35).

An interest in coincidence, frequent portrayals of an ascetic life, a sense of imminent disaster, obsessive characters, a loss of the ability to understand combined with depictions of the importance of daily life and ordinary moments — these are all concerns that Auster and DeLillo share. One important difference is that in DeLillo it is the media that befuddles characters, whereas in Auster it is language itself; hence in DeLillo's *Americana* one character sits for hours in the locked room of the family basement watching TV ads with his father. In Auster's *City of Glass,* on the other hand, Peter Stillman locks his infant son in a closed, small, lightless room so that his son might learn the original, prelapsarian language. Most of all, however, DeLillo's novels are concerned with actual events of the world today, are concerned with what Auster calls "the sociological moment" (Irwin 118) whereas at the center of Auster's writing is a "preoccupation with the possibilities of *telling,* of making a de facto 'reality' which can meld with the reality we otherwise know" (Creeley 35).

A better comparison than Auster and DeLillo might be Auster and Toby Olson, for both authors foreground story and narrativity, not "the sociological moment." Olson's most recent novel, *At Sea,* has a self-referentiality and intertextuality that reminds one of the interweavings of Auster's work. Near the start of the novel a character reads an informative essay on the Truro area of Cape Cod, Massachusetts, published in the travel section of the *New York Times.* Olson wrote that essay. Near the novel's end the five main characters of Olson's past novels reappear (vacationing on the Cape) to help solve the crime: Jesus, Allen, Paul, David, and Jack. These characters form a sort of community even as they accentuate the work's fictionality, thus, questioning its realism. Like Auster, then, one can say that Olson is a postmodernist who uses what I've called earlier in this introduction a sufficient realism. Both Auster and Olson at times destabilize and problematize realism from within some of its conventions. In both writers there is more than first meets the eye, yet both novelists meet the novel-reading audience halfway. Both authors problematize such aspects of humanism as reason, self, and the communicative efficacy of words, yet neither author wholly abandons them.

Neither Auster nor Olson abandons what might be called the moral case: what if . . . ? Auster has said in interviews and in his essay "The Red Notebook" that *City of Glass* (which Olson reviewed enthusiastically for the *New York Times Book Review*) quite literally began with a "what if . . ." situation. The phone rang. He answered it. The other person wanted the Pinkerton Detective Agency. He told the other party that he was not a detective, but soon after this he thought what if I had said "yes, this is the Pinkerton Agency"? Actions have their consequence even if motives are impenetrable, and this is a fact Auster explores in each of his works.

In both Auster and Olson narratives often move from closed spaces to wanderings, and this movement parallels characters' understanding of actions and their consequences. Characters are paradoxically most free when confined and least free when openly rambling.[2] Freedom, for both, means being responsible for the welfare of others. Auster told Mark Irwin that Jim Nashe in *The Music of Chance* "crisscrosses America for an entire year, and yet, in some sense, he's a prisoner. He's imprisoned in his own desire for what he construes to be a notion of freedom. But freedom isn't possible for him until he stops and plants himself somewhere and takes on responsibility for something, for some other person" (111–112). In Olson's *Seaview* the brief second section ends with "a kind of lawn party atmosphere" that holds back "the encroaching darkness" (175), whereas the constant travel of the novel's first part brings on that darkness.

In a world of simulations that lack an original the difficulty of attaining any authentic connection increases, and if there is no longer a stable, centered human subject, then any depiction of postmodern character will be either an exercise in nostalgia or the writer must confront difficulties that earlier writers could not have imagined. Both Auster and Olson confront these difficulties in order to demonstrate the continuing importance of an authentic connection between people. Marco Stanley Fogg (whose name itself is a sort of simulacrum) starves in Central Park (one of Auster's hunger artists) in order to return to the world, but he can't make this return without the help of others. In *At Sea* the narrator says of the villain Cal Rush that she denied history "and through that both place and self lose their anchoring" (222). Fogg's friends rescue him and then he discovers his past. Both Auster and Olson anchor characters through their connection to others and through their searches of the past.

This is not the fiction of decentered ahistorical pastiche. This is not the fiction of *just* nihilism and despair. "At bottom," Auster has said, "I think my work has come out of a position of intense personal despair, a very deep nihilism and hopelessness about the world, the fact of our own transience and mortality, the inadequacy of language, the isolation of one person from another. And yet, at the same time, I've wanted to express the beauty and extraordinary happiness of feeling yourself alive, of breathing in the air, the joy of being alive in your own skin" (Irwin 118). Or as A. puts it in *The Invention of Solitude:* "He finds it extraordinary that on some mornings, just after he has woken up, as he bends down to tie his shoes, he is flooded with a happiness so intense, a happiness so naturally and harmoniously at one with the world, that he can feel himself alive in the present, a present that surrounds him and permeates him, that breaks through him with the sudden, overwhelming knowledge that he is alive" (121).

In Sherwood Anderson's story "Unlighted Lamps" a father is about to die. He has "a disease of the heart." There is a secret from the past that he must tell his daughter. If she knows what he knows, she will be redeemed. He has never touched her. He dies before he tells her, before he touches her. He meant to of course. But this is the fiction of modern alienation and fragmentation. In this small town where Mary and Doc Cochran live, no one understands or connects with anyone else.

In the large house in which Sam Auster died the situation seems much the same as that in Anderson's story. Sam, like Doc Cochran, does not truly speak to, touch, or engage his children. However, if Sam Auster is the epitome of the decentered postmodern man, Paul Auster does not present him in *The Invention of Solitude* as the norm, but rather as a defective character. Furthermore, the younger Auster of this book gets the answer that the younger Cochran never receives. And yet while that answer explains something, it does not explain everything as it would have in "Unlighted Lamps." The younger Auster finds out that his father's mother killed his father's father. The papers that contain this information "explain a great deal. A boy cannot live through this kind of thing without being affected by it as a man" (36). The information, however, does not "explain everything." Paul Auster understands his father to have been a cold, silent, detached man who when he first saw his grandson could only poke "his head into the carriage for a tenth of a second" and say, "a beautiful baby. Good luck with it" (19). Yet, others who knew his father thought he was the warmest, kindest, most wonderful man. In going through his father's possessions after his death Paul Auster is "happiest to have retrieved" a complimentary letter to his father from one of his father's former tenants for the letter "somehow balances the ledger" (57). It is hard to believe that the Sam Auster who received the letter and the Sam Auster who looked quickly into the baby carriage were the same man.

> The rampant, totally mystifying force of contradiction. I understand now that each fact is nullified by the next fact, that each thought engenders an equal and opposite thought. Impossible to say anything without reservation: he was good, or he was bad; he was this or he was that. All of them are true. (61)

The Invention of Solitude may not be a continuation of modernist fragmentation and alienation, but it does not offer the metaphysical first cause of all things either.

"Whereas a mythology was given to the artist in the past by tradition and the patron," Charles Jencks has observed, "in the Postmodern world, it is chosen and invented" (41). *The Invention of Solitude* may be read as Auster's chosen and invented mythology, as the first cause of all his subsequent works. But to do so leads to a certain danger in the consideration of his writing. To understand his first prose work in this way may cause one to misread his other prose works, to see too much continuity and not enough change. "Who cares about finding the right label for my books?" Auster said to me in a letter. Critics, he said,

> confuse the thoughts and statements of the characters in my books with my own beliefs. . . . Just because Quinn thinks these things doesn't mean I do. As far as I was concerned, Quinn's approach to writing was an example of his alienation — his terrible distress and sadness as a man. Or — just to sound off a bit — doesn't anyone see that the things "Paul Auster" says to Quinn in *City of Glass* are in fact just the opposite of what I myself stand for? Can't a writer poke fun at himself — make himself appear ridiculous and stupid — without being misunderstood? (Personal correspondence, 19 January 1994)

Yet, it is difficult for nascent Auster criticism not to make such confusions when events from his memoir reappear in his novels; when pages of the prose poem *White Spaces* appear in *The Locked Room* as having been written by Fanshawe (91–92); when Auster's *Art News* essay on Blakelock appears as the words of Marco Stanley Fogg in *Moon Palace* (137–139); when a passage from an interview in which Auster describes financial difficulties in his early career (*Art of Hunger* 281–283) becomes part of Peter Aaron's biography in *Leviathan* (59–60).

On the other hand, self-referentiality should not be taken as autobiography. For example, in *The Invention of Solitude* Auster describes Van Gogh's *The Bedroom,* a painting he saw while in Amsterdam. He describes it as depicting "a prison. . . . The bed blocks one door, a chair blocks the other door, the shutters are closed: you can't get in, and once you are in, you can't get out" (143). Auster does not describe Van Gogh's painting of the house in Arles. These paintings hang next to each other in the museum. Auster is creating art in *The Invention of Solitude,* not writing autobiography. If one painting is all inside, the other is all outside. Auster has exercised here one of the most basic methods of art, selection, and what he has selected he turns into a metaphor that merges an external object and the mind's interior.

Are we to take Fanshawe's words or Fogg's words as Auster's? I think not. Flower in *The Music of Chance* describes the aesthetic terms of Stone's model City of the World. Flower's commentary on self-reference, on the mixture of the real and the imaginary, could be mistaken as describing Auster's own understanding of these things:

> If you bend down, you'll see Willie's daughter holding his hand on the front steps. That's what you might call the private backdrop, the personal material, the inner component. But all these things are put in a larger context. They're merely an example, an illustration of one man's journey. (79–80)

Auster tells this story in a third-person narration from Jim Nashe's perspective, and we know quite clearly that Nashe hates both Flower and Stone. So much for reading these aesthetic commentaries as the author's own beliefs.

Furthermore, although Peter Aaron's biography (and initials) match Paul Auster's, a central fact of Sachs's life comes out of Auster's. In *The Invention of Solitude* Auster "remembers visiting the Statue of Liberty with his mother and remembers that she got very nervous inside the torch and made him go back down the stairs sitting, one step at a time" (169). In *Leviathan* Mrs. Sachs, Ben's mother, tells a story about a visit to the Statue of Liberty and how "we all went down the stairs sitting, one step at a time" (39). In postmodern investigations of human subjectivities the self can be split into selves to probe the peculiarities of self. One autobiographical detail of the author's life can become a detail in a character's life that a narrator records in the story that he tells. Instead of a unified self we have then a self that can radiate toward infinite possible relations. As it radiates, it questions those relations. In *The Deep North,* another novel of initials and shifting subjectivity, Fanny Howe says that her main character, Gemma (or "G"), "was not, as it turned out, what she said she was to anyone but him, not black or white, but a mystery, which rhymed with history" (138). Certainly, Auster's works are rich in mysteries which rhyme with history. "Paradox, I think," he has said, "gets very much to the heart of what novel writing is for me. It's a way for me to express my own contradictions" (Irwin 113). Questions, paradoxes, mysteries: these, and not autobiographical verities, are at the heart of Auster's writing.

If Quinn's words are not Auster's own, whose are they? They are the words of "the real Mr. Sad," as Peter Stillman, Jr. calls him at one point (28). In Quinn we see the contradictions of a destabilizing and shifting postmodern subjectivity. All of Auster's characters are not one and the same. If Quinn wants "to be nowhere" and has ceased to "exist for anyone but himself" (9), the Auster of *The Invention of Solitude* realizes "he was not alone" (139) and gives himself up for Daniel, his son. Quinn does not "feel responsible" for what he writes (9). Responsibility, old-fashioned as this may sound, is a virtue in Auster's works. Quinn is a "triad of selves" (11) and this fractured subjectivity is a sad thing. Since he isn't who he is, it is so easy for him to become someone else: "Paul Auster." Quinn, who "had privately celebrated his birthday" (18), is so desperate for contact with some other, any other, person that he waits three nights for the phone to ring — even though when it rings the voice will not ask to speak to Quinn.

Quinn accepts his identity as "Paul Auster" the detective, but not without difficulty. His new identity gives his life new meaning and purpose, but it is a usurped meaning and purpose. "It wasn't his appointment, it was Paul Auster's" (21). One can not borrow purpose and meaning as one would a hat. Quinn at this point speaks of himself as other, but not to find himself as the "A." of the second section of *The Invention of Solitude* does. Rather, Quinn speaks of himself as other to lose himself.

In this state of subjective flux and abandonment things begin to break down. Words begin to fall freely and fast from the things to which they normally attach themselves. "And if a tree was not a tree, he wondered what it really was" (59). He reminds himself to look at his "watch more often" (59), a pathetic attempt to forestall the breakdown. He buys a red notebook with the hope that if he writes everything down he'll be able to stabilize the situation. He signs his own name in the notebook, yet since under the pen name William Wilson he writes mystery novels about a detective named Max Work, "it was the first time in more than five years that he put his own name in one of his notebooks. He stopped to consider this fact for a moment but then dismissed it as irrelevant" (64). Of course, nothing could be more relevant, but Quinn is a fool, and so soon after this Quinn writes in the red notebook: "And then, most important of all: to remember who I am. To remember who I am supposed to be. . . . My name is Paul Auster. This is not my real name" (66). And thus his fate is sealed.

Franz Kafka's "The Hunger Artist," according to Maud Ellmann, shows that the power of starvation depends on visibility. The presence of spectators is what makes fasting art, just as readers justify the work of the starving poet. The Auster of *The Invention of Solitude* has his audience of readers, but the character Quinn has no audience within the fictive world created by the author. When there is no audience, according to Ellmann, starvation becomes a pathology. Auster's books are about the search for identity which sometimes results in the permanent loss of one's own identity through a search for someone else's. This is the situation for Quinn, but not for the narrator of *The Locked Room* or Marco Stanley Fogg. Quinn so obsessively searches for Stillman that he irrevocably misplaces himself, whereas the narrator of *The Locked Room* and Fogg eventually recover themselves. When a character loses self-identity it is as if that character has been overfed on the character of another. In her recent book *The Hunger Artists: Starving, Writing, and Imprisonment,* Ellmann has said that if someone has their mouth so full of food that they cannot chew or swallow, that person will go hungry. In order to digest, some of the food must be taken away. The same principle applies to knowledge: too much is just as dangerous as not enough. Hence, Blue in *Ghosts* knows everything about Black: when he will eat, when he will sleep, when he will go out, when he will stay at home. Yet precisely because he knows everything he knows nothing. When first writing a report he considers including the stories he has made up about the case. He decides against this, however, and sticks just to the facts, the endlessly divisible minutiae of facts. He is devoured by the case because he will take no fact out of his gorged mind and replace it with the airy space of make believe. He is haunted by the ever-present, unceasing real. Hence, he does not consume the object, but the object invades him.

Similarly, as a sarcophagus consumes the corpse within, the building superintendent where Fogg lives tells him that his apartment reminds him "of a coffin" (45). In other words, Fogg creates his own sarcophagus, and therefore the books of his Uncle Victor that he reads consume him. As Fogg empties his apartment of words he creates his tomb. Fogg's fast turns his body into a dungeon. "The stomach is a place almost as private as the grave" (39), Ellmann says, and if "the very need to eat reveals the 'nothing' at the core of subjectivity" (30), then "starvation . . . has become the last remaining recipe for authenticity" (34).

Anna Blume, imprisoned in the "City of Destruction," begins to write her letter after the death of her friend Isabel as a substitute for personal contact. And if imprisoned and starving, and if writing is the only connection and release, then what happens when there is no more ink and no more paper?

America in the 1980s was no longer a consumer society. It had crossed an important boundary. It became the consumed society. A recent ad for Camel cigarettes illustrates this. We see a party like scene of people who have the heads of camels: we don't smoke Camels, Camels smoke us. Or, as for words, we don't speak language, language speaks us. If we are the consumed society, are we then used up, kaput? This is a question we must live with daily, but not obsess over endlessly. As Auster has said of the narrator of *The Locked Room,* "But in the end, he manages to resolve the question for himself—more or less. He finally comes to accept his own life, to understand that no matter how bewitched or haunted he is, he has to accept reality as it is, to tolerate the presence of ambiguities within himself" (*Art of Hunger* 264). At the start of the final chapter of this novel the narrator says: "To the extent that we were able to act, we did" (160). To do anymore than this is not possible; to do anything less than this is unconscionable.

It may be appealing to readers in a world where words and representations are out of our control, a world where institutions beyond our control formulate such important things as the very words we speak, and in a world in which irreconcilable stories comprise our history to read of the struggles of others to attain and maintain some semblance of control. Both Jim Nashe of *The Music of Chance* and Peter Aaron of *Leviathan* attempt to control situations before they get out of hand. Many of Auster's characters speak of chances for redemption: blow one chance, try again. This is so for Nashe. On the first page Auster mentions one of these attempts, but as soon as five pages later, "Nashe realized that he was no longer in control of himself" (6). Try, try again. And so Nashe sees the stone wall that he and Pozzi must build to pay off a gambling debt "as a chance to redeem himself in his own eyes" (127). But is redemption possible in a world dominated by "an atmosphere of suspicion and mistrust" (125), a world in which Nashe and Pozzi must work "under the threat of violence" (144)? Nashe and Pozzi live under that fundamental law of discipline common to the insane asylum or prison, what Michel Foucault has called "the docility and utility of all elements of the system," an internal — not external — surveillance (218). So certain is Nashe of being monitored that he monitors himself and Pozzi. The imprisoned watches the other prisoners. One night a drunken Pozzi throws pebbles at Flower and Stone's mansion, breaking a window. "After that night, Nashe understood that he would have to keep a closer watch over the kid" (135).

After Pozzi's departure and/or death Nashe works alone on the wall. He is still under the watchful, controlling gaze of Calvin Murks and Murks still wears a gun. One day Nashe asks him, "What's with the gun, Calvin?" and the next morning Murks comes to the meadow without it. "Nashe didn't know what to think anymore. Was Murks telling him that he was free now, or was this simply another twist in an elaborate strategy of deception" (182). Such are the questions that plague us all in America in the 1990s. How can any of us maintain control of our lives in a world of constant deception?

FBI agents surround the narrative of Auster's next novel, *Leviathan,* like bookends. As Peter Aaron hurries to tell his story before the agents find out the truth on their own and come to his house for a second time, he speaks of a number of attempts at redemption — especially for his best friend Benjamin Sachs — and how with each attempt a person only gets further and further into a mess. He writes the book, in fact, as a way to redeem Sachs (but in doing so probably gets himself into trouble with the FBI for withholding information). In a world of disinformation he wants to be sure that someone knows the true information about his friend at least as he sees it. In *Moon Palace,* unlike the prior novels where words fall apart, Fogg eventually is able to put them back together again. In *Leviathan* they fall apart for Sachs (a writer who stops writing) as his life also falls apart. Aaron puts his life together and, of course, like Fogg in *Moon Palace,* he's the one who tells the story.

But it is not easy. The truth shifts with every few pages, and yet Aaron tells it — even if he must lie to do so. (He breaks a promise to Sachs — culpability and responsibility again.) Aaron presents events from a number of different perspectives. He recalls both Ben and Maria's explanation for Ben's fall off the fire escape of an apartment building. He recalls both Ben and Fanny's explanation for Ben's infidelity. In such uncertainty, what action can one take? Though Aaron acts now in writing the book, he feels that he failed his friend because he failed to act four years ago:

> Looking back on it now, I believe I would have served him better if I had told him what I thought. I should have laughed in his face. I should have told him he was crazy and made him stop. If there was ever a moment when I failed Sachs as a friend, it was that afternoon four years ago. I had my chance to help him, and I let it slip through my fingers. (132)

But Aaron did not know then what he knows now. His failure to act can be forgiven as can any of ours. For what can we know? And if we cannot know all, how can we act? And if we did know all, would we be as immobile as Blue in *Ghosts,* would we be ghosts? "Knowing what I know now," Aaron says a few pages later, "I can see how little I really understand. I was drawing conclusions from what amounted to partial evidence, basing my response on a cluster of random, observable facts that told only a small piece of the story" (141). When is this not the case; how is this not so for any of us? Sachs for Aaron "was no longer just" his "missing friend, he was a symptom of" his "ignorance about all things, an emblem of the unknowable itself" (164). Aaron, much like the narrator of *The Locked Room,* concludes that the struggle ultimately is "to coexist with the forces of my own uncertainty" (272). Is this not the condition we must live in — to coexist with our own uncertainty?

Auster stated in an interview, "In the strictest sense of the word, I consider myself a realist" (*Art of Hunger* 269). "And yet," he continued, "there's a widely held notion that novels shouldn't stretch the imagination too far. Anything that appears 'implausible' is necessarily taken to be forced, artificial, 'unrealistic' " (270). Sachs becomes the Phantom of Liberty, the mysterious person who destroys publicly displayed models of the Statue of Liberty. Is this "implausible" in a world in which the Barbie Liberation Organization switches the voices of G.I. Joe and Barbie, in a world in which the city of Philadelphia hosts a parade during the celebration of the two-hundredth anniversary of the U.S. Constitution that the city's residents can't watch in person (they were told to go home and watch it on television so that there would be no interference with CBS's camera crews)? In this parade of a reality stranger than any fiction, postmodern or otherwise, Merrill Lynch sponsors a float called "Manifest Destiny."[3]

Auster's most recent novel, *Mr. Vertigo,* is the story of a boy who could fly. A great joy and pleasure in reading this book is that Walt, the narrator and "wonder boy" who could fly, describes this seemingly implausible act with complete seriousness, complete plausibility. *Leviathan* can be read as a consideration of the place of a sort of 1960s commitment in the 1980s, but *Mr. Vertigo* encompasses more than just a decade, it traverses the entire twentieth century. Rather than the sparse narrative style of some of his earlier work, this novel uses an expansive first-person colloquial voice. The narrative is discursive, as in *Moon Palace,* but the voice is more particularized than Fogg's and more reminiscent of Pozzi's wise-cracking style of speech in *The Music of Chance.* Like *Moon Palace,* Walt narrates *Mr. Vertigo* from a point distant in time from much of the action. Fogg is a middle-aged man looking back on his late youth; Walt is an elderly man looking back on his early youth and its consequences. Because of this narrative position, both narrators are able to poke fun at themselves. This reminds me of Franklin's method in *The Autobiography,* and like poor Benjamin's tale, *Mr. Vertigo* can be read as an American success and failure story.

From *The Invention of Solitude* to *Mr. Vertigo* characters must "die" in order to live; they must lose themselves in order to know and possess themselves. Some — Quinn, Sachs — go spinning out of control; others — Anna Blume, Marco Stanley Fogg — succeed. Walt, however, dies a thousand deaths and reinvents himself a thousand times (or, perhaps, it's one thousand and one times). From *The Invention of Solitude* to *Mr. Vertigo* characters have searched for a home. Home eludes all others — Anna Blume, Jim Nashe — but does not elude Walt, who finds and makes in the course of his long life several meaningful and stable ones. From *The Invention of Solitude* to *Mr. Vertigo* Auster has investigated postmodern subjectivity. *The New York Trilogy* depicts shifting subjects while *The Invention of Solitude, Moon Palace, The Music of Chance,* and *Leviathan* attempt to locate and establish stable subjects. *In the Country of Last Things* depicts the externals that impinge on and threaten to dislodge the centrality of the self or to decompose the subject. *Mr. Vertigo,* on the other hand, presents a stable subject rather than a shifting one.

Mr. Vertigo is a novel of four sections. The first part describes Walt's training by Master Yehudi and his life with Aesop, Mother Sioux, and

Mrs. Witherspoon. In the second section Walt goes on tour, gets kidnapped by his Uncle Slim, escapes, loses his power to fly, and then heads to Hollywood with Master Yehudi. Just before reaching the coast Uncle Slim reappears, robs them, and leaves them stranded in the desert. Master Yehudi then kills himself so that Walt can live. In the third section Walt plans his revenge on Uncle Slim. After he kills Slim he becomes an employee of a mobster, Mr. Bingo, in Chicago. He opens his own nightclub, the Vertigo Club, meets a fading Dizzy Dean and tries to talk him out of continuing to embarrass himself with his dismal pitching. Walt's speech doesn't go as planned. He takes out a gun and threatens to shoot Dean in order to save him. Because of this assault he loses his club, joins the army (his "eyes were too weak for flight school" [263]), and moves to New Jersey after his discharge where he works in a bakery. He marries Molly Quinn (her nephew is Daniel Quinn), and after she dies of cancer he returns to Saint Louis, back where he started at the century's beginning. There he lives with the now elderly Mrs. Witherspoon. She dies. He stays on in the house and one morning begins writing the story of his life.

Like Fogg and other Auster characters, Walt, too, makes a number of aesthetic statements. This is a very different sort of novel from those that comprise *The New York Trilogy*. If destructive acts tied to a confused aesthetics and moral sense dominate the trilogy, in this novel creative acts sprung from a shared purpose predominate. Aesop and Walt, for example, though divided by race, are among the closest of Auster's pairs. Whereas Fanshawe doesn't invite his friend, the narrator of *The Locked Room*, into his box, Aesop does invite Walt into his imaginative world of words. Even though Aesop and Mother Sioux die horrible deaths, made so especially because of their closeness to the narrator and to one another, Aesop opens a world for Walt that enables him many years later to write the story of his life.

Walt's full name is Walter Claireborne Rawley. He is both an explorer and an artist, this boy who could fly, this elderly man who writes. What Auster said of Philippe Petit's *On the High-Wire* can be applied to *Mr. Vertigo:* "When read carefully, the book is transformed into the story of a quest, an exemplary tale of one man's search for perfection. . . . It seems to me that anyone who has ever tried to do something well, anyone who has ever made personal sacrifices for an art or an idea, will have no trouble understanding what it is about" (*Art of Hunger* 247).

Postmodern fiction or, more precisely, historiographic metafiction is about "issues such as those of narrative form, of intertextuality, of strategies of representation, of the role of language, of the relation between historical fact and experiential event, and, in general, of the epistemological and ontological consequences of the act of rendering problematic that which was once taken for granted by historiography — and literature" (Hutcheon xii). Paul Auster's fiction is about all of these issues, too. His writing is a unique and important synthesis of postmodern concerns, premodern questions, and a sufficient realism. Yet, he says it is the story itself that matters most to him: "stories are crucial. It's through stories that we struggle to make sense of the world. This is what keeps me going — the justification for spending my life locked up in a little room, putting words on paper" (Irwin 119).

* * *

This collection of essays grew out of the Paul Auster half-issue of the *Review of Contemporary Fiction* (14.1, 1994) that I guest-edited. There is so much interest in Auster's work that it seemed necessary and even urgent to me to organize a separate and longer collection. As I said at the start of this introduction, one has the sense that just as Auster's fiction exploded on the world scene in the late 1980s, Auster scholarship will witness an exponential growth in the late 1990s. This volume in Penn Studies in Contemporary American Fiction will help form that growth.

Auster's interests have been European as much as American: writing on Knut Hamsun's novel *Hunger,* translating Joseph Joubert, compiling the Random House anthology of twentieth-century French poetry, and so forth. Perhaps these concerns and efforts of his in some way account for the immediate enthusiastic response to his work in Europe. He is as well-known in Europe as he is in America. A walk down the avenues of Paris or London will reveal this fact. In every bookstore window, there are the works of Paul Auster. But this should not come as a surprise, for his works are a pleasure and a wonder. Furthermore, as Malcolm Bradbury has written, "We live in a late twentieth-century phase in which the arts are, as they were at the century's turn, in international intersection" (327). Contributions for this collection have come from Wales, the Netherlands, France, and Japan as well as the United States.

Two essays from France open the volume. Pascal Bruckner's "Paul Auster, or The Heir Intestate," ably translated by Karen Palmunen, describes Auster's writings as nomadic wanderings and inventions of solitude that attempt to create connection with the outside world. Bruckner demonstrates the importance of *The Invention of Solitude* to a thorough understanding of Auster's subsequent writings. Marc Chénetier's translation of his afterword to the French edition of *The New York Trilogy* is about sound in Auster, as well as about naming, identity, and solitude. In this collection of essays Chénetier's afterword, which ranges across a number of Auster's fictions, serves as a foreword to the more specific readings that follow.

Norman Finkelstein's essay connects Auster's poetry to his fiction and in doing so places Auster's poetry in the tradition of Oppen and Reznikoff, thus suggesting Auster's relation to the poetics and thematics of "open poetry." Derek Rubin offers an analysis of the theme of hunger and in doing this he develops a point suggested in Finkelstein's essay: the relationship of Paul Auster's writing to the Jewish-American tradition.

The essays in this volume can be read as groundwork essays, essays whose ideas can be taken in myriad other directions. It is interesting to note, for example, the way an "open poetry" aesthetic that places much importance on process can be seen in many of Auster's writings, not just in his poetry. In *The Invention of Solitude* there is a voice or tone that carries one forward, a "projective voice," and there are many phrases used to make the narrative felt as present: "I remember a day very like today" (22). Process is apparent in *Leviathan*'s conclusion. The fifth chapter is the shortest because Aaron wrote a short draft of the whole story and then went back to expand each chapter, but had to stop in the middle of the fourth chapter; hence, the fifth chapter did not go through the expansion process and is by far the shortest.

It is interesting to note that while Auster does not provide an explicit centrality for Judaism in his work, the Jewish tradition is ever present. Auster is not Philip Roth and yet in a metaphoric manner Auster asks questions similar to those Roth probes in a more explicit way. Sometimes Judaism makes a surprising, sudden, and important appearance. In *In the Country of Last Things,* when Anna Blume enters the library she encounters a group of Jewish scholars. "I'm Jewish, too," she blurts out (95). During part of her stay in the library she has a number of conversations with the rabbi who leads the group. "[T]he fact was that I felt on solid ground with him," Anna says (96). Yet in *Moon Palace,* Rabbi Green, who officiates at Solomon Barber's funeral, thinks that Fogg is crazy and Fogg feels sorry for the rabbi (301). There is no "solid ground" between Fogg and Rabbi Green. Fogg has managed, however, to have his father buried next to his mother. "It took some doing to get him into Westlawn Cemetery, a lone Gentile in a sea of Russian and German Jews" (300).

Madeleine Sorapure in her essay "The Detective and the Author" looks at *City of Glass* in relation to detective fiction. She sees this novel as a "meta-anti-detective story" in which Auster uses and parodies detective novel conventions to comment upon processes of signification. Unreliability, uncertainty, contingency, and "Auster's powerful refusal to accede to the traditional category of closure" in *The Locked Room* are the concerns of Stephen Bernstein's essay. Bernstein's sophisticated, theoretically well-informed essay compellingly argues that the deployment and problematization of closure in Auster's fiction is connected to his representation of the postmodern sublime.

Tim Woods's essay on *In the Country of Last Things* and the "reproduc-

tion of space" continues Bernstein's examination of closure and antici-
pates Steven Weisenburger's consideration of temporality, chance, and
genealogy in *Moon Palace*. Weisenburger cogently demonstrates the ways
in which fictional structure and technique are connected to Auster's
themes of fatality and the immutability of time. The improbability and
limitations of freedom within the confines of an all-pervasive power is the
subject of Tim Woods's essay on *The Music of Chance*.

Arthur Saltzman shows in his contribution on *Leviathan* that Auster has
not abandoned ambiguity, indeterminacy, mystery, and poetry for a conventional realism. This novel, which unsettles us with more shifts from
the absurd push of coincidence, radiates, according to Saltzman, between the poles of belief and doubt. In developing a critical assessment of
the limitations of Auster's project, Eric Wirth discusses the philosophical
contexts of Auster's fiction. The volume concludes with a brief essay in
which Motoyuki Shibata outlines his experience translating Auster's work
into Japanese.

The essays in this volume move from West to East, they lay a groundwork for further discussion of Auster's fiction, they say important (and at
times contradictory) things about this intriguing author. In "The Philosophy of Composition" Poe said that writers should begin with their effect
in view (1459). In writing on Paul Celan, Auster said that "the poem . . . is
not a transcription of an already known world, but a process of discovery"
(*Art of Hunger* 87). Auster's writing has its effect in view and is at the same
time an art of discovery. It is, also, at times a prose of near perfect poetry.
The essays included in this book will help readers appreciate Auster's
"poetry" and encourage them to return to it again and again.

*   *   *

I thank William Drenttel for preparing an excellent bibliography for
this volume. This will be very useful for those who wish to read further in
and about Auster. I also thank John O'Brien and Steven Moore of the
Dalkey Archive Press for accepting my offer to edit a half-issue of the
Review of Contemporary Fiction on Paul Auster, Emory Elliott for encouraging me to proceed in the present project, and the students in the Auster
seminar at Saint Joseph College, spring 1994, for their joyful engagement
with the texts.

Notes

1. *The Music of Chance* may be about chance, may have chance as its content, but
the novel does not have chance as its form or use chance as a generative method.
Auster is not William Burroughs or John Cage.

2. Both Auster and Olson have a number of scenes in different books that take place in caves or other tight, cave-like enclosures. This fact reminds me of the importance of such spaces to one of the best early American novels, Charles Brockden Brown's *Edgar Huntly.* The narrator of *The Locked Room* says that "this room . . . was located inside my skull" (147). This sort of melding of exterior geography and interior psychology is also central to Brown's novel. I am often struck by the similarities between American novels of the 1790s and 1990s. Certainly, the breakdown of signification and the lack of a coherent self in some way dominates both. (One may think of the *Federalist Papers* in this context, too.) Consider this passage from Brown's less well-known novel, *Jane Talbot,* a passage that constantly undermines and erases its own speaking:

> I am ashamed of myself, Henry. What an inconsistent creature I am? I have just placed this dear letter of yours next my heart. The sensation it affords, at this moment, is delicious; almost as much so as I once experienced from a certain somebody's hand, placed on the same spot. But that somebody's hand was never (if I recollect aright) so highly honored as this paper. Have I not told you that your letter is deposited *next* my heart? (52)

3. See Davis ("Set Your Mood to Patriotic"). Paul Auster lived for a number of years (he has since moved around the corner) on the same street in Brooklyn as my grandparents had. In fact, Auster lived on the same side of the street and less than one block away from the house I visited often as a young child. Until the day I met with Auster in Brooklyn, I had not been on this street for more than thirty years. New York is a city of millions of streets, and of all the streets in this city, why did Auster live on this one? Once Auster went to Rome and on the way home seated next to him on the plane was the American poet, fellow New Yorker Charles Bernstein. As Auster says, "chance is a part of reality" (*Art of Hunger* 269).

Works Cited

Anderson, Sherwood. "Unlighted Lamps." In *The Sherwood Anderson Reader.* Ed. Paul Rosenfeld. Boston: Houghton Mifflin, 1947. Pp. 36–52.

Auster, Paul. *The Art of Hunger: Essays, Prefaces, Interviews.* Los Angeles: Sun & Moon Press, 1992.

———. "Auggie Wren's Christmas Story." *New York Times,* 25 December 1990, A31.

———. *City of Glass.* Los Angeles: Sun & Moon Press, 1985.

———. *Ghosts.* Los Angeles: Sun & Moon Press, 1986.

———. *In the Country of Last Things.* New York: Viking, 1987.

———. *The Invention of Solitude.* New York: Penguin, 1988.

———. Letter to author. 19 January 1994.

———. *Leviathan.* New York: Viking, 1992.

———. *The Locked Room.* Los Angeles: Sun & Moon Press, 1986.

———. " 'Moonlight' in the Brooklyn Museum." *Art News* 86.7 (September 1987): 104–105.

———. *Moon Palace.* New York: Viking, 1989.

———. *Mr. Vertigo.* London: Faber and Faber, 1994.

———. *The Music of Chance.* New York: Viking, 1990.

———. "The Red Notebook." *Granta* 44 (1993): 236–253.

———. *White Spaces.* Barrytown, N.Y.: Station Hill, 1980.

Baudrillard, Jean. *America*. Trans. Chris Turner. London: Verso, 1989.

Bawer, Bruce. "Fiction Chronicle: Doubles and More Doubles." *The New Criterion* 7.8 (April 1989): 67–74.

Birkerts, Sven. "Paul Auster." In *American Energies: Essays on Fiction*. New York: William Morrow and Co., 1992. Pp. 338–346.

Borges, Jorge Luis. *Labyrinths: Selected Stories and Other Writings*. Ed. Donald A. Yates and James E. Irby. New York: New Directions, 1962.

Bradbury, Malcolm. "Modernism/Postmodernism." In *Innovation/Renovation: New Perspectives on the Humanities*. Ed. Ihab Hassan and Sally Hassan. Madison: University of Wisconsin Press, 1983. Pp. 311–327.

Brown, Charles Brockden. *Jane Talbot*. Boston: S. G. Goodrich, 1827.

Creeley, Robert. "Austerities." *Review of Contemporary Fiction* 14.1 (1994): 35–39.

Davis, Susan G. " 'Set Your Mood to Patriotic': History as Televised Special Event." *Radical History Review* 42 (1988): 122–143.

DeLillo, Don. *Mao II*. New York: Viking, 1991.

Ellmann, Maud. *The Hunger Artists: Starving, Writing, and Imprisonment*. Cambridge: Harvard University Press, 1993.

Foucault, Michel. *Discipline and Punishment: The Birth of the Prison*. Trans. Alan Sheridan. New York: Pantheon, 1977.

Howe, Fanny. *The Deep North*. Los Angeles: Sun & Moon Press, 1988.

Hutcheon, Linda. *A Poetics of Postmodernism: History, Fiction*. New York: Routledge, 1988.

———. *A Theory of Parody*. New York: Metheun, 1986.

Irwin, Mark. "Memory's Escape: Inventing *The Music of Chance*—A Conversation with Paul Auster." *Denver Quarterly* 28.3 (1994): 111–122.

Jameson, Fredric. "Postmodernism and Consumer Society." In *Postmodernism and Its Discontents: Theories, Practices*. Ed. E. Ann Kaplan. London: Verso, 1988. Pp. 13–29.

Jencks, Charles. "Postmodern and Late Modern: The Essential Definitions." *Chicago Review* 35 (1987): 31–58.

Lavender, William. "The Novel of Critical Engagement: Paul Auster's *City of Glass*." *Contemporary Literature* 34.2 (1993): 219–239.

Maltby, Paul. *Dissident Postmodernists: Barthelme, Coover, Pynchon*. Philadelphia: University of Pennsylvania Press, 1991.

McPheron, William. "Remaking Narrative." *Poetics Journal* 7 (1987): 140–149.

Melville, Herman. *Moby-Dick or, The Whale*. New York: Penguin, 1975.

Olson, Toby. *At Sea*. New York: Simon and Schuster, 1993.

———. *Seaview*. New York: New Directions, 1982.

Perloff, Marjorie. *Radical Artifice: Writing Poetry in the Age of Media*. Chicago: University of Chicago Press, 1991.

Poe, Edgar Allan. "The Philosophy of Composition." In *The Norton Anthology of American Literature*. Ed. Nina Baym et al. Vol. 1. 3rd ed. New York: Norton, 1989. Pp. 1459–1467.

"Reverse English." *New York Times*, 30 August 1992, E14.

Paul Auster, or The Heir Intestate

Pascal Bruckner

The Invention of Solitude is both the *ars poetica* and the seminal work of Paul Auster. To understand him we must start here; all his books lead us back to this one. Novel-manifesto in two parts, "Portrait of an Invisible Man" and "The Book of Memory," this work immediately sounds the theme of remorse.

Paul Auster was able to become a writer because his father left him a small inheritance that spared him a life of poverty. The father's death not only liberated his son's writing but literally saved his life. The son would never stop repaying this debt, would never finish reimbursing the deceased, in prose, for his fearsome gift. As payment Auster seeks to revive the image of this man he barely knew. The elder Auster, landlord by profession, was an absent character, "a block of impenetrable space in the form of a man" (7), an invisible being, "tourist of his own life" (9). One had the feeling that he never could be located, and he masked this evanescence with perpetual chatter. How could you be yourself in a world where your father was disengaged? This father remained a stranger to Auster, and made Auster a stranger to himself. His father had denied him the usual outlet of youth: rebellion, because one can't rebel against a phantom. And the author, who had to lose his father in order to find him, would respond by filling his novels with figures of weak, colorless, pitiful parents, overwhelmed by their offspring and incapable of assuming fatherhood. Like Pinocchio snatching Geppetto from the jaws of the shark, Paul Auster would save his father from oblivion and, by giving him new life, justify his own existence.

As the story unfolds, sketching an increasingly more complex image of the deceased, one truth becomes evident: reaching one's father requires work. By giving birth to his own parent through words, the author repairs a broken communication and makes it possible for himself, in turn, to become a father. In short, a subtle dialectic directs this plot. According to Auster, proximity is deceptive, and anonymity is not only the misfortune of the masses, or of the cities, but also a cancer gnawing away at the family and marital unit. Human contact often masks a gulf that only death or distance can bridge. We are separated from others by those very things that also connect us; we are separated from ourselves by the illusion of self-knowledge. Just as we must forget ourselves in order to reach a certain level of self-truth, we must also leave others in order to find them in the prism of memory or separation. That which is closest is often the most enigmatic, and distance, like mourning and wandering, is also an instrument of redemption.

In the beginning, therefore, are sin and dispossession. Only an accident, a rupture, will shake the self from its apathy, from the pseudo-intimacy it maintains with itself. It is here that Auster's series of staggering paradoxes begins.

For Auster, confinement is a form of exile. *The Invention of Solitude* can be read as a celebration of rooms and closed spaces. This enclosure has nothing to do with the so-called panegyric of private life, or "cocooning." There is neither public nor private in this novelistic universe since the individual does not own himself. His center is located outside himself. This penchant for narrow spaces, where the spirit can project itself against the walls (the examination of this theme in Hölderlin, Anne Frank, Collodi, Van Gogh, or Vermeer is fascinating) makes the room a kind of mental uterus, site of a second birth. In this enclosure the subject gives birth, in essence, to himself. From mere biological existence he now attains spiritual life. This confinement transforms him into a voluntary castaway, a Robinson Crusoe run aground in the middle of the city, wedged into a tiny fissure of the urban habitat. This shipwreck is necessary, even if it resembles a deferred suicide. The self must die, Auster seems to say, in order to live; there is a redemptive sense to annulment; hence Auster's heroes push themselves to the limit of hunger and physical deprivation. This self-destructive passion, which barely avoids total annihilation (in a way similar to that analyzed by Auster in Knut Hamsun's *Hunger*), transforms this confinement in one's room into a sort of secular asceticism without transcendence, without God. As if the fathers' actual death required the fictitious death of their sons, Auster's character is always ready to offer himself in sacrifice. The only valid existence is that which has experienced extinction.

Auster's work explores a second paradox: death is the first step toward resurrection. Since this life given us by another is invalid, descent into hell is the only way to reclaim an authentic existence, to kill the old man within. Our room is a prison that opens the gates of freedom; the self is a dungeon we must voluntarily enter in order to find escape. If confinement leads to nomadism, the latter in turn will guide the protagonists toward self-reconciliation.

Auster also examines a third paradox: wandering is intimacy's help-mate. In his work, it is fate, ironic and mischievous providence, that breaks down the false barrier between the near and the far, between mine and yours, ours and theirs. No matter how far he roams, the individual will ultimately meet himself; he is inclined to be at home everywhere, since he is not at home in his own house:

> During the war, M.'s father had hidden out from the Nazis for several months in a Paris *chambre de bonne*. Eventually, he managed to escape, made his way to America, and began a new life. Years passed, more than twenty years. M. had been born, had grown up, and now was going off to study in Paris. Once there he spent several difficult weeks looking for a place to live. Just when he was about to give up in despair, he found a small *chambre de bonne*. Immediately upon moving in, he wrote a letter to his father to tell him the good news. A week or so later he received a reply: your address, wrote M.'s father, that is the same building I hid out in during the war. He then went on to describe the details of the room. It turned out to be the same room his son had rented. (80)

All of Auster is there in this love of coincidences that rhyme the most remote, improbable events. He excels at sprinkling his characters' adventures with correlations, which have no a priori meaning, but to which the story gives unexpected consequences. Noting the signs that fate strews along our path is the only way to combat the arbitrary: suddenly, in the randomness of existence, a certain order appears just below the surface, an order which seems mysteriously to control us. There is meaning in the world, but this meaning is only suggested, never clearly expressed. There-fore, everything in Paul Auster's work occurs by chance; and what better image of chance than an inheritance — an event as harmful as it is benefi-cial. It is as if money of the deceased were an oppressive gift that could drag us, with its donor, beyond the grave. The novelist's challenge here is to endow this image of the unexpected with the weight of necessity, to continue converting the improbable into the inevitable, to avoid gra-tuitousness. The novelist must also be a bit of an acrobat: plunging his characters into confusing situations, then weaving among them a fabric of dense analogies, linking the episodes together in such an inevitable manner that the reader cannot imagine the story occurring any other way. This penchant for reversals, for sudden about-faces, also places Paul Auster in the picaresque tradition, at the opposite extreme from his avowed masters, Kafka and Beckett.

Wandering, in Auster, has this original aspect: rather than pitting the individual against a cold, hostile world, it forces him to confront himself and the scattered fragments of his existence. Everything relates back to the self, and, while the closed room serves as a microcosm, the outer world itself becomes an enclosure, which speaks in veiled tones. "Home" is everywhere since the self is not at home with itself. *The Invention of Solitude* announces a theme that Paul Auster will raise to the level of a true obsession: nomadism as a means of cloistering oneself; introspection as a means of escape. (Hence the appeal of pseudonyms and non-places in *City of Glass,* the characters' capacity to take on other identities, the kaleidoscope of doubles, of contingent selves, the suspended moments when a person almost chooses to become someone else, illusions that bathe this trilogy in a kind of subdued Platonism.) "Exiling himself in order to find out where he was" (16). This formula that Auster applies to Thoreau suits Auster perfectly. He is able to reverse the language of mobility and immobility, of the wanderer and the sedentary. Through escape, we experience intimacy; through confrontation, estrangement. And this reversal may be rooted in the experience of a young boy who, in the presence of his father, felt total absence and solitude.

It is easy to see what distinguishes Paul Auster from other contemporary writers and to see why he is so successful. There is no one less narcissistic than this novelist obsessed with the self. This is because he challenges two attitudes that are common today: the proud, in-control self with no ties and no past, and the traditionalist or minority, proud of his identity, his roots, his people. Auster's point of view is different: he recognizes his connection to a family, a tradition, a culture, but he also realizes that this is a highly problematic link. In short, to paraphrase the famous verse of René Char, the legacy is ambiguous: the will is missing. Since nothing has a priori meaning — this, the very curse of modernity — the self, like solitude and tradition, must literally be invented and recreated. Auster is not an advocate of difference; he claims no particular status, does not ghettoize himself in any group. He does not seek what separates people, but, rather, what brings them together; and what they have in common is a similar confusion about their identity. But he has also avoided what has been killing French literature for the past twenty years: the invasive proliferation of autobiography, of the diary, of self-preoccupation as a genre in and of itself. This literature, which tends to narrow rather than broaden experience, is most frequently reduced to a bitter whine, since it conveys above all the impossibility of escaping the self. And it is the unfortunate irony of these books, devoted to revealing the individual's most intimate essence, their subjectivity unparalleled, that they all end up resembling each other, as if written by the same person. With these publications writing becomes an isolating activity, which contradicts its intended universality. And its fanatical celebration of the writer's uniqueness or interiority repels the reader, who is reluctant to let himself be trapped or fascinated. Instead of creating a world where all might live together, the writer takes from the community its common tool, language, which he then uses to distance himself from the group and to express his own uniqueness. All these voices raised in soliloquy, detailing their petty problems, create a universe of mutual deafness where each person, talking about himself, no longer has the time to listen to others.

Unlike this orgy of egotism, Auster's *The Invention of Solitude* is a story whose strength lies in its very simplicity. Through this apparent banality the reader finds himself, and the novel regains its true identity. It is once again a homeland open to all without distinction, a place of welcome: "I don't feel that I was telling the story of my life so much as using myself to explore certain questions that are common to us all" (292), Auster says in an interview. Auster's hero is not someone who prefers himself, to repeat Brecht's definition of the bourgeois, but someone who doubts and communicates this doubt to the reader. Readers identify less with the protagonists' adventures than with the strangeness they feel about themselves — for whom being or becoming someone constitutes the ultimate difficulty. Auster does not condemn, like classical writers, the self's wretchedness in the face of God's grandeur. He does worse: he dissolves this self, declares it a nonentity. Uncertainty eats into the core of our being; our heart is empty or cluttered with so much static that it seems to hold nothing.

This work clearly also expresses the genealogical passion of the uprooted, and it is not insignificant that Auster is an American entirely oriented toward Europe. But this proximity is misleading. A reading of Auster produces a double sensation of familiarity and disorientation, for Auster, deeply anchored in the New World, does not write European books in America; he enriches the American novel with European themes. *The Invention of Solitude,* a tribute to Auster's departed father, continues in the second part with a warm greeting to all those poets and thinkers who have influenced the author. Through writing we can choose other fathers to compensate for our own, discover a spiritual link, go beyond ourselves. Memory is immersion in the past of all those others who comprise us. The narrator distinguishes, one by one, these voices that speak through him that must be quieted before his true inner voice can be heard. But this goal is impossible to attain: the palimpsest self, like an ever-unpeeling onion, resists categorization. This peregrination through the continents of memory may be a marvelous journey, but it does not succeed in easing the pain. No matter how far it roams, the self is always haunted and tortured by the others; it is a room full of strangers and intruders who speak in his place. Auster's approach is not, of course, the same as Proust's anamnesis, an attempt to compensate for life's imperfections by fixing the flight of time in a work of art. It is an eternal quest, without guaranteed results, which can never achieve closure. A detective of the self, Paul Auster applies an uncompromising narrative skill to a metaphysical quest: Why is there a self rather than nothing? To facilitate this task, he presents his fiction in the protective guise of the detective novel. In the end, however, nothing is resolved. Each book is a collective work, the tribute of a writer to all those, past and present, who have helped him create. But this courtesy toward the dead, calling them to his bedside, inviting them to a vast, cross-century symposium, does not expunge the debt. Just as a son can never stop paying for the death of the father who gave him life, so, too, the self can never stop paying its due. It could even define itself this way: the eternal debtor always under obligation to others. That is why this literature must tirelessly rewrite its missing testament. And if, as the famous saying goes, a prophet is someone who remembers the future, the writer, according to Auster, is someone who predicts the past in order first to capture and then to free himself from it. But memory's archives are both chaotic and infinite, and the clerk who attempts to record them will soon get lost in the maze.

Paul Auster completely renews the coming-of-age novel. With unusual talent he reveals how painful it is to be an individual today thrust out from the protective shell of a belief or tradition. After these extensive investigations he offers no final wisdom. Each of his novels outlines the beginning of a redemption, which it subsequently rejects. The lack of response, or of comfort, the stubborn refusal to abandon the pain of this issue, that is the strength of these works. As each plot is unraveled an increasingly more obscure enigma is revealed. His literature is like a brief burst of sunshine between a hidden and an exposed mystery, a glimmer between two shades of darkness. "Just because you wander in the desert, it does not mean there is a promised land" (*Solitude* 32). All his characters — vagabonds, gamblers, semi-tramps, magnificent losers, failed writers — are under way. Like Marco Stanley Fogg at the end of *Moon Palace*, facing the ocean in the hazy moonlight, these characters are more serene at the end of the day, but they are never sovereign. Their chaotic odyssey never ends in peace, and they always fail to regain their lost innocence. Writing never removes the agony, but, rather, alters and deepens it. Writing is futility because it fails to express the experience of loss and renunciation. Perhaps Paul Auster's rich works already prefigure what certain historians foresee as the religion of the future: Christian-Buddhism, that is, a concern with personal salvation linked to an acute awareness of uncertainty and the void.

— *Translated by Karen Palmunen*

Works Cited

Auster, Paul. "Interview with Larry McCaffery and Sinda Gregory." In *The Art of Hunger: Essays, Prefaces, Interviews*. Los Angeles: Sun & Moon Press, 1992. Pp. 269–312.

———. *The Invention of Solitude*. New York: Penguin, 1988.

Paul Auster's Pseudonymous World

Marc Chénetier

In *City of Glass*, Quinn, who writes popular detective novels under a pseudonym, is waiting for his train. Seated next to him, a sheep-like young woman grazes one of his books: "He did not like [her] and it offended him that she should be casually skimming the pages that had cost him so much effort" (85). In *Ghosts*, Blue feels at first little inclined to share Black's reading, but he eventually enters chapter 3 of Thoreau's *Walden* with great attention: "Books must be read as deliberately and reservedly as they were written" (48). Let us read, then, not casually, but with deliberation and reserve, this once at least.

Let us first rid the trilogy of the tinsel that weighs it down. Just as Mallarmé's "dancer" could not possibly be "a woman dancing" for the double reason that she was "not a woman" and that "she did not dance," two simple enough details make this something other than a detective trilogy in New York: it does not take place in New York and it is not a detective story. Such a statement is not generated by some perverse attraction to paradox but by mere facts. See how Quinn himself, a makeshift detective as well as specialized genre-author, is perfectly alien to his job: he has never killed anybody, does not know a thing about crime, does not fear for his own life; no corpse whatsoever provides the motive for this private eye's stalking of a non-existent culprit; and, in the end, no dénouement intervenes. In a word, see how the hallowed springs of the genre nowhere get strained. An enigma, there indeed is; a mystery even, shall we say, but a detective novel? No. *Very* soft-boiled is Paul Auster's work; Mr. Auster works on more austere mystery, even if he once wrote the real thing—but "not for real"—under a borrowed moniker. And then, listen to the narrative voice of *Ghosts*, telling us where Blue is going to operate: "The address is unimportant. But let's say Brooklyn Heights, for the sake of argument" (9). "For the sake of argument"—that is, so that the plot as well as the genre may be given a chance to work—is an "argument" as in "theatrical argument." A street, then, in Brooklyn

Heights. In this street, Whitman "hand set the first edition of *Leaves of Grass*" and H. W. Beecher "railed against slavery from the pulpit of his red-brick church. So much for local color" (10). So much for whoever demands that a novel should contain the usual decor and normal ingredients. So much, also, for whoever wants to be invited to read this as part of the literary corpus and is willing to admit that this author does not quite go by the sacred rules of the genre—pattern Auster, pray. René Magritte would tell you himself: "This is not a private eye novel." The mere "stenophonic" reminder of a theme will allow Eric Dolphy or John Coltrane to hang from it their own chords and improvisations. An alibi, in other words, a fake nose. Literary parasitism. New York and the detective novel are to this book, if you will, what the human face was to Arcimboldo: a pretext whereon to play with carrots and cabbages. Leaves.

By not being casual, one also gets rid of elements that might too easily attract in Auster's work and, thereby, delude one into believing him facile. Gone are the enticing bewitchments of a temperate exoticism to which the foreign readership might all too easily succumb (New York!— would the readers rush to buy "The Dubuque Trilogy," "The Iowa City Trilogy," even though these are identically "gridded" cities, in which characters might just as easily be shadowed?); gone is all the glamour of the hard-boiled novel that Chandler, Chase, and others have, "postmortem," loaned to Brautigan's *Dreaming of Babylon,* Charyn's Isaac pentaptych, Thomas Berger's *Who Is Teddy Villanova?* All of this being swept out of the way, one can, for far better reasons, show Auster a consideration that hurried, ready-made superlatives tend paradoxically to deny him, and to point out what, profoundly, matters in his work. Auster has been too much and badly praised for providing a certain readership with the exact bill of fares it expected. Hit a man too hard with a swinging censer, you kill him dead.

Let us, therefore, go back to sources, and we shall see that the detective's investigations do no more than clothe a narrative skeleton with ancient obsessions, that the walls of the "city of glass" reflect other surfaces and hide other depths, that what haunts it comes from way back, and that "the secret chamber" (as *The Locked Room* is referred to in the French version) can only be called so inasmuch as the ardent center of a suffering consciousness (James did talk of the "chamber of consciousness") becomes indeed visible to the naked eye.

If an assumed arbitrariness allows Paul Auster to nest at the heart of his fictions a number of autobiographical notations under the pretext of character painting (without straining or even demanding our credulity), if his taste for playing obliquely with personal references muddles the tracks the reader follows while making them clear for the private eye, then Auster unrelentingly filigrees the traces of an authorial presence that his ironical or humorous confessions cannot altogether erase. As we turn the pages, everything invites us not to take too seriously what we recognize of the author himself under the features of his characters. These are false clues for superficial conclusions, investigations leading to as many dead ends. For example, as a young man, Quinn wrote several collections of poems and critical essays and published a number of translations; a woman by the first name of Auster's wife can be seen passing by — she has the same national origin and comes from the same state and town; the narrator of *The Locked Room* once held jobs similar to the precarious ones its creator once held himself; the name of Paul Auster's son is on loan to one of his heroes, when he does not lend his own to yet another: "Schiff," the name of a character who goes by the first name of Paul, may well bear the name of one of the author's parents — to whom *Moon Palace* will later be inscribed — but the word may refer one's imagination to the name of the ship on which Auster worked, as well as to his art, come to think of it, should we read "craft" under "ship"; and the preference of the author for spiralled notebooks is one shared by Quinn. Such blatant confessions proliferate to such an extent that, in the last analysis, they have no more importance than the gratuitous tricks to which another protagonist confesses he owes his own creations. If the narrator of the third volume of the trilogy invites us to read an approximate anagram of the name of the author under that of one of his relations ("Stuart"), then the "Paul Austers" that intervene here and there are only brutal manifestations of the arbitrary nature of names. In the world of the pseudonym, real names are turned gangrenous by the uncertainties of identity. Lures or lime-twigs — all manifest references to the life of the author — merely end up tightening on his features a mask that more subtle allusions alone could lift or remove. Autobiographical winks are banalized in order to dissimulate another cluster of worthy similarities, namely, those that have to do with the work itself, its interrogations, the writing activity, the portrait of Paul Auster as creator of "the lost ones."

Should one superpose the titles of Paul Auster's works that preceded the trilogy, one would indeed end up with a cheaply conceived Galton photograph showing the principal thematic hinges of his *oeuvre*. From *WALL Writing* and *FACING the Music* to *WHITE Spaces* and *FRAGMENTS from COLD*, via *UNearth, The Art of HUNGER* and *The Invention of SOLITUDE*, the accents can be heard in an enterprise placed under the multiple sign of silence, deprivation, whiteness, cold light, lack, and loss.

The Invention of Solitude remains the most important book by this writer. It is also the matrix of everything he has written since. Who, in effect, could miss, in a trilogy that stages a pseudo-private eye, the anguished echoes of a private "I" who invents his solitude by insinuating himself in the gap open at the heart of filiation and inscribes in all a relation to the

Other, who stalks the real with powerless words? "Solitude became a passageway into the self, an instrument of discovery," says the narrator of *The Locked Room* (125). It is precisely the heuristic power of solitude that innervates and organizes the narrative of self-discovery produced by Auster's investigators of identity: "Turning off the light and locking the door" (*Ghosts* 57); "I locked up the secret inside me" (*Locked Room* 69); "this room, I now discovered, was located inside my skull" (*Locked Room* 147); "his interior brother, his comrade in solitude" (*City of Glass* 12). All are indications that the investigation cannot possibly concern the world, that it can only refer the investigator to his own interiority, where the unconscious bubbles up.

Over all the previous titles of Paul Auster prevail the atmospheric characteristics of the trilogy: in front of the Frick Gallery, it is "austere and white"; in the Stillmans' flat, with its white partitions, is where "Virginia," as white as the rest, welcomes Quinn. In front of dumb walls that merely reflect the meager rays of a wintry sun, everything is bathed by the omnipresent raw, ruthless light that filters through transparent, impalpable air. This is the light that isolates Edward Hopper's wan figures on the reservation of their uncertain selves, accentuates their vulnerability under the pale sun; it is the light that outlines the grain elevators and the city roofs of Precisionist Charles Sheeler, the "used up air" in which Ieurre, the grammarian protagonist placed by Pascal Quignard at the center of his novel *Carus,* sees the very nature and substance of speech and words. A harsh, glaring light, overwhelming, but one that lights up the world toward no revelation: a slipcover, a lid of a light. The air itself is "full of light," Peter Stillman says; it is the air that swathes the paltry snorts and flutters of a man whose very name spells paralysis, atonia, immobility, a name that would mean quietism if the air his mouth exhales as crazy words did not somehow manage to make him agitated. A covering light, an internal air breathed upon the world from the obscurity of chests, winds of the soul, exhaustion: "petering out," indeed.

Already, from these violent contrasts of glare and shadow, there emerges the double of a more intimate night where ephemeral illuminations weakly flicker. To the clear lines of a world that has been cut out from primary colors, to the neat drawing of forms and objects, are opposed the meanderings and drifts of beings whose destiny, then only hope, is to go back inside themselves. Their hope is to enter the womb of the "salutary emptiness within," of non-encumbered space, solitude, vacuity, a place with no line or mark where it becomes *ipso facto* impossible to get lost, where the feeling of "lostness" Auster's protagonists may feel in front of the world is compensated by the absence of all Law. Whence the love they feel for protective places: "All he ever asked of things: to be nowhere. New York was the nowhere [Quinn] had built around himself"

(*City of Glass* 9). Or else, they may endeavor to become nobody. In the first pages of each novel, an abundant rhetoric of negation and deprivation is put in place; they all end after a gradual process of stripping body and soul bare, an intimately figurative or literal process that tends toward an end by mere evanescence. Austerity means nudity, silence, dereliction, the pure and simple stoicism. Diogenes in his barrel. Quinn on his bare floor. And Blue in his garbage can, "a saint of penury." Ah, happy days!

Still, the Other — that gaping hole, that absence at the heart of oneself which narratives must fill up, furnish, clothe — remains. Even as Auster does everything he can to destabilize and deconstruct his narratives (through stylization; the arbitrariness presiding over the choice of narrative instances; the mix of real and borrowed names; the absence of a resolution or of any clarification of the original enigma, by making sure the programmed frustration induced by disappointing would-be "dénouements" immediately triggers a hunger for the newly discovered "openings" into the unknown), his taste for story-telling is nourished by the conviction that, outside the Other, there is no definition of the self. Fanshawe "is the place where everything begins" for the narrator of *The Locked Room* and "without him [he] would hardly know who [he is]" (7). Watching, stalking, turning into a voyeur, everything becomes an attempt at discovering one's identity by default. Whence the improbable series of doubles, so often explored by commentators, that people the pages of the trilogy. Mirrors, twins, innumerable fathers and sons, reflections, ghosts, and eponyms are all instruments that enable one "to understand the connectedness of inner and outer," "to bring the outside in and thus usurp the sovereignty of inwardness" (*City of Glass* 97). No one can face himself anywhere but outside of himself: "My true place in the world, it turned out, was somewhere beyond myself, and if that place was inside me, it was also unlocatable. This was the tiny hole between self and not-self, and for the first time in my life I saw this nowhere as the exact center of the world" (*Locked Room* 58). This gap, this intermediary zone — what we might call a "no-self-land" — keeps growing and the white space it defines is the place where everything — destiny, meaning, relation to the Other, language — reaches a vanishing point: this is where the unassignable reigns, the Real. The action of such an instrumental couple is centrifugal and it never ceases to drill the abyss. If the Other fascinates, it is because it seems to provide a mode of access to the self, "no one can cross the boundary into another — for the simple reason that no one can gain access to himself" (*Locked Room* 80–81). For one to be, there must be two. But if the One is always dependent on the Other, in order to know that Other, One would have to know One's self.

The official thematics of the double is therefore itself reproduced by a "double" metafictional doubling, one internal to the work itself, the other internal to it, based on the literary surroundings. The trilogy keeps recycling references to itself until, at the end of the third volume, it confesses its unity through the voice of a narrator—one would have sworn was totally alien to the first two. Beside the systematic—however diffuse—cross-referencing between volumes, beside the permanent recourse to an aesthetics of whiteness, absence, and emergence, a large number of *mises en abîme* fold the text back over its processes and groupings. We have not only the writing activity that keeps busy protagonists who seem permanently occupied by the redaction of some report or other, nor an enormous (Max) task (Work) that hides under the name of a narrator, but also the pen bought from a deaf mute, a manuscript as "heavy as a man" (*Locked Room* 21), the name of a publisher ("Walter J. Black, Inc.") that may be read as more than a simple tag (*Ghosts* 32). The circulation of identical signs is not merely playful: it reinforces the effect of collapse and fold over, illustrates the inescapable self-enclosure of the symbolic, its incapacity to utter the real, and shows the grotesquely vain efforts deployed by underlining, repetition, insistence, the closure of a world that language forces to stutter along with itself. Black, here a publisher, becomes a character there; Quinn circulates in a volume that is not really his; the book of Thoreau commented upon in *Ghosts* provides the patronym of Dennis Walden in *The Locked Room;* a Stillman who is no longer the Stillman appearing in *City of Glass* lends a fake identity to a Fanshawe who is not Fanshawe (*Locked Room* 153); the name of Henry Dark, falsely historical in the first volume, is used by the actual Fanshawe as an alias while hiding in Boston. . . . Signals sent from volume to volume, the intrication of similar but distinct references, the recycling of phony true informations and of true false details are not mere authorial coquetry, they in fact serve as commentary upon a conviction Quinn is entrusted with confessing: "What interested him about the stories he wrote was not their relation to the world but their relation to other stories" (*City of Glass* 14).

If the world is not made up of texts, none can talk about it and, if it is made up of stories, one can only discuss it through them. *The Invention of Solitude* already says the same thing: Auster can only define himself through writing, establishing relations, and vanquishing solitude by talking of writing to other writings. As an American, he speaks of and to all of classical American literature and tells it of Beckett; as a living American, he talks of and to those of his contemporaries, whether American or not, who speak to him. *The New York Trilogy* has as its fundamental objects literature and language, the only modes of explorations of the subject.

At first, Blue gets bored reading *Walden,* as our own contemporaries have difficulty re-reading essential American texts. Under the pretext of a detective novel, Auster presents a synthesis of their ancestral questioning.

Truth to tell, little of a braggart himself, he does not claim for himself the status of an original or prodigy writer.

Stevenson, Dickens, Cervantes, hidden under the name of a Madame Saavedra's husband (Michael), make more or less significant appearances (the latter, in particular, underlines the regressive nestings inherent to any literary work that is fully conscious of its processes and objectives). That Daniel Quinn's initials should refer us back to Don Quixote's should not surprise the reader of a text in which author and protagonists repeatedly meet, as in the opening of Book II in the Spanish master's work. Because, snugly nested within *Don Quixote,* there is also the other book that Cervantes thought of writing while he was writing the first, and there is little risk in discovering, under the trilogy, the great book of American literature, the most significant chapters of which were written — beside the already mentioned Whitman and Thoreau — by Hawthorne, Melville, and Poe.

Leaving aside the fact that Hawthorne's "Wakefield" lends its argument to Blue's adventures, Fanshawe is borrowed from the first book of the romancer whose wife's name, Sophie, becomes that of the female protagonist of *The Locked Room.* As for Melville, he is everywhere: first, because he provides the patronyms of characters that are fictitious in the second degree; second, because an ironical "Call me Redburn" comes to relay, in a letter from Fanshawe to his sister Ellen (*Locked Room* 117), the recurrent use of the "let's suppose," or "let's say" which, under the invocation of Ishmael, the wanderer, factorizes uncertainty; third and most important, because of the obstinate walls on which characters more than a little reminiscent of Bartleby attempt, as full-fledged scriveners themselves, to read or inscribe the signs of their identity and of their obscure desire. As for Poe, he governs from afar the aesthetics of the double by way of a "William Wilson," direct from his celebrated story, as well, of course, as the double investigative and metaphysical dimension of the trilogy. Dupin, "The Pit and the Pendulum," "El Araf," "Eureka": Poe's works underpin a creation which, much like his, carries us ever forward toward the dissolution of signs and the great white empty spaces of the end of *The Narrative of Arthur Gordon Pym.* Witness the "southward trek to oblivion" that announces the end of the narrator's quest in *The Locked Room* (144).

Auster's trilogy constitutes a summary-cum-commentary of classical American literary reflections on the nature and meaning of the words to be inscribed on the white walls of consciousness: what would it mean to understand? It is not indifferent that, here, Pym's runes be replaced by a reference to H. D. who, more than being a pretext for speculating on the letter and the ironical meaning of signs (Heraclitus or Democritus? Humpty Dumpty?), refers us to the hieroglyphic part of Hilda Doolittle's work. As a poet, she would not have denied the pertinence of a research concerning the links that exist between constellations and names — inherited from the Kabalah — mentioned in *City of Glass*. The names that matter, the trilogy thereupon insists, can only be found "in the white pages," even if, as it happens, they are those of a phone book. (Let hermeneutics do the walking.) One, at any rate, should not look for them in any book, for their status compares with Melville's notion of "true places." They should not be looked for on maps, as we remember, for "true places never are."

It must be clear at this point that calling upon the most radical and most essential segment of the American tradition makes it possible to call, in its wake, upon a large fraction of the literary and philosophical preoccupations of our own time. If it was suggested earlier on that one could think of Paul Auster as the novelist of "the lost ones," the reason is, of course, that naturally enough the Beckett of "For to End Yet Again," of "Enough," or of "Lessness" serves him as indispensable reference, that Blanchot's meditations spring up here and there as situations demand, and that an obsessional theme of contemporary letters — the non-adequation of language to the world — is ever present in his writings. The unnameable . . . the feeling of loss directly issues from it; linked to it are the allied themes of negation, absence, dereliction and uncertainty, all reflections on the dissemination and proliferation of meaning. It may well be that an allusion to Peirce's mad semiological classifications is simply an effect of the present writer's imagination or wishful thinking — so, what else is new? — but may it be suggested here that an identical relation links, on the one hand, Peirce's reflections on the relative motivation of signs and Auster's own in the trilogy and, on the other hand, the last sentence of the memoir on which the narrative of *City of Glass* is founded ("What will happen when there are no more pages in the red notebook?" [*City of Glass* 200]) and the sentence which Peirce, by then nearly mad, once sent in a letter to William James, along with a call for help: "Soon the ink will freeze in my inkwell. Then, what?"

To read Paul Auster is to hear a number of his immediate contemporaries echo his preoccupations. Such a quest for *some* coherence in the chaos of events, be it at the cost of a more or less acute paranoia, such a quest for an unstable, elusive meaning among resemblances and possible narratives, such an Oedipa Maas–like intransitive investigation, such descriptions of "preterites" run out from among the Elect for refusing Meaning. How could they not invite one to re-read Pynchon once more, and more particularly *The Crying of Lot 49*? How, then, can one not find more than a complicitous wink in the trilogy, even though Paul Auster will readily say he had never read Pynchon before writing these books? How could one not succumb to the temptation of tracing the extraordinary linguistic manipulation that presides over the destiny of "the Kenosha Kid," in *Gravity's Rainbow,* under the use, in the trilogy, of the name of that little-known town where Paul Auster's own father was born? In these three books one can follow the movements of disorder and entropy so central in the work of Pynchon, for whom "fictioneering" alone will allow the slightest mastery over the world. Pynchon's epiphanies are perceptible here under this or that "brief scald, a weird synapse of recognition" (*Locked Room* 151) (the immense shadow of William Gaddis also looms here). One thinks of William H. Gass when Auster declines in his turn the harmonics of the word "blue" in the American language, of Rudolph Wurlitzer, who himself owes so much to Beckett, when a prolonged stress falls upon the vanishings and the deliquescence of being and consciousness, of Don DeLillo, finally, whose *The Names* practically constitutes a necessary gloss on the trilogy of his friend Paul Auster, and who, because he knows how to read "means" under "names," also knows that the real is a direct function of the tools used to utter it. Of course, neither Wurlitzer, nor Pynchon, nor DeLillo can be considered as what ancient literary history used to call "influences," as Auster had not read them before the composition of his trilogy. But whoever stalks the intertext cannot help but note that an enormous and essential sector of contemporary American fiction explores the mysteries of "making sense," that it tracks down patterns and motifs that might confer an order upon things before placing them under accusation as pure effects of language. (Joseph McElroy and Richard Powers be my witnesses.) Thus, to the naive cratylism of Blue in the early stages of his quest, one could oppose the linguistic nature of utopia in the works of Henry Dark ("his wordhood," Stillman says).

In the last analysis, in the work of Paul Auster language is stripped of all transcendence and only finds its motivations in power play. Short of poetic rebellious attempts, the language of the Father imposes its authority, forbidding any construction of the self. Once the Father's authority has been removed, such phenomena as Peter Stillman's glossolalia can emerge; whenever it exerts itself anew, it dictates the normative clichés of father-son conversations. In Auster's work, language, words, and writing are less a matter of black and white than superpositions of "blank and want" — as land-artist Robert Smithson once put it, thus prolonging the meditations of Melville and Poe. The specter of meaning still haunts a literature that has understood, with Hoffmannsthal, that "depth must be hidden on the surface," that between the lines nothing ever hides but the white, insistent obscenity of a nonsense, which words clumsily attempt to cover up, and that runes and signs, mysterious and senseless, suggest all the better as they do not name it. Whence the "certain pleasure" that the narrator feels when abroad, due to the fact of experiencing "language as a collection of sounds, [of being] forced to the surface of words where meanings vanish" (*Locked Room* 140). Peter Stillman's bliss has no other source: "Wimble click crumblechaw beloo. Clack clack bedrack. Numb noise, flacklemuch, chewmanna. Ya, ya, ya" (*City of Glass* 29). As Molly would put it, "all I know is what the words know." And Auster is not so sure they know very much. Even when attempting to refound language into a world, one cannot read out of reality any more than what one inscribes on it, nor decipher any more of the real than what one has fed into it: the world is always pseudonymous, since names do not correspond to things and names create for the world a reality that it may not have ("To say is to invent," Malone said). As for Being, it is but a miserable Spanish inn where one filches discourses from the neighbor's plate, the Other, who, since he never comes, does not allow anyone to recognize himself in him. Godot may not be God but, while waiting for him, meaning deliquesces, language moves in rounds and becomes impoverished, night falls. Only chance remains . . . But that, as someone said, "is another story."

*   *   *

I see people at the back of the room who look disappointed. So, all right, let's read, let's read again, as usual, if that's what you want. All right, it *is* a detective trilogy, it *does* take place in New York. But if André Malraux could detect in Faulkner's *Sanctuary* "the intrusion of Greek tragedy into the police novel," can we not understand that any enigma is in itself a tragedy, that the sphinx, the he/she "of dubious smile and ambiguous voice," always means death? Fortunately, the Knight of the Sad Countenance, Auster is here to remind us, already wondered, way back then, "to what extent would people tolerate blasphemies if they gave them amusement" (*City of Glass* 154).

Works Cited

Auster, Paul. *City of Glass*. Los Angeles: Sun & Moon Press, 1985.
———. *Ghosts*. Los Angeles: Sun & Moon Press, 1986.
———. *The Locked Room*. Los Angeles: Sun & Moon Press, 1986.

In the Realm of the Naked Eye: The Poetry of Paul Auster

Norman Finkelstein

I

Paul Auster the novelist came into print later than Paul Auster the poet, essayist, and translator, and presently eclipses all of his other personae, at least in the eyes of a general literary audience. *The New York Trilogy* has tantalized readers for some time now; more recent novels have also been well received. But while Auster notes that the poet and the writer of prose grew up together (personal correspondence, 15 October 1988), perhaps like the protagonist and Fanshawe, his alter ego in *The Locked Room,* the last book of the *Trilogy,* we can say with equal confidence that Auster first offered his readers poetry but reached a wider audience with his fiction. The publication of *Disappearances: Selected Poems* (1970–1979) did not change Auster's current reputation as one of the very best of a new generation of novelists, but this volume does round out our view of his work and deepen our appreciation of a writer who instinctively understands Susan Sontag's dictum that "*transparence* is the highest, most liberating value in art — and in criticism — today" (13; italics in the original).

This is not to say that Auster's poetry presents the same sort of glassy surface as does the degree-zero writing of his fiction. Auster's "white" prose (and indeed, there is a revealing prose poem in *Disappearances* called "White Spaces") studiously avoids interpretation, and in the very passion of that avoidance lies whatever hope readers have of fulfilling their secret interpretive desires. *The Locked Room* ends with its autobiographically obsessed protagonist, after publishing Fanshawe's works and marrying the widow of the man he presumed is dead, reading and throwing away each page of his old friend's last notebook: "Each sentence erased the sentence before it, each paragraph made the next paragraph impossible. It is odd, then, that the feeling that survives from this notebook is one of great lucidity" (370). If this is how Auster's *hypocrite lecteur* is meant to consume his prose, coming away oddly satisfied, perhaps even enlightened, by the brilliance of such reflexivity, what are we to make of this?:

> To see is this other torture, atoned for
> In the pain of being seen: the spoken,
> The seen, contained in the refusal
> To speak, and the seed of a single voice,
> Buried in a random stone.
> My lies have never belonged to me.
> 			(*Disappearances* 14)

This is reflexivity of a different order, and if it is an art of transparence, we see through it only so much as we can see through a one-way mirror. But we are not really being observed; rather, the mirror is confessing to us. The poet always implicates his readers in the most intimate of his psychic examinations, which is to say that he makes us a gift of the lies—the inadequacies of his speech—which he tells to himself.

The mirror games of Auster's poetry, played for such high stakes as these, produce verbal textures that both attract and repel. Some of his poems are as brittle as broken glass, and like glass they can splinter and embed themselves in the reader's flesh. But their mineral beauties lure us back, and we are gradually convinced by the insistence of Auster's unmaking:

> Vatic lips, weaned
> of image. The mute one
> here, who waits, urn-wise,
> in wonder. Curse overbrims
> prediction: the glacial rose
> bequeaths its thorns to the breath
> that labors toward eye
> and oblivion.
> We have only to ready ourselves.
> From the first step, our voice
> is in league
> with the stones of the field.
> 			(*Disappearances* 21)

Our voice: the poet is not merely speaking in the first-person plural here; he is offering his readers a contract, and though he is frank about what we will get, he urgently wants us to sign:

> . . . You ask
> words of me, and I
> will speak them — from the moment
> I have learned
> to give you nothing.
> (*Disappearances* 28)

Unearth, which was Auster's first book (the version in *Disappearances* is shorter than the original), establishes the terms of the poet's relationship to his readers. No, they are not quite *hypocrites lecteurs,* but Auster's obvious discontent with the easy consumerism of the contemporary lyric, already apparent by the early seventies, leads him to a raw vatic stance that has nothing to do (despite all the stones) with the more self-satisfied shamans of that period:

> Rats wake in your sleep
> and mime the progress
> of want. My voice turns back
> to the hunger it gives birth to,
> coupling with stones
> that jut from red walls: the heart
> gnaws, but cannot know
> its plunder; the flayed tongue
> rasps. We lie
> in earth's deepest marrow, and listen
> to the breath of angels.
> Our bones have been drained.
> Wherever night has spoken,
> unborn sons prowl the void
> between stars.
> (*Disappearances* 36)

This is perhaps the harshest poem that Auster has ever written, and if readers can assent to *these* hungers, then more genial ambivalences are in store.

After *Unearth,* Auster's poems, although they remain mostly "weaned / of image," are less hermetic, less obsessive in their treatment of the self. Despite such poems as "White Nights" ("I am no longer here. I have never said / what you say / I have said" [43]) or "Interior" ("In the impossibility of words, / in the unspoken word / that asphyxiates / I find myself" [45]), the dominant note is struck, however grudgingly, in "Scribe": "A flower / falls from his eye / and blooms in a stranger's mouth" (47). The other is no longer merely a reflection of the self or an imagined reader upon whom the poet can project his doubts and anxieties. Reader and poet continue their dialogue, but they are joined by other voices, especially those of earlier poets. Furthermore, the reflections and disjunctions that actually constitute the self for a writer like Auster come to be accepted, or at least tolerated, with more ready grace.

In *City of Glass,* the first volume of *The New York Trilogy,* a case of mistaken identity leads the mystery writer Quinn, the novel's protagonist, to impersonate a detective named "Paul Auster." When "Auster" himself shows up toward the book's end, he is no detective at all, but a writer, leading the comfortable life (beautiful wife, happy child, modest, serious career) for which the tortured and confused Quinn desperately longs. "Auster" can offer Quinn little in the way of help or solace, and in the very last pages of the book, the unnamed narrator whom we learn is telling the tale bluntly declares that "as for Auster, I am convinced that he behaved badly throughout" (202–203). In short, the real Auster's facility for narrative mirror games (and this is only one of innumerable examples in his fiction) simplifies the problem of the self: attitudes and identities continually oscillate, and finally we are forced to conclude that the sum of these identities both is and is not a unified image of the writing subject. The "truth" of the self's identity is, if not beside the point, at least to be found only in the circumambulations of plot, the walking, following, or searching that occupy so much of *City of Glass* and other Auster novels.

But in Auster's mature poetry (which for me begins after *Unearth,* with *Wall Writing,* probably his richest collection), mirror games tend to exhaust themselves much more quickly. The self cannot be put to the same uses in poetry as it can in fiction. The formal demands of lyricism are such that if the "I" is going to be preserved as a centered voice, eventually it must speak directly to its object. With various strategies some contemporary poets deliberately attempt to expunge the "I" from their writing (with mostly unsuccessful results). Auster has never been among these. More an heir of Charles Reznikoff and George Oppen than Charles Olson or Jack Spicer, Auster seeks to renew the balance between the writing subject and the world outside; the stormy loss of the self (or as is now fashionable, its smooth deconstruction) never interests him, despite the obvious pain involved in achieving the desired equilibrium. From the impacted syntax and agonized doppelgangers of the earlier work, we move to the measured beauty of "White," written for Paul Celan:

For one who drowned:
this page, as if
thrown out to sea
in a bottle.

So that
even as the sky embarks
into the seeing of earth, an echo
of the earth
might sail toward him,
filled with a memory of rain,
and the sound of rain
falling on the water.

So that
he will have learned,
in spite of the wave
now sinking from the crest
of mountains, that forty days
and forty nights
have brought no dove
back to us.
                    (*Disappearances* 61)

The poet gives himself over completely to his elegiac task. To do so, he must be wholly in touch with his feelings, and yet subordinate them entirely to the tropes that will best memorialize the "one who drowned." Hope and despair mingle in the images of water and earth, and the muted allusion to the story of Noah seals the poem as Auster saves his least tentative gesture for the end. In the last line comes the well-deserved "we": poet, reader, and the one who drowned are joined in the sad wisdom of loss.

II

In "Hieroglyph" (*Disappearances* 60), another crucial poem in *Wall Writing*, Auster calls his work "Blood Hebrew." It is an apt phrase in that it names both Auster's relation to Judaism and to poetic tradition, which often become congruent in his poetry. At the end of his essay on his friend Edmond Jabes, Auster quotes Marina Tsvetaeva: "In this most Christian of worlds / all poets are Jews" (*Art of Hunger* 106). True enough: what poet, even the most geographically rooted, cannot identify with the themes of the Exile and the Book which Jabes has made his own? And further: what poet, in the experience of otherness that virtually defines the poetic identity, has not felt at least a bit like the Jew in a Christian world? But the Jewish poet writing in tongues compounded by exile (the

Egyptian French of Jabes, the American English of Auster, the German —
unspeakable irony! — of the Romanian-born Celan): this is a special instance of otherness and a more pressing crisis of identification.

In *The Book of Questions,* Jabes writes: "First I thought I was a writer.
Then I realized I was a Jew. Then I no longer distinguished the writer in
me from the Jew because one and the other are only torments of an
ancient word" (195). The irony here is that only a writer who is a Jew
would trace the two conditions back to the same source. This vaguely
tautological situation is inherited by Auster. Like Jabes, Auster is haunted
by Jewish themes, and perhaps more importantly, by the Jewish attitude
toward writing: to witness, to remember, to play divine and utterly serious
textual games. Consider the Celan-like "Fore-Shadows," which I take to
be addressed to victims of the Holocaust generally, but perhaps to lost
Jewish writers in particular:

I breathe you.
I becalm you out of me.
I numb you in the reach
of brethren light.
I suckle you
to the dregs of disaster.

The sky pins a vagrant star
on my chest. I see the wind
as witness, the towering night
that lapsed
in a maze of oaks,
the distance.

I haunt you
to the brink of sorrow.
I milk you of strength.
I defy you,
I deify you
to nothing and
to no one,

I become
your most necessary and most violent
heir.
          (*Disappearances* 54)

Here, the "unborn sons" of *Unearth* (a title which, in retrospect, takes on the weight of exile) come into their own. The "necessary and most violent / heir" of a lost Jewish culture inevitably defies and deifies these "fore-shadows," haunting them as much as they haunt him. It is just this exchange of spiritual energies, this ghostly confrontation in the domain of tribal memory, which inspires the poem.

This is even more apparent in "Song of Degrees," which is virtually a midrash on the story of Jacob:

> . . . Tents,
> pitched and struck: a ladder
> propped
> on a pillow of stone: the sheer
> aureole rungs
> of fire. You,
> and then we. The earth
> does not ask
> for anyone.
>   (*Disappearances* 64)

Again Auster moves to the first-person plural. When God appears to Jacob in the dream of the angelic ladder, he reaffirms the covenant made with Abraham and Isaac to make the Jews a great nation: "Your children will be like the dust of the earth. They will spread west and east and north and south. The nations of the earth will be blessed because of you, for I am with you" (Gen. 28:19). So from a modern Jewish perspective, "You, / and then we." But almost by definition, after thousands of years of exile and disaster, a modern Jewish perspective entails a profound ambivalence toward the covenant. As Auster declares:

> . . . Even
> if you crawled from the skin
> of your brother,
> you would not go beyond
> what you breathe: no
> angel can cure you
> of your name.
>   (*Disappearances* 65)

After Jacob wrestles with the angel, his name is changed to Israel, a positive representation of the entire people. His original name, associated with fraud and deceit in his dealings with Isaac and Esau, is relegated to a secondary status, and it is after the wrestling match at Peniel that

Jacob is reconciled with his brother. But for Auster, the onus of that original name cannot be removed. The secular Jewish writer can contemplate ancient tales or recent (literary) history, but he is fated to doubt the very strength he draws from such encounters.

Not that he can dispense with them. There is a somewhat contrived but nonetheless moving episode in *In the Country of Last Things* in which Anna Blume, the questing narrator, takes refuge in the National Library, one of the few institutions in Auster's postapocalyptic "City of Destruction" that is not in a state of total chaos. She chances into a room where a rabbi is studying with his disciples. As Anna tells it:

> Then I looked into his eyes, and a flicker of recognition shuddered through me.
>   "I thought all the Jews were dead," I whispered.
>   "There are a few of us left," he said, smiling at me again. "It's not so easy to get rid of us, you know."
>   "I'm Jewish, too," I blurted out. (95)

Anna's sudden admission of her hitherto unrevealed Jewish origins is due to the instinctive trust she puts in the rabbi, for "he reminded me of how things had been when I was very young, back in the dark ages when I still believed in what fathers and teachers said to me." This almost miraculous sense of connection in a world that is literally falling apart leads to a major turning point in the narrative, since it is with the rabbi's help that Anna meets her lover Samuel Farr, a colleague of her brother for whom she is searching. In her last meeting with the rabbi, he tells her that every Jew "believes that he belongs to the last generation of Jews. We are always at the end, standing on the brink of the last moment, and why should we expect things to be any different now?" (112).

The rabbi's observation is reminiscent of Walter Benjamin's angel of history: "His face is turned toward the past. Where we perceive a chain of events, he sees one single catastrophe which keeps piling wreckage upon wreckage and hurls it in front of his feet" (257). Blown backward into the future by a storm from paradise, the angel can only bear witness to the continued disaster which is human history. Like the rabbi's generations of Jews, like Anna Blume, and like Auster in his most Jewish poems, the angel's task, regardless of the pain, is to remember. *In the Country of Last Things* takes the form of a letter, and at the end of the novel, despite — or because of — all that Anna has lived through, she promises to write again. In *Wall Writing*, the scribe writes of the other who is himself, casting the poem into the sea of memory like a letter in a bottle or a prayer to an absent god:

. . . these
hammer-worshipped
spew-things
cast
into the zones of blood.
                    (*Disappearances* 74)

III

If Paul Auster's work were concerned only with the past, however, or with
the flickering self, it would not have achieved the tensile strength and
jagged expressivity that mark it as among the best American writing of
the last twenty years. In poetry especially, a concern solely for tradition or
solely for the vicissitudes of the ego will severely limit a writer's range of
expression. Even when such concerns are simply combined—as in the
case of Robert Lowell, for example—one can expect only limited success.
"Its past was a souvenir," Wallace Stevens says in "Of Modern Poetry";
and then, echoing Whitman, "It has to be living, to learn the speech of
the place / It has to face the men of the time and to meet / The women of
the time" (174–175). If such Romantic optimism, such broad extrover-
sion, is less accessible in recent years, it is due to the equally Romantic
pull of interiority, which becomes increasingly difficult to resist when the
men and women of the time prove to be somewhat more banal than
Stevens believed. Given such circumstances, modern lyric interiority risks
triviality, as does a poetry devoted only to exteriors.

The objectivists are some of the few poets who manage to avoid this
impasse. Scrupulously measuring even minimal encounters of self and
world, and dedicated to finding the linguistic strategies necessary to ren-
der their measurements into a verse both abstract and sensual, poets such
as Louis Zukofsky, Charles Reznikoff, and George Oppen become increasingly important to a younger generation that values integrity—in
thought, in feeling, in craft—above all else. The objectivists share the
general modern distrust of tradition, but grow strong through secret
affinities to the past (Oppen, author of the paradigmatic "Psalm," once
admitted that Blake was more important to him than was W. C. Williams).
These poets, paying such close and thoughtful attention to the present
moment, in turn provide the new generation with links to a usable past.
As Auster says in "The Decisive Moment," his essay on Reznikoff, "Each
moment, each thing, must be earned, wrested away from the confusion of
inert matter by a steadiness of gaze, a purity of perception so intense that
the effort, in itself, takes on the value of a religious act" (*Art of Hunger* 36).

This piece, dated "1974; 1979," is written during the years when Auster's poetry is most strongly influenced by the objectivists. For Auster,

Reznikoff's insistence on the poem as a "testimony" to the individual's perceptions of the world, or Oppen's belief that poetry should be a "test of truth," does indeed take on the value of a religious act. As the objectivists themselves understood, such a poetic both confirms and supplants an older form of devotional poetry, though as Harold Bloom often points out, it is difficult in this context to make a clear distinction between secular and religious literature.[1] The older religious poem, at least in the Jewish tradition, is predicated on a preexisting text as a manifestation of transcendental presence, however remote. Frequently the poem is in some sense a midrash or commentary. In *Wall Writing* Auster subverts but still depends on this strategy, given the aura of some previously inscribed source or "prooftext" that hovers around many of the poems. But the devotional quality of the objectivist poem depends on a complete sense of absence, for only then can direct encounters with the material world take on the value previously reserved for encounters with mediating sacred texts. The poet is thus doubly exiled: from the homeland, to be sure, but from what George Steiner calls the homeland of the text as well. "For as long as he remains in the realm of the naked eye," Auster announces in *White Spaces,* "he continues to wander" (*Disappearances* 107).

This "realm of the naked eye" differs from the world of the original objectivists in that it is far more barren and rendered with greater abstraction. Like Auster's *In the Country of Last Things,* it is a realm in which objects seem to "disappear and never come back" (1). The glinting pieces of broken glass, the twigs and buds growing in urban lots, the sparrows and children hopping about the stoops and alleys — in short, all the reassuring materials of the objectivist lyric, quietly celebrated for their mere being — are gone. In *White Spaces,* all that is left is "a landscape of random impulse, of knowledge for its own sake — which is today a knowledge that exists, that comes into being beyond any possibility of putting it into words" (*Disappearances* 103–104). Speaking a language that is almost prior to language, a language of bare consciousness that methodically eschews the enumeration of objects, the poet, invoking the "invisible God of the Hebrews," states flatly that "It is sometimes necessary not to name the things we are talking about" (105).

Readers familiar with the tenets of objectivism may wonder how a poetry based upon acts of testimony and reportage can become transformed, in Auster's hands, into a poetry made out of "letters from nowhere, from the white space that has opened up in his mind" (106). What are these spaces into which the objective world has disappeared, and more importantly, how could the same impetus behind objectivism lead to such resolute unmaking? In fact, it is a logical progression. Objectivism, as these poets themselves came to understand it, is primarily concerned not with objects per se, but with a language of objectification

derived dialectically from an honest apprehension of a subjective response to the world. The term that the objectivists so often privilege in
discussing their work is *sincerity,* and it is sincerity as the force behind the
poet's reportage that also operates in Auster's work. If a white space
opens in the poet's mind, if he is continually faced with "the supreme
indifference of simply being wherever we happen to be" (104), he must
keep faith with himself by finding a discourse that will objectify even so
subjective a state of experience. Furthermore, while Auster admires, perhaps even envies the objectivists' ability to give themselves (though not
without a struggle) to the simple grace of the object world, he understands that he cannot give himself to the world in quite the same way. The
quasi-religious optimism of the objectivists' careful gaze finally is remote
from the bleaker perspective of Auster's naked eye.

A helpful comparison could be drawn between *Disappearances* (1975),
the title sequence of Auster's volume, and the poetry of Oppen, especially *Of Being Numerous* (1968). Auster's poem bears the clear influence
of Oppen's work from the sixties: the same dry, clipped phrasing; the
deliberately measured lines of varied lengths, expressive of concerned
mental activity; the uncanny abstraction in the face of what is obviously
a wildly sprawling urban sensorium.[2] Oppen's great theme, "the shipwreck / Of the singular" (151), and the consequent social and political
exploration "of being numerous," opens outward, despite his persistent
skepticism and frequent horror, into a vision of community:

> Which is ours, which is ourselves,
> This is our jubilation
> Exalted and as old as that truthfulness
> Which illumines speech.
> (173)

Although the "meditative man" has been subsumed by the crowd, the
potential for "clarity" — in poetry as much as in social existence — is preserved.

But in *Disappearances* (and the very title can be opposed to Oppen's
precariously balanced but still hopeful *Of Being Numerous*), although Auster acknowledges that he too is "beyond the grasp / of the singular," a
brooding counter-narrative develops:

> He is alive, and therefore he is nothing
> but what drowns in the fathomless hole
> of his eye,

and what he sees
is all that he is not: a city

of the undeciphered
event,

and therefore a language of stones,
since he knows that for the whole of life

a stone
will give way to another stone

to make a wall

and that all these stones
will form the monstrous sum

of particulars.
                (77–78)

The stones in the wall, the people of the city, produce "the monstrous sum / of particulars" — a horror of anonymous multiplication against which the poet can only oppose "his nostalgia: a man." Later in the poem, Auster, understanding his subjectivity is lost within such monstrosity, elaborates on his predicament:

It is nothing.
And it is all that he is.
And if he would be nothing, then let him begin
where he finds himself, and like any other man
learn the speech of this place.
                (83)

Language may be our only recourse, but it does not offer the same regenerative promise of clarity as in Oppen's work. Auster's conclusions are more limited, tentative, guarded:

. . . For the city is monstrous,
and its mouth suffers
no issue
that does not devour the word
of oneself.

Therefore, there are the many,
and all these many lives
shaped into the stones
of a wall,

and he who would begin to breathe
will learn there is nowhere to go
but here.
                    (85)

Here, not elsewhere: no longer a discourse of the other, Auster's poetry resignedly takes up residence in the familiar, for it has nowhere else to go. But if a primal rediscovery of self and world (however historically determined) offers his objectivist fathers renewed poetic opportunities, for Auster such chances have already been exhausted.

IV

It is difficult not to read the last sections of *Disappearances* as a protracted farewell to poetry, though it could also be said that Auster's entire poetic output, as represented by this volume, consists of nothing but such a farewell. By this I do not mean simply that Auster's work marks the end of one or another poetic tradition: not only are such pronouncements risky, since they reflect more on the critic than the poet, but they are of limited historical value, since the features of one or another type of poetry tend to recur at odd times and when they are least expected. No, Auster's poems constitute a farewell to poetry in that they can be read as an extended meditation on the impossibility of writing poetry in our time — at least for Paul Auster. From the beginning, when the centered subject, the lyric "I" speaks, it is aware that it is and is not the author of its discourse: the language comes from self and other, here and elsewhere, past and present. Auster finds this situation increasingly intolerable:

. . . Do not
forget
to forget. Fill
your pockets with earth,
and seal up the mouth
of my cave.
                    ("Clandestine," 99)

Because what happens will never happen,
and because what has happened
endlessly happens again,

we are as we were, everything
has changed in us, if we speak
of the world
it is only to leave the world

unsaid.
            ("Narrative," 116)

Simply to have stopped.

As if I could begin
where my voice has stopped, myself
the sound of a word

I cannot speak.
            ("In Memory of Myself," 122)

When a writer of such proven integrity and ability makes these statements, they should be taken seriously, and not merely as a fashionable
pose. Fiction, no matter how difficult the march through its hills and
valleys, must provide relief after this, for the conventions of fiction are
such that the authorial voice will in most instances obliterate itself will-
ingly, giving over entirely to narration. Plot, character, setting, and dialogue are the givens of an "elsewhere" against which author and reader
do not struggle. *The New York Trilogy* is, as they say, metafiction, and it is
close to Auster's poetry because it still obsessively walks the line between
the unity of the self and the freedom of self-dispersal, which fiction offers
its most skillful practitioners. *In the Country of Last Things* and *Moon Palace*
are somewhat more traditional, coherent, first-person narratives, and are
perhaps more "realistic" novels than most readers would prefer to believe. Thus Auster's trajectory seems to be taking him away from the
agonized debate that marks his poetry from start ("My lies have never
belonged to me" [14]) to finish ("myself / the sound of a word / I cannot
speak" [122]).

Finish? Now in his late forties, Auster, despite his current devotion to
fiction, could certainly turn to poetry again, as he himself admitted to me
(personal correspondence, 15 October, 1988). Nevertheless, *Disappearances* is a sealed book, ten years of unified effort, a single, indispensable

statement for contemporary poetry. Looking at the thin chapbooks collected in this volume, I am reminded that Auster is not the only important writer of his generation who has apparently left poetry behind. Ross
Feld's splendid *Plum Poems* appeared in 1972; since then he has published
almost nothing but his meticulously crafted fiction and criticism. Although the terms of his argument are articulated more by Jack Spicer
than the objectivists, Feld too is a writer who agonizes over the role of the
self in poetry — and turns to the novel with an almost audible sigh of
relief. "I don't learn from my own poems" says Feld sadly in *Plum Poems*
(29). Whether one "learns" from writing literature of any genre is debat-
able, but perhaps that is beside the point. The distinction that can be
made is that lyric poetry expresses a kind of measured truth about the
conditions of the self, while the novel, despite all the high-minded claims
for its moral seriousness, does not. "The tongue," says Auster in his final
poem,

> is forever taking us away
> from where we are, and nowhere
> can we be at rest
> in the things we are given
> to see, for each word
> is an elsewhere, a thing that moves
> more quickly than the eye . . .
>   ("Facing the Music," 125)

Perhaps this is a general description of the state of poetry today. If so, the
poet's disappearance is one honorable response.

Notes

1. As Bloom says, "The scandal is the stubborn resistance of imaginative literature to the categories of sacred and secular. If you wish, you can insist that all high
literature is secular, or, should you desire it so, that all strong poetry is sacred.
What I find incoherent is the judgment that some authentic literary art is more
sacred or more secular than some other. Poetry and belief wander about together
and apart, in a cosmological emptiness marked by the limits of truth and of
meaning" (4).

2. Another collection of poems from about the same time which reveals a
similar objectivist influence is Michael Heller's *Knowledge*.

Works Cited

Auster, Paul. *The Art of Hunger and Other Essays: Essays, Prefaces, Interviews.* Los
    Angeles: Sun & Moon Press, 1992.

———. *City of Glass*. Los Angeles: Sun & Moon Press, 1985.

———. *Disappearances: Selected Poems*. Woodstock, N.Y.: Overlook Press, 1987.

———. *In the Country of Last Things*. New York: Viking, 1987.

———. Letter to the author, 15 Oct. 1988.

———. *The Locked Room*. Los Angeles: Sun & Moon Press, 1986.

———. *Unearth*. Weston, Conn.: Living Hand, 1974.

Benjamin, Walter. "Theses on the Philosophy of History." In *Illuminations*. Trans. Harry Zohn. New York: Schocken Books, 1968. Pp. 253–264.

Bloom, Harold. *Ruin the Sacred Truths: Poetry and Belief from the Bible to the Present*. Cambridge: Harvard University Press, 1989.

Feld, Ross. *Plum Poems*. New York: Jargon Society, 1972.

Heller, Michael. *Knowledge*. New York: Sun, 1979.

Oppen, George. *Collected Poems*. New York: New Directions, 1975.

Sontag, Susan. *Against Interpretation and Other Essays*. New York: Farrar, Straus and Giroux, 1966.

Steiner, George. "Our Homeland, the Text." *Salmagundi* 66 (Winter–Spring 1985): 4–25.

Stevens, Wallace. *The Palm at the End of the Mind*. New York: Knopf, 1971.

"The Hunger Must Be Preserved at All Cost": A Reading of *The Invention of Solitude*

Derek Rubin

> It was once rumored that the Messiah was about to appear. So the Chelmites, fearing that he might bypass their town, engaged a watchman, who was to be on the lookout for the divine guest and welcome him if he should happen along.
>
> The watchman meanwhile bethought himself that his weekly salary of ten gulden was mighty little with which to support a wife and children, and so he applied to the town elders for an increase.
>
> The rabbi turned down his request. "True enough," he argued, "that ten gulden a week is an inadequate salary. But one must take into account that this is a permanent job."
>
> — Yiddish folktale (Howe and Greenberg 626)

The future of Jewish-American literature has been a controversial issue for some time. It goes back at least to the publication of Philip Roth's *Goodbye, Columbus* (1959), when Irving Howe argued in a review of the book that Roth "is one of the first American Jewish writers who finds . . . almost no sustenance in the Jewish tradition" ("The Suburbs of Babylon," 37). Howe suggested that, since for a younger writer like Roth memories of the Jewish-immigrant culture and way of life were fading, "[i]t is possible that [his book] signifies . . . the closing of an arc of American Jewish experience" (37). He concluded that if that was indeed the case it was "a saddening thought, since it is hard to see what new sources of value are likely to replace the Yiddishist tradition and the American Jewish *milieu* at its best" (37–38). In saying this, however, Howe seems to have forgotten that, as rich a literary source as the experience of first- and second-generation American Jews might have been, the Yiddishist tradition and the Jewish-immigrant milieu to which he refers constituted just one brief, if fascinating, moment in the long history of Jewish life and culture.[1] In fact, the sensibility of writers like Daniel Fuchs, Henry Roth, Saul Bellow, and Bernard Malamud was arguably shaped, at least partly, by age-old Jewish values and ideals that ran far more deeply than the immediate experiences that figured in their fiction. Given this, there would seem to be no reason to expect that third- and fourth-generation American Jews, in spite of their vastly different experience, would not find sustenance in some of the same values that underlie the work of their predecessors. A brief look at Paul Auster's *The Invention of Solitude* (1982) will bear this out convincingly.

Auster, as we learn in this autobiographical work, is a third-generation American Jew whose grandparents immigrated to the United States from Eastern Europe. Like most of the members of his generation, he is on the surface fully Americanized. He tells us that he was "brought up as an American boy, who knew less about my ancestors than I did about Hopalong Cassidy's hat" (28). And yet Auster's Jewishness figures in a variety of prominent ways in *The Invention of Solitude*. For example, there is the centrality of the past: "[T]he Auster of *Solitude* centers himself through a historical search," writes Dennis Barone (32) — and crucial to that historical search is Auster's Jewish past: his own private past, that of his family, and that of the Jewish people as a whole. There is also the importance of Scripture — of specific texts from the Old Testament, but also of the concept of the Book itself, and of the act of commentary or interpretation, all of which are central to Jewish life, religion, and culture. And then, at the core of Auster's character, of his perception of the self and of the individual's relation to the world around him, is the characteristically Jewish trait of longing, of yearning, of "hunger."[2] It is upon this latter quality that I will focus here, since, perhaps more than any of the other aspects of the book, it links Auster in a fundamental way to his Jewish past and to earlier Jewish-American writers.

Hunger, in the sense in which it figures in *The Invention of Solitude,* is probably best defined by looking briefly at an essay by Isaac Rosenfeld entitled "The Fall of David Levinsky" (1952). Rosenfeld's essay, which is a review of Abraham Cahan's novel, *The Rise of David Levinsky* (1917), is particularly relevant to my argument, not only in that it helps us to understand a key Jewish quality in Auster's work, but also in that it defines this quality in relation to one of the earliest Jewish-immigrant novels, thereby emphasizing the link with an author of a later generation like Auster. In his discussion of *The Rise of David Levinsky* Rosenfeld describes the central trait of the protagonist as that of "hunger, in [a] broader, rather metaphysical sense of the term" (155). He explains how physical, spiritual, emotional, and sexual deprivation in Levinsky's youth made dissatisfaction an integral part of his character. This, he says, expresses itself in his adulthood both as "a yearning for fulfillment," and as "an organic habit" as a result of which "no satisfaction is possible" (155). In short, "[b]e-cause hunger is strong in him, he must always strive to relieve it; but precisely because it is strong, it has to be preserved" (155). Hunger, in the sense he is using it here, Rosenfeld explains, is thus

> not only the state of tension out of which . . . desires . . . spring; precisely because the desires are formed under its sign, they become assimilated to it, and convert it into the prime source of all value, so that the man . . . seeks to return to his yearning as much as he does to escape it. (156)

Now, it is this same kind of hunger that is also central to Auster's book, and which, one might argue, constitutes in it the "prime source of all value." I will first examine how this quality figures in *The Invention of Solitude,* and then discuss briefly in what way it can be said to be charac-teristically Jewish.

    *   *   *

As to how this kind of hunger figures in *The Invention of Solitude,* to begin with, each of the two sections of Auster's book, "Portrait of an Invisible Man" and "The Book of Memory," grows out of a profound dissatisfaction, which, as with David Levinsky, gives rise to a powerful yearning.

The immediate occasion for the first section is the sudden death of Auster's father. Auster's need to write this part of the book, however, goes back to his childhood, which was dominated by a lack of fatherly love and attention. His earliest memory, he tells us, is of his father's absence. "For the first years of my life he would leave for work early in the morning, before I was awake, and come home long after I had been put to bed. . . . From the very beginning," he writes, "it seems, I was looking for my father, looking frantically for anyone who resembled him" (20–21). His later memories, he tells us, are dominated by a craving for love, approval, and attention, which his father withheld from him. He describes how "I mulishly went on hoping for something that was never given to me — or given to me . . . rarely and arbitrarily. . . . It was not that I felt he disliked me," he writes. "It was just that he seemed distracted, unable to look in my direction. And more than anything else, I wanted him to take notice of me" (21). It is thus Auster's longing for a father who was often absent and whom he felt he never got to know that prompts him to write about him after his death. "If, while he was alive," he says, "I kept looking for him, kept trying to find the father who was not there, now that he is dead I still feel as though I must go on looking for him. Death has not changed anything. The only difference is that I have run out of time" (7).

If the driving force behind Auster's writing "Portrait of an Invisible Man" was his yearning to find his father, in "The Book of Memory" it was his yearning to find himself. This section of *The Invention of Solitude* springs from a crisis. It begins on Christmas Eve, 1979, not long after his father's death, with Auster in a state of extreme demoralization. Referring to himself in the third person, he describes how he was so at odds with himself that "[h]is life no longer seemed to dwell in the present . . . that even the horrors of the day, which ordinarily would have filled him with outrage, seemed remote to him" (76). At this point, he had been living alone in New York in a small room at 6 Varick Street for approximately nine months. In the course of the book we learn that not only his father, but his maternal grandfather, whom he loved dearly, also died recently. Moreover, he and his wife were separated not long ago, so that he fears that he has lost his beloved son Daniel, too. Indicative of his isolation and alienation is his reluctance to go out: he lives on the top floor and the elevator has been out of service for the last three days. He describes how, on the rare occasions that he does leave the building, upon returning he feels "as if he were being forced to watch his own disappearance, as if, by crossing the threshold of this room, he were entering another dimension, taking up residence inside a black hole" (77). Dissatisfied with the dark, aimless, and isolated existence he is leading in this small room, Auster longs to come to terms with himself. "These four walls hold only the signs of his own disquiet," he writes, "and in order to find some measure of peace in these surroundings, he must dig more and more deeply into himself" (78–79). To which he adds:

> The world has shrunk to the size of this room for him, and for as long as it takes him to understand it, he must stay where he is. Only one thing is certain: he cannot be anywhere until he is here. And if he does not manage to find this place, it would be absurd for him to think of looking for another. (79)

And so begins the process of self-examination that constitutes "The Book of Memory."

We have thus seen that the two sections of *The Invention of Solitude* have their origin in a sense of dissatisfaction, or deprivation, which gives rise to a yearning for fulfillment. But in what way can this yearning be said to be so strong that Auster strives to preserve it as much as he does to relieve it?

This becomes evident when we see how the concept of "solitude" figures in Auster's book. In order to do that, however, we first have to understand what he means by the term solitude.

Auster himself has explained this in an interview. His starting point in defining the term is a fundamentally solipsistic view of man, whereby he argues that "even if we're surrounded by others, we essentially live our lives alone: real life takes place inside us. . . . In the end," he explains, "we know who we are because we can think about who we are. . . . And this takes place in absolute solitude. It's impossible to know what someone else is thinking" ("Interview," 299). Auster argues, however, that, although we live alone, each man locked, as it were, within his consciousness, we still have a sense of belonging, of community, because "everything we are comes from the fact that we have been made by others" ("Interview," 300). Self-consciousness, he explains, is the act of "looking at ourselves. But we can only see ourselves because someone else has seen us first. In other words, we learn our solitude from others" ("Interview," 300). This implies, he says, "that you don't begin to understand your connection to others until you are alone. And the more intensely you are alone, the more deeply you plunge into a state of solitude, the more deeply you feel that connection. It isn't possible," he adds, "for a person to isolate himself from other people. No matter how apart you might find yourself in a physical sense . . . every thought in your head has been born from your connection with others" ("Interview," 301).

Turning now to how this concept figures in *The Invention of Solitude,* we see that each of the parts of the book focuses upon one aspect of the experience of solitude. The first part revolves around the idea of solipsism, of each person ultimately being alone. Or as Auster puts it: "It's about the question of biography, about whether it's in fact possible for one person to talk [about] another person" ("Interview," 292). The second part focuses upon the self, upon what one's solitude, or inner world, consists of. "I felt as though I were looking down to the bottom of myself," Auster says about this section of the book, "and what I found there was more than just myself—I found the world" ("Interview," 301). In both cases, Auster's book incorporates a concept, or fundamental perception, of human experience the consequence of which is that the yearning that forms the heart of each section must, by definition, remain unfulfilled.

As to the first section, its very title, "Portrait of an Invisible Man," reflects both Auster's yearning for fulfillment and his denial of its possibility as a means of preserving it. Within the narrative itself he states explicitly that his desire to know his father cannot be satisfied. "Impossible, I realize, to enter another's solitude" (19), he writes. And a little further on: "To recognize, right from the start, that the essence of this project is failure" (20). Of course, the task Auster has set himself is all the more elusive because of his father's extreme detachment, and inability or refusal, as Auster says, "to reveal himself under any circumstances" (7). Again and again Auster tries to capture the essence of this man who, as he puts it, "had managed to keep himself at a distance from life, to avoid immersion in the quick of things. He ate, he went to work, he had friends, he played tennis," Auster tells us, "and yet for all that he was not there. In the deepest, most unalterable sense, he was an invisible man" (7). It is precisely this extreme detachment of his father's which makes Auster's desire both to satisfy his hunger and to preserve it all the stronger.

In fact, this contradictory desire is so strong that it dominates, or perhaps one should say fuels, Auster's entire effort to write about his father before his memory fades away. For one thing, as he becomes increasingly aware of the absurdity of the task he has set himself, he writes,

> I have begun to feel that the story I am trying to tell is somehow incompatible with language, that the degree to which it resists language is an exact measure of how closely I have come to saying something important, and that when the moment arrives for me to say the one truly important thing (assuming it exists), I will not be able to say it. (32)

It is, however, not only in what Auster calls "the rift between thinking and writing" (32) that his yearning both to satisfy and to preserve his hunger is felt, but also in the dilemma posed by the act of writing itself. If he began writing "Portrait of an Invisible Man" in order to fulfill his yearning for his father, in time he finds that, because of the impossibility of his task, the actual process of writing has only increased the pain that gave rise to that yearning:

> There has been a wound, and I realize now that it is very deep. Instead of healing me as I thought it would, the act of writing has kept this wound open. . . . Instead of burying my father for me, these words have kept him alive, perhaps more so than ever. I not only see him as he was, but as he is, as he will be, and each day he is there, invading my thoughts, stealing up on me without warning. (32)

Yet, painful as the act of writing may be, Auster also dreads the moment when he will have to stop writing:

> The closer I come to the end of what I am able to say, the more reluctant I am to say anything. I want to postpone the moment of ending,

and in this way delude myself into thinking that I have only just begun, that the better part of my story still lies ahead. No matter how useless these words might seem to be, they have nevertheless stood between me and a silence that continues to terrify me. When I step into this silence, it will mean that my father has vanished forever. (65)

Thus, because of his need both to satisfy his hunger and to preserve it, Auster finds himself caught between his inability to assuage his pain through writing about his father and his fear of the pain of losing him when he stops writing about him. Hunger, both as the source of yearning and as its object, is clearly — to use Rosenfeld's phrase again — the prime source of all value in "Portrait of an Invisible Man."

This also holds for "The Book of Memory," where in his "attempt," as he puts it, "to turn myself inside-out and examine what I was made of" ("Interview," 292), Auster discovers not some core sense of self, but his past: memories of the people, the books, the events, and the places in his life that make up this self, and from which he had felt so detached. Just as in "Portrait of an Invisible Man" his father's "invisibility" made Auster's desire both to fulfill and to preserve his yearning for him all the stronger, so in "The Book of Memory" his demoralization and his sense of emptiness and purposelessness have the same effect. The worse he feels, the more intensely he yearns to come to terms with himself; yet the deeper he digs, the more elusive the self becomes as he increasingly discovers more of the outside world of which the self is made. "The Book of Memory" is therefore, indeed, as Auster has pointed out, both about being alone and about community ("Interview," 301). But just as his conception of the self makes it impossible for him to feel totally isolated, so it is also impossible for him to attain a sense of real community, predicated as it is upon the idea that man is ultimately alone. Here is how Auster formulates the lesson he learned:

As he writes, he feels that he is moving inward (through himself) and at the same time moving outward (towards the world). What he experienced, perhaps, during those few moments on Christmas Eve, 1979, as he sat alone in his room on Varick Street, was this: the sudden knowledge that came over him that even alone, in the deepest solitude of his room, he was not alone, or, more precisely, that the moment he began to try to speak of that solitude, he had become more than just himself. Memory, therefore, not simply as the resurrection of one's private past, but an immersion in the past of others, which is to say: history — which one both participates in and is a witness to, is a part of and apart from. (*Invention* 139)

A part of and apart from — Auster strives both to satisfy his great hunger and to preserve it.

*   *   *

Having seen how the kind of hunger that Rosenfeld identifies in *The Rise of David Levinsky* figures in *The Invention of Solitude,* the question now arises as to the sense in which this trait can be said to be particularly Jewish. Again Rosenfeld's essay is useful, for in it he explains how the "whole history [of the Jews] is marked by this twist" (157). Its significance, he says, lies in the fact that "it is not confined to single personalities like Levinsky, but is exactly repeated on an impersonal and much larger scale in Jewish history, religion, culture — wherever our tradition and its spirit find expression" (157). He gives as an example *Galut,* the Diaspora, which, he rightly points out, has played a dominant role in Jewish life throughout the ages: "the theme of the Return, of yearning for Eretz Israel, to which are linked Cabala and Messianism, modes of prayer and worship as well as modern political and social movements, so that the whole becomes," he says, "a compendium of Jewish activity per se" (157). Rosenfeld argues, however, that "the yearning for Israel runs through the Diaspora in no simple sense, as of a fixed desire for a fixed object" (157). Rather, "[i]t is a reflexive desire, turning on itself and becoming its own object. . . . Otherwise," he asks, "why the proscription of temporizing in *Galut,* of making any compromise with desire, no matter how small, even down to the obdurate and seemingly ridiculous prohibition of shaving the beard?" (157). And the answer to this is, of course, clear: "The hunger must be preserved at all cost" (157).

This age-old Jewish trait, which is so prominent in an immigrant like David Levinsky, also played a significant role in the experience of Cahan's successors, the authors of the second generation. Never entirely at home, whether in the world of their immigrant parents or in present-day America, their predicament as Jews and as intellectuals was also typically that of the exile. Yet, as various critics have argued, it was precisely by virtue of their not belonging that they became insiders. Paradoxically, their familiarity with the experience of alienation linked them in fundamental ways to their Jewish past, to the predicament of many Americans in the postwar era, to other modern writers and intellectuals, and indeed to a central aspect of the plight of modern man in general.[3] In short, as "specialist[s] in alienation" — to borrow Rosenfeld's telling phrase ("The Situation of the Jewish Writer," 123) — they too had to preserve their hunger at all cost.

This also holds for a third-generation American Jew like Auster; however, being fully Americanized and further removed from his immigrant roots, Auster certainly does not experience as acute a sense of difference and exclusion as did many of his predecessors. Yet, as we have seen in *The Invention of Solitude,* he still feels the same kind of hunger. It is interesting to note in this connection that in "Portrait of an Invisible Man" Auster himself suggests a link between this hunger and the Jewish experience of dispersion or exile. Referring to the impossible task he has set himself of finding his father, he writes: "Just because you wander in the desert, it does not mean there is a promised land" (32).

Needless to say, in arguing that this trait which Auster shares with his predecessors is particularly Jewish, it is important to bear in mind that it is not exclusive to the Jews. In fact, Rosenfeld points out that what he identifies as Levinsky's characteristically Jewish hunger is also found in the *American* attitude toward financial success. Because of this, he says, the story of the emptiness, of the sense of loss, and of the spiritual long-ing that Levinsky feels as he rises from poverty to great wealth in America, is at one and the same time a treatment both of the age-old Jewish theme of hunger, and, as Rosenfeld puts it, "of one of the dominant myths of American capitalism — [namely] that the millionaire finds nothing but emptiness at the top of the heap" (153). Indeed, Auster himself seems to be aware of a similar parallel between the yearning typical of the Dias-pora Jew and that characteristic of many Americans. Talking about the importance of baseball in his life, and about the depth of the dreams and longing it arouses in American children, Auster writes in "The Book of Memory" that

> In his own Jewish childhood, [he] can remember confusing the last words of the Passover Seder, "Next year in Jerusalem," with the ever-hopeful refrain of disappointed fandom, "Wait till next year," as if the one were a commentary on the other: to win the pennant was to enter the promised land. (117)

This hunger is, of course, a quality shared not only by Jews and Ameri-cans but by others as well. In the title essay of his book *The Art of Hunger* Auster identifies the same trait in the hero of *Hunger* (1890), a novel by the Norwegian writer Knut Hamsun. Discussing this character's self-imposed hunger Auster explains that:

> His fast . . . is a contradiction. To persist in it would mean death, and with death the fast would end. He must therefore stay alive, but only to the extent that it keeps him on the point of death. The idea of ending is resisted in the interests of maintaining the constant possibility of the end. ("The Art of Hunger," 13)

Auster argues that preserving our hunger, in a spiritual or metaphysical sense, is the only means we have of facing "death as we live it today: without God, without hope of salvation. Death as the abrupt and absurd end of life" (20). The hero of Hamsun's novel achieves this by "systematically unburden[ing] himself of every belief in every system, and in the end," says Auster, "by means of the hunger he has inflicted upon himself, he arrives at nothing. There is nothing to keep him going — and yet he keeps on going. He walks straight into the twentieth century" (20).

So, if the hunger at the center of *The Invention of Solitude* links Auster in a fundamental way to his Jewish past and to earlier Jewish-American writers, it also arguably lends to this book a wider significance as a work of contemporary literature. Or to put it another way: When Auster speaks to us of hunger in *The Invention of Solitude*, he is addressing us as a twentieth-century man and as an American, but he does so with such urgency, such insight, and such poignancy because he is addressing us also as a Jew.

Notes

1. Almost twenty years later Howe still expressed the same skepticism about the future of Jewish-American writing in an otherwise excellent introduction to a book he edited entitled *Jewish-American Stories* (16–17).

2. These Jewish aspects are certainly not unique to Auster's work. In his recent book, *The Ritual of New Creation*, Norman Finkelstein discusses them as characteristic of contemporary Jewish literature.

3. To the best of my knowledge, Isaac Rosenfeld was the first person to develop this idea in his comments on "The Situation of the Jewish Writer" (1944). For other interesting discussions of the subject, see Leslie Fiedler, "Saul Bellow"; Irving Malin, *Jews and Americans;* and Ruth R. Wisse, *The Schlemiel as Modern Hero.*

Works Cited

Auster, Paul. "The Art of Hunger" [1970]. Rpt. in *The Art of Hunger,* pp. 9–20.

———. *The Art of Hunger: Essays, Prefaces, Interviews.* Los Angeles: Sun & Moon Press, 1992.

———. "Interview." In *The Art of Hunger.* With Larry McCaffery and Sinda Gregory. Pp. 269–312.

———. *The Invention of Solitude.* New York: Penguin, 1988.

Barone, Dennis. "Auster's Memory." *Review of Contemporary Fiction* 14.1 (1994): 32–34.

Fiedler, Leslie. "Saul Bellow" [1957]. Rpt. in *The Collected Essays of Leslie Fiedler,* 2 vols. Vol. 2. New York: Stein, 1971. Pp. 56–64.

Finkelstein, Norman. *The Ritual of New Creation: Jewish Tradition and Contemporary Literature.* Albany, N.Y.: State University of New York Press, 1992.

Howe, Irving. "Introduction." In Howe, ed., *Jewish-American Stories.* New York: Mentor-NAL, 1977. Pp. 1–17.

———. "The Suburbs of Babylon" [1959?]. Review of *Goodbye, Columbus,* by Philip

Roth. Rpt. in Howe, *Celebrations and Attacks: Thirty Years of Literary and Cultural Commentary.* London: Deutsch, 1979. Pp. 35–38.

Howe, Irving, and Eliezer Greenberg, eds. *A Treasury of Yiddish Stories* [1954]. New York: Schocken, 1973.

Malin, Irving. *Jews and Americans.* Carbondale, Ill.: Southern Illinois University Press, 1965.

Rosenfeld, Isaac. "The Fall of David Levinsky" [1952]. Review of *The Rise of David Levinsky,* by Abraham Cahan. Rpt. in Shechner, *Preserving the Hunger.* Pp. 152–159.

———. "The Situation of the Jewish Writer" [1944]. Rpt. in Shechner, *Preserving the Hunger.* Pp. 121–123.

Shechner, Mark, ed. *Preserving the Hunger: An Isaac Rosenfeld Reader.* Detroit: Wayne State University Press, 1988.

Wisse, Ruth R. *The Schlemiel as Modern Hero* [1971]. Chicago: University of Chicago Press, Phoenix Edition, 1980.

The Detective and the Author: *City of Glass*

Madeleine Sorapure

> The form trusts too much in transcendent reason.
> — Geoffrey Hartman, "The Mystery of Mysteries"

Readers of detective fiction typically admire the interpretive skill of the detective, who, in the midst of mysterious, misleading, and disparate clues, is able to discern logical and necessary connections leading invariably to the solution of the mystery. Part of the strong appeal of detective fiction, critics have suggested, is that readers can identify with the detective and achieve interpretive victory alongside him, or closely on his heels. Glenn W. Most, for example, comments that the detective serves as "the figure for the reader within the text, the one character whose activities most closely parallel the reader's own" (348). In the method he applies to the puzzling text that confronts him, the detective is indeed a kind of exemplary reader, correctly interpreting ambiguous or misleading signs and establishing what Frank Kermode has described as a tight "hermeneutic fit" (187).

And yet, the emphasis on the correctness of the detective's interpretation clearly indicates that it is the author who functions in detective fiction as the exemplary figure, the true master. The author constructs the puzzle that the detective eventually solves, and while we are guided by the detective and may marvel at his superior interpretive skills, the detective's success is, of course, measured by the accuracy with which he recuperates the "transcendent reason" of the author, composing the events he has experienced into a comprehensive plot that matches that of the author. Often in detective fiction we see precisely this at the end of the story: the detective recaps the entire proceedings, charting the true significance of the clues and characters he has encountered. Establishing causality and eliminating ambiguity, the detective presents his own "authorial" ability to unite disparate elements into a formal coherence. Indeed, we can say that the detective is successful only insofar as he is able to attain the position of the author, a metaphysical position, above or beyond the events in the text.

No doubt, the satisfaction of reading traditional detective fiction — of both the classic British and the "hard-boiled" American type — derives from the implicit assurance that detective and reader will eventually ascend to the position of the author. Recent anti-detective fiction, however, denies this satisfaction and instead portrays the detective's frustrated pursuit of authorial knowledge. William Spanos, in "The Detective and the Boundary," describes the anti-detective story (and its psychoanalytic analogue) as "the paradigmatic archetype of the postmodern literary imagination"; its purpose is "to evoke the impulse to 'detect' . . . in order to violently frustrate it by refusing to solve the crime" (154). In Thomas Pynchon's *The Crying of Lot 49*, for example, Oedipa Maas doggedly pursues leads, constructs plots, analyzes seemingly insignificant clues. In short, she does everything a good detective should do, but is unable to solve the mystery, and is left at the end to simply wait for a solution that may or may not present itself. This novel, like most anti-detective fiction, calls into question not the abilities or efforts of the individual detective, but rather the methodology of detection itself, a methodology that valorizes the powers of reason in the face of mystery, that validates the hermeneutic enterprise, and most importantly, that allows for an authoritative position outside the events themselves from which omniscient knowledge is attainable: in short, the position and knowledge of the author, toward which detective and reader strive.[1]

Spanos and others have elaborated the critique, offered in anti-detective fiction, of the methodology and presuppositions of the traditional detective novel.[2] Paul Auster's *City of Glass*, the first novel in *The New York Trilogy*, refocuses this critique on the function of the author in the discourse of detective fiction. Like other reflexive or self-conscious novels, *City of Glass* incorporates a formal and thematic questioning of authorship and authority, analyzing what Michel Foucault, in "What Is an Author?," has described as the "author-function," the particular position the author occupies within a discourse and the particular kinds of knowledge made available by the author's position and activity.

City of Glass could be awkwardly described, then, as a "meta-anti-detective" story. Within the novel are several characters who are simultaneously authors and detectives, or more precisely, who are authors who choose to play the role of detective. This configuration — professional author–amateur detective — is not unusual. Indeed, we perceive a certain continuity between the activities of writing and investigating, which may explain the frequency with which, in fiction, authors find themselves playing detective and detectives find themselves "playing author" by writing about their adventures. The two pursuits are, we assume, complementary. In *City of Glass*, however, author-characters who take on the role of detective are forced to radically revise their understanding of both authorship and detection.

A schematic description of the plot of *City of Glass* makes clear its focus on the relationship between authorship and detection. The main character, Daniel Quinn, is an author of conventional, moderately popular detective stories. Through a chance event — he is mistaken for "Paul Auster," who, in the novel, is an author who is mistaken for a detective — Quinn becomes involved in what initially seems to be a fairly simple case. He is hired (as "Auster") by Peter and Virginia Stillman to guard them from Peter's father, recently released from jail. It seems that the elder Peter Stillman had served twenty years in prison for abusing his son in a bizarre language deprivation experiment: he had wanted to discover the "original language of innocence" (76), and so for seven years he kept his son isolated from human speech and contact. Now Virginia and Peter fear that he plans to kill them, and Quinn's job is simply to keep the elder Stillman away from them. However, Quinn soon realizes that Stillman has no intention of menacing his son and daughter-in-law; instead, Stillman pursues investigations for a treatise on the establishment of a new Tower of Babel. His investigations consist of collecting broken items off the sidewalks of New York and giving them names, and Quinn's investigations consist of following Stillman and recording his activities. At a point when Quinn is particularly troubled by Stillman's odd behavior, he contacts "Paul Auster," who is unable to help with the Stillman case and who instead describes his own project of literary detection, his inquiry into the true authorship of *Don Quixote*. Quinn keeps a record of his detective pursuits in a red notebook, which another writer, the narrator (a friend of "Auster"), pieces together into what promises but ultimately fails to be a hard-boiled detective novel, *City of Glass*.

All of the author-characters in the novel — Quinn, Stillman, "Auster," and the narrator — try to apply the logic of the traditional detective story to their experiences as detectives, and instead realize, in varying degrees, the inadequacy and inaccuracy of the genre's presuppositions. Thus, rather than depicting detectives who invariably attain authorial omniscience, the novel presents author-characters whose experiences return them to the detective's ground-level, fragmented, and imperfect understanding.

The opening lines of *City of Glass* initiate its consistent critique of authorship in traditional detective fiction. Typically, the beginning of a detective story offers a piece of information whose significance is that it sets in motion the series of meaningful events that make up the detective story; the plot is already contained, as a germ or seed, in the beginning. The beginning of *City of Glass* draws out these expectations in order to examine their implications.

> It was a wrong number that started it, the telephone ringing three times in the dead of night, and the voice on the other end asking for someone he was not. Much later, when he was able to think about the things that happened to him, he would conclude that nothing was real except chance. But that was much later. In the beginning, there was simply the event and its consequences. (3)

Perhaps the most striking feature of this beginning is the way it draws attention to the distinction between retrospection — "much later . . . he would conclude" — and the experience in the present — "In the beginning, there was simply the event and its consequences." Typically, this distinction would indicate that although the significance of the wrong number isn't apparent when it actually takes place, its full importance will become clear in retrospect, after the mystery has been solved. As Quinn observes, theorizing from his own experience of writing detective novels, "a sense of plenitude and economy" (15) converge in the detective story because all details, and particularly those in the opening pages, have the potential to be significant. He comments that, "since everything seen or said, even the slightest, most trivial thing, can bear a connection to the outcome of the story, nothing must be overlooked" (15).

In *City of Glass*, however, the authority invested in the retrospective view is undermined at the same time as it is evoked. As the narrator comments, Quinn's retrospection causes him to conclude that "nothing was real except chance" (3). In other words, the beginning, and much that transpires after the beginning, is pure chance, not the fortuitous coincidence that we typically encounter in detective stories. For example, William Stowe observes that in the works of Raymond Chandler "coincidences don't just happen. Marlowe puts himself in the right place at the right time and opens himself to them" (378). In *City of Glass*, however, chance events are not redeemed by eventual fulfillment in a final, well-plotted solution. An event that is pure chance can neither be predicted by prior events nor prefigure subsequent events. Retrospection, which establishes causal connections from a perspective outside or beyond the events themselves, stumbles over a chance event, which is neither result nor omen.

Thus, from the start, the connection between events in *City of Glass* differs from that which we would expect to find in a detective story. Consider Sherlock Holmes's comments to Watson at the end of *The Hound of the Baskervilles*:

"The whole course of events," said Holmes, "from the point of view of the man who called himself Stapleton was simple and direct, although to us, who had no means in the beginning of knowing the motives of his actions and could only learn part of the facts, it all appeared exceedingly complex." (235)

Chance, which governs Quinn's adventures, plays no part in Sherlock Holmes's understanding of mystery. For Holmes there is a fundamental, "simple and direct" pattern underlying the only apparently complex or random events. And so, with the solution inherent in the beginning, the detective plays the part of an archaeologist, charting the significance of the crime's clues or artifacts, items that cannot *not* be meaningful and that call out to be interpreted and fit into their proper pattern. The narrative of detection directs us to a mode of interpretation that operates, in a sense, in reverse — from the corpse back to the criminal.

Read in reverse, however — with the end of the story providing the explanation for the myriad details and diversions along the way — *City of Glass* presents a new complication. Toward the end of the novel we realize that the story has been told not by an omniscient author but by a narrator who is himself a character in the story, and who is, like Quinn, engaged in a detective's activity of piecing together the facts of a case, Quinn's case. The narrator, although present throughout the novel in its particular style and construction, explicitly reveals his part only toward the end, when he begins to address the reader directly to comment on the difficulty of confirming certain facts and dates in Quinn's experiences. The narrator's comments at the end of the novel reveal him to be a detective who follows the clues closely and claims to avoid making any personal interventions or distortions in the case. He is the kind of detective that Quinn was at the beginning of the Stillman case. The narrator comments, "There were moments when the text was difficult to decipher, but I have done my best with it and have refrained from any interpretation" (202). And again, "Since this story is based entirely on facts, the author feels it his duty not to overstep the bounds of the verifiable, to resist at all costs the perils of invention" (173). But what he is unable to discover and unwilling to invent are crucial matters in the context of the detective story he writes; it is not simply a matter of tying up loose ends and resolving marginal issues. Left unanswered are decisive questions: Is a crime committed? What happens to the potential victim? What happens to the suspected criminal? Finally, what happens to the detective himself? *City of Glass* dramatizes the thorough failure of the narrator-detective to answer these centrally important questions and to solve the mystery. He fails, in essence, to become the author of a detective story. Having discovered the narrator's inability to pose a solution or even a crime, we return to the beginning of the novel and see not the inevitability of the solution but the inevitably widening horizon of the mystery. There is not, as with Sherlock Holmes, apparent confusion or seeming complexity at the start; instead, relative clarity and stability mark the onset of Quinn's experiences and their narration.

With the unpromising material from Quinn's red notebook, the narrator has attempted to tell Quinn's story in the mode of a hard-boiled detective novel, a mode that is clearly better suited to Quinn's predicament than the puzzle format of classic detective fiction. Critics have commented on the difference between hard-boiled and classic detective fiction, between Chandler and Doyle, in terms of the way they approach mystery. William Stowe remarks that Chandler's fiction moves away from "the methodical *solution* of 'mysteries' toward the philosophical understanding of mystery" (382). The classic detective novel glorifies the powers of reason in overcoming a mystery that is always only apparent. The hard-boiled novel, on the contrary, portrays its hero as, in Stefano Tani's words, "a man who accepts and endures absurdity, the sudden twists to which an unpredictable reality subjects him in his unrewarding job, which he sticks to anyway, Sisyphus-like" (24).

Though this description suits Quinn perfectly, his experiences and attributes take the features of the hard-boiled detective to curious extremes. His commitment to the case is absolute, but so much so that he continues working on it, "Sisyphus-like," even after the potential criminal is probably dead and after the client has apparently left town. In addition, one of Quinn's most distinguishing characteristics, and one which immediately suggests the difficulties he will have as a hard-boiled detective, is his desire to "lose himself," to imagine and assume alternative identities. The mystery is, in this sense, in Quinn himself, in his "lost" self, or rather, in his efforts *not* to find himself, to keep his thoughts only on the surface of himself and his world. This is, of course, highly incongruous with the behavior of the traditional detective, whose persona is a generally consistent one. Part of the tension of the hard-boiled style is that the detective's intervention seems to inaugurate violence and additional crime, so that the detective seems linked to both the legal and the criminal sides of society. But the hard-boiled detective remains on the side of the law, and the tension is resolved in his ultimate commitment to right over wrong. The detective must, it is clear, be a fairly consistent figure with conventional and predictable values in order for him to be able to focus on the mystery that exists outside of him. If a degree of uncertainty exists in the detective's very identity, as it does to a great extent with Quinn and other "anti-detectives," it will interfere with his ability to resolve the mystery at hand.

In this sense, Auster's *City of Glass*, like *The Crying of Lot 49*, would fit into Stefano Tani's category of the "deconstructive anti-detective novel," in which

> reality is so tentacular and full of clues that the detective risks his sanity as he tries to find a solution. In a very Poesque way, the confrontation is no longer between a detective and a murderer, but between the detective and reality, or between the detective's mind and his sense of identity, which is falling apart, between the detective and the "murderer" in his own self. (76)

Detection becomes a quest for identity, as the mystery outside releases the mystery inside the detective. Ultimately, as Tani observes, the deconstructive anti-detective novel calls into question the very notion of a stable, consistent self upon which detection and authorship are both predicated.

In Quinn's description of the "triad of selves" through which he writes detective stories, we see his desire to assume different identities and thus "lose" himself. Quinn publishes under the pseudonym William Wilson, a name which, in itself and in its reference to Edgar Allan Poe's short story, reverberates in terms of doubled and potentially antagonistic identities. Tani comments that Poe's "William Wilson" highlights the doubled, divided status of the artist, the paradox of creativity in which "creation implies destruction, ultimately destruction of the artist himself" (14). By "becoming" William Wilson, itself a fractured persona, Quinn creates his detective hero, Max Work. And just as the narrator of *City of Glass* feels a close affinity and admiration for Quinn ("He will be with me always" [203]), Quinn feels closely allied to Max Work:

> Whereas William Wilson remained an abstract figure for him, Work had increasingly come to life. In the triad of selves that Quinn had become, Wilson served as a kind of ventriloquist, Quinn himself was the dummy, and Work was the animated voice that gave purpose to the enterprise. And little by little, Work had become a presence in Quinn's life, his interior brother, his comrade in solitude. (11–12)

For Quinn, writing involves not only multiplication of his "selves" but also self-negation, as he becomes a ventriloquist's dummy through which other forces speak. As an author, Quinn identifies strongly with his detective, Max Work, and even feels Work "working" and speaking through him.

> It was not precisely that Quinn wanted to be Work, or even to be like him, but it reassured him to pretend to be Work as he was writing his

books, to know that he had it in him to be Work if he ever chose to be, even if only in his mind. (16)

What happens to Quinn, of course, is that he *is* called on to be a detective in a hard-boiled novel, to play the role of Max Work. In the process of becoming a detective in an "actual" mystery, and in attempting to apply the methods of his fictional hero to a "real" situation, Quinn comes to realize the inadequacy of the principles that inform Work's actions and ideas.

Quinn's author-detective persona becomes even more fragmented as he gets involved in the Stillman case. He is hired as "Paul Auster," and Quinn soon discovers that the effect of operating as "Auster" is similar to the effect of writing as William Wilson/Quinn/Max Work. The narrator tells us that although Quinn "still had the same body, the same mind, the same thoughts, he felt as though he had somehow been taken out of himself, as if he no longer had to walk around with the burden of his own consciousness" (82). For Quinn, the name "Auster" is a "husk without content. To be Auster meant being a man with no interior, a man with no thoughts" (98). There is clearly a certain amount of self-conscious play here on the effect of being "Auster," as the name of the author is charac- terized by emptiness and anonymity. But perhaps more importantly, as Quinn assumes another identity it serves to keep him operating entirely on the surface, to prohibit any introspection. "As Auster he could not summon up any memories or fears, any dreams or joys, for all these things, as they pertained to Auster, were a blank to him. He consequently had to remain solely on his own surface, looking outward for sustenance" (98–99). Part of the work of the detective is, of course, to attend to the surface, to clues and appearances, but only in order to arrive at the true meaning which appearances disguise. The methodology of detection corresponds to a mode of reading predicated on the metaphorics of "depth," a semantic or symbolic depth that the interpreter brings to the surface. As a writer of detective fiction, Quinn had always assumed that "the key to good detective work was a close observation of details. The more accurate the scrutiny, the more successful the results" (105). As a detective, though, Quinn seems satisfied to attend to the surface, seeing it as an end in itself, a means of escape from his troubling memories. When he is compelled to go beyond the surface, to derive some insight from his observations, to hypothesize about underlying meaning, Quinn finds that things don't "yield themselves" in reality as easily as they are made to in fiction.

To be sure, Quinn's knowledge about crime and detection is wholly conditioned by their representations in films, books and newspapers, but while this knowledge serves him well as an author, Quinn's reliance on the literary model of detection gradually declines as he sees its inadequacy in an "actual" situation. At first, Quinn doesn't feel handicapped by the fact that he has no knowledge of real crime and detection, for "what interested him about the stories he wrote was not their relation to the world but their relation to other stories" (14). He approaches the Stillman case as if it were more or less another story, and he feels that he can solve it by applying the same principles that he applied in the fictional world of his detective stories. In a certain sense, he can best be a detective by remaining an author.

But in Quinn's first act as a detective he encounters a situation in which the fictional detective's tools of observation, deduction, and intuition are thoroughly inoperable. Quinn goes to Grand Central Station to meet Stillman's train and to begin tailing him. Things go smoothly, and Quinn soon sees Stillman, recognizing him from an old photograph that Virginia Stillman had provided. But then, in a bizarre twist, Quinn sees a second man who is also Stillman, or who looks as much like Stillman as the first man. The first Stillman is dressed shabbily and seems slightly dazed, whereas the second Stillman has a prosperous and confident air about him, but both are or could be Stillman, and Quinn must decide which of the two to follow as they begin to go off in different directions. "There was nothing he could do now that would not be a mistake. Whatever choice he made — and he had to make a choice — would be arbitrary, a submission to chance. Uncertainty would haunt him to the end" (90). This first decision Quinn faces as a detective is one in which, while it seems that there can be a correct choice, there can be no choice based on the logical or rational procedures typical of the detective. The principles of Max Work with which Quinn had armed himself simply don't apply in a "real" dilemma, nor does intuition come to the rescue. Quinn follows the second Stillman for a few steps, then abruptly decides to follow the first Stillman, not for any reason but "acting out of spite, spurred on to punish the second Stillman for confusing him" (90). After this, the novel contains no more references to the mysterious second Stillman, although he haunts the subsequent proceedings in the form of a continually menacing alternative to Quinn's entire enterprise.

After a number of days of following the man who he has decided is Stillman, and unable to see any sense in his strange behavior, Quinn begins to realize that the case isn't developing as it should, or rather, that the case isn't developing as a story would. As Quinn knows from writing and reading detective fiction, "the detective is one who looks, who listens, who moves through this morass of objects and events in search of the thought, the idea that will pull all these things together and make sense of them" (15). But Quinn finds himself unable to do this in the midst of Stillman's truly puzzling behavior. Stillman's daily activity is to walk in a seemingly aimless manner — or rather, to shuffle or stumble — through the streets of New York. He stops every now and then to pick up an object lying on the sidewalk, examine it closely, and either put it in a large bag he carries with him or put it back on the sidewalk. Those objects that Stillman decides to keep — among them a broken umbrella, the head of a rubber doll, a torn photograph, leaves and twigs, and "sundry other clumps of flotsam" (95) — he also writes about in a small red notebook that he carries with him. Stillman's behavior confounds Quinn's belief that "human behavior could be understood, that beneath the facade of gestures, tics, and silences, there was finally a coherence, an order, a source of motivation" (105).

After thirteen days of shadowing Stillman, in a manner reminiscent of the narrator in Poe's "The Man of the Crowd," Quinn begins to question the purpose of the entire project. "Little by little, Quinn began to feel cut off from his original intentions, and he wondered now if he had not embarked on a meaningless project" (95). If Stillman is, as he indeed seems to Quinn, a slightly demented but harmless old man, then following him on a junk-collecting tour of New York is a waste of Quinn's time. But if Stillman's actions are motivated by some extremely complex and devious plot, then Quinn's skills as a detective are being greatly tested. Quinn's dilemma recalls that of Oedipa Maas in *The Crying of Lot 49*: either connections and correspondences are purely accidental, or they are evidence of a massive, extravagant plot. Finally, Quinn decides to believe that Stillman's actions are motivated by some larger and perhaps menacing design. "This view of the situation comforted Quinn, and he decided to believe in it, even though he had no grounds for belief" (97). He realizes that in deciding on this interpretation he is, in effect, coercing the potentially random and arbitrary facts of Stillman's behavior into a pattern, "ransacking the chaos of Stillman's movements for some glimmer of cogency" (108). That is, he acknowledges that detection is a form of "paranoia," the imposition of order or meaning on what may be pure accident. Quinn reads Stillman's actions as significant simply because he wants them to be significant: "He wanted there to be a sense to them, no matter how obscure. This, in itself, was unacceptable. For it meant that Quinn was allowing himself to deny the facts, and this, as he well knew, was the worst thing a detective could do" (108–109).

However, once Quinn decides to believe that Stillman's behavior is intentional, he seems to have little trouble discerning an underlying pattern. "For no particular reason that he was aware of" (105), Quinn begins to draw a map of Stillman's movements each day, relying on the extensive notes he had begun to keep four days into the case. Each day's map resembles a letter, and eventually the letters spell "OWER OF BAB." "The solution seemed so grotesque that his nerve almost failed him.

Making due allowances for the fact that he had missed the first four days and that Stillman had not yet finished, the answer seemed inescapable: THE TOWER OF BABEL" (111). "Discovering" this pattern has the effect not of satisfying Quinn but of horrifying him. "The whole thing was so oblique, so fiendish in its circumlocutions" (112) that it seems more an accident or a fluke than a consciously plotted and executed design by Stillman. Perhaps what is most disturbing to Quinn about this pattern is that, while intricate and seemingly premeditated, it seems to be completely without purpose.

Quinn does eventually learn Stillman's rationale for his strange behavior, but this does little to clear up the mystery. It seems that Stillman takes as his "project" to discover the principle by which words could correspond absolutely to the things they name; his goal is to fill the gap between signifier and signified by, in effect, reinstating the instrumental function of language. When things are no longer able to perform their functions, language as an instrument through which man names his world is distorted and falsified; when an umbrella breaks and is no longer able to function as an umbrella, to use one of Stillman's examples, we should not call it an umbrella, but we do. Because language has lost its instrumental function in a fallen or "broken" world, people can no longer master their words or their world; post-Edenic language "can no longer express the thing. It is imprecise; it is false; it hides the thing it is supposed to reveal" (122). So as Stillman traces out the letters "THE TOWER OF BABEL" on his walks through New York, he creates a symbolic new Tower as he retrieves and renames the broken and useless items he finds. He tells Quinn, "My samples now number in the hundreds — from the chipped to the smashed, from the dented to the squashed, from the pulverized to the putrid" (123). And Stillman gives these things names that reflect their new state, inventing "new words that will correspond to the things" (123) in order to reinstate man's mastery over language and over his world.

As an author, Stillman attempts to infuse words with meaning, and to secure that "real" meaning and guarantee the connection between the word and what it means by virtue of his "genius" (123), his God-like ability to endow broken things with their new and proper names. Of course, the absurdity of his project of renaming the garbage found on a particular configuration of New York's streets highlights the impossibility of an authorial practice that presupposes a true and instrumental language to which the author, as *deus artifex*, has special access. Stillman's project also calls into question the activity of the traditional detective, in his attempts to penetrate to the truth or essence behind appearances and to reform the corruption brought about by the introduction of evil into an otherwise benign world. The detective works to restore order and truth, to establish the correspondence between people's actions and their motivations, between the outward sign and its hidden or disguised signified. He searches for and always discovers a plot that infuses the world of the crime and gives meaning and coherence to the events within it. In solving the crime and re-establishing order, the detective relies on what Stillman has revealed as a certain conception of language that presupposes its adequacy to what it names. But the absurdity of Stillman's project reveals the extremes to which man will go — extremes that the novel suggests are naturalized in the form of the detective story — to escape his position in the midst of a broken world, operating with a broken language.[3]

Quinn's experiences as a detective, together with his exposure to Stillman's project, lead him to a very different understanding of detection and authorship by the end of the novel. Soon after his encounters with Stillman, for example, Quinn muses on the implications of the word "fate," a word that obviously has some importance in terms of the retrospection of the detective novel. Rather than thinking of fate as indicative of a predetermined, overarching design that directs actions, promises causality and inevitability and can be discovered retrospectively, Quinn comes to define fate as the condition of things as they are:

> Fate in the sense of what was, of what happened to be. It was something like the word "it" in the phrase "it is raining" or "it is night." What that "it" referred to Quinn has never known. A generalized condition of things as they were, perhaps; the state of is-ness that was the ground on which the happenings of the world took place. He could not be any more definite than that. But perhaps he was not really searching for anything definite. (170)

Quinn here reconceives of fate in a way that displaces the belief in a controlling or omniscient authority and instead sees it as descriptive of a ground-level perspective, characterized in this instance by the detective's immersion in the world of the text rather than the author's position above or beyond it. It is significant, too, that Quinn suggests his uneasiness with a model of detection that is satisfied only with definite answers and with fate in the traditional sense, as he comments that he may no longer be "searching for anything definite" (170).

Indeed, Quinn never does discover anything definite. For several months, he performs a twenty-four-hour-a-day stakeout of Virginia and Peter Stillman's apartment, even though they seem to have left town. In fact, Quinn soon loses interest in the Stillman case and instead applies his detective skills to his surroundings in the alley in which he now lives. He spends many hours staring up at the sky, measuring and deciphering the movements of the clouds, the changing colors of the sky, the effect of the wind. "These all had to be investigated, measured, and deciphered" (180). Again in an extreme version of detection, Quinn tries to connect truly unrelated ideas and to see some significance in their connection. For instance, he recalls that the center-fielder for the New York Mets, Mookie Wilson, has the real name of William Wilson, Quinn's own pseudonym as a writer. "Surely there was something interesting in that. Quinn pursued the idea for a few moments but then abandoned it. The two William Wilsons cancelled each other out, and that was all" (196). Or again, he tries to connect the fact that Stillman was arrested in 1969, the same year as America's first landing on the moon, and the same year as Christopher, the patron saint of travel, had been de-canonized by the pope. It seems that Quinn becomes drowned by the case, swamped by myriad, disparate, and unrelated details. He can no longer even distinguish those details that would be traditionally defined as significant from those that are insignificant and useless to his understanding of the case "as a case." Quinn's experiences highlight what William Spanos describes as the "ontological invasion,"

> a growing recognition of one of the most significant paradoxes of modern life: that in the pursuit of order the positivistic structure of consciousness, having gone beyond the point of equilibrium, generates radical imbalances in nature which are inversely proportional to the intensity with which it is coerced. (158)

For Quinn as well as for the narrator and Stillman, the impulse to establish order and certainty backfires, instead generating disorder and anxiety for the positivistic detective.

On a number of levels, then, *City of Glass* calls into question the presuppositions of the traditional detective novel, in which the detective aspires to and achieves a perspective above or beyond the case. Finally, the character of "Paul Auster" and the particular activity that this "Auster" performs in the novel contribute to its critique of authorship and detection. "Auster" is working on a speculative, imaginative, even "tongue-in-cheek" (150–151) interpretation of *Don Quixote,* focusing, as one might guess, on the issues of authorship that the work raises. As is well known, Cervantes insisted that he was no more than the editor of a translation of a text written in Arabic by Cid Hamete Benengeli. But according to "Auster" 's theory, "Benengeli" was actually the pseudonym for a collective of four characters in *Don Quixote*—Sancho Panza, the barber, the priest, and Samson Carrasco, the bachelor from Salamanca—who work together to cure Don Quixote of his madness by recording his absurd delusions, hoping to reveal to their friend the error of his ways by chronicling them for him. But in a final twist, "Auster" speculates that Don Quixote orchestrated the whole thing—his madness, the efforts of his friends—in order to have his name and his actions recorded for posterity. "Auster" even suggests that Don Quixote was himself the one who translated the tales from Arabic: "I like to imagine that scene in the marketplace at Toledo. Cervantes hiring Don Quixote to decipher the story of Don Quixote himself. There's a great beauty to it" (154).

"Auster"'s speculations about the authorship of *Don Quixote* clearly have reverberations for the model of authorship enacted in *City of Glass*. His theory, in effect, writes Cervantes entirely out of the picture. In place of the imaginative and complex structure attributed to Cervantes, "Auster" poses an equally imaginative and complex scheme of authorship contrived and executed by Don Quixote himself. In this scheme, Don Quixote serves as a kind of "center elsewhere" in the world of the work: completely visible throughout the work as its enigmatic main character, yet nowhere visible as its mastermind and master plotter.[4] In *City of Glass*, too, the author, like Don Quixote/Cervantes, disappears within a multilayered maze of fictional embodiments, the author-characters. Narrative authority is displaced, undermining the privileged path of access for the critic who attempts, much like the detective, to follow the author's intentions and design, but who finds instead Auster/Quinn fragmented within the text. At the same time, though, "Auster" as author/detective is able to chart a new path through *Don Quixote*. His activity as literary critic and "master reader" foreground the connections between detection and interpretation, revealing the critic as one who reconstructs an elusive text by uncovering an author-based plot that informs its structure.

"Auster"'s elaborate reading of *Don Quixote* suggests, in fact, that when one has discovered the *true* author of a work, one possesses the key to understanding the work. His interpretation can, in this sense, be applied to *City of Glass* itself to suggest an equally elaborate scheme in which "Auster" is the true author of the work. In this scheme, "Auster," perhaps to test his theory of *Don Quixote,* invented Quinn and wrote Quinn's red notebook himself, and then brought it to the narrator, with fictitious background information, in order to have him write a novel. It seems a perfectly plausible plot, and one that, like "Auster"'s interpretation of *Don Quixote,* would solve the mystery of *City of Glass* itself, neatly tying up the loose ends throughout the novel by suggesting that they are there because they are supposed to be there, as part of an elaborate parody of the detective novel in which, despite the narrator's best intentions and efforts, there is no crime, no solution, and, by the end, no hero. In this interpretation, the author ("Auster") seems to be situated in a position of even greater mastery and authority than in the traditional detective story — a kind of metamastery — standing behind not only the events and characters in the novel but the writing of the novel itself. However, this interpretation, suggested by the text of *City of Glass,* also implies that what the author knows and withholds from the reader is not the redeeming truth — the solution which puts the mystery to rest — but instead the fact that the whole thing is a sham, built on nothing, with Auster representing "Auster" constructing an elaborate hoax.

Finally, though, *City of Glass* is more than a sophisticated puzzle. The novel undermines a reading that would reinforce the interpretation of detective fiction in terms of a master plot, master plotter, and master reader. Here the space between Auster and "Auster," between the author and the author-character, is crucial. In that "meta" space — the space of metafiction, as it were — Auster stages a complex play with his name, simultaneously associating and dissociating himself and his mode of authorship with an author-character who is either a marginal character or the major figure, the master plotter.

Michael Holquist has suggested that "postmodernism exploits detective stories by expanding and changing certain possibilities in them" (165). But *City of Glass* doesn't merely expand or change a possibility, one among many, in detective fiction. As I've suggested, and as I think the novel demonstrates, the author-function in detective fiction provides the basis on which detective and reader can move with assurance through the text; positioned beyond the events of the text, the author, in effect, guarantees that there is such a position. *City of Glass,* however, insistently frustrates the efforts of its author-characters to achieve an author's perspective on the events in which they are engaged. The novel frustrates, as well, the reader's or critic's attempt to locate the real Paul Auster behind the scenes. The "Paul Auster" in the text is either (or simultaneously) a manipulative master plotter or a playful minor character. How, then, are we to figure the activity of his real-life model? Finally, the implications for criticism of detective fiction are clear: if, as Dennis Porter comments, "[t]he critic's essay is the report of an investigation leading up to the (re)construction of a literary work" (226), an essay on *City of Glass* is the report of the work's (de)construction of the investigation.

Notes

1. In this sense, Michael Holquist's characterization (in "Whodunit and Other Questions") of anti-detective fiction as "metaphysical" seems inaccurate. The defining characteristic of anti-detective fiction is, rather, that it refuses the detective access to a metaphysical position, a position, above or beyond the events he experiences, from which to discover their true meaning.

2. Spanos, "The Detective and the Boundary." See also Stefano Tani, *The Doomed Detective;* Michael Holquist, "Whodunit and Other Questions"; Frank Kermode, "Novel and Narrative"; and Dennis Porter, *The Pursuit of Crime,* especially chapter 13, "Antidectection" (245–259).

3. See Norma Rowen's "The Detective in Search of the Lost Tongue of Adam: Paul Auster's *City of Glass.*" Rowen reads *City of Glass* as a novel in which "the detective's quest becomes overtly and inextricably mingled with the search for the prelapsarian language" (225). In "Deconstructing *The New York Trilogy:* Paul Auster's Anti-Detective Fiction," Alison Russell offers a similar interpretation of the trilogy as a deconstruction of logocentrism, of a "language grounded in the metaphysics of presence" (72).

4. In "Structure, Sign and Play in the Discourse of the Human Sciences," Jacques Derrida describes this "center elsewhere" in terms which are quite resonant for a discussion of detective fiction:

> The concept of centered structure is in fact the concept of a play based on a fundamental ground, a play constituted on the basis of a fundamental immobility and a reassuring certitude, which itself is beyond the reach of play. And on the basis of this certitude anxiety can be mastered, for anxiety is invariably the result of a certain mode of being implicated in the game, of being caught by the game, of being as it were at stake in the game from the outset. (279)

As I have suggested, an anti-detective novel such as *City of Glass* calls into question the function of the author as "fundamental ground" and "reassuring certitude" in the world of the fiction. In doing so, it places detective and reader back in the game, implicated and at stake.

Works Cited

Auster, Paul. *City of Glass.* Los Angeles: Sun & Moon Press, 1985.

Derrida, Jacques. "Structure, Sign and Play in the Discourse of the Human Sciences." In *Writing and Difference.* Trans. Alan Bass. London: Routledge, 1978. Pp. 278–293.

Foucault, Michel. "What Is an Author?" In *Language, Counter-memory, Practice.* Ed. Daniel Bouchard. Trans. Bouchard and Sherry Simon. Ithaca, N.Y.: Cornell University Press, 1977. Pp. 113–138.

Doyle, Arthur Conan. *The Hound of the Baskervilles.* New York: Grosset and Dunlap, 1901.

Holquist, Michael. "Whodunit and Other Questions: Metaphysical Detective Stories in Postwar Fiction." In Most and Stowe, eds., *The Poetics of Murder.* Pp. 149–174.

Kermode, Frank. "Novel and Narrative." In Most and Stowe, eds., *The Poetics of Murder.* Pp. 175–196.

Most, Glenn W. "The Hippocratic Smile: John LeCarre and the Traditions of the Detective Novel." In Most and Stowe, eds., *The Poetics of Murder.* Pp. 341–365.

Most, Glenn W., and William Stowe, eds. *The Poetics of Murder: Detective Fiction and Literary Theory.* San Diego, Calif.: Harcourt Brace Jovanovich, 1983.

Porter, Dennis. *The Pursuit of Crime: Art and Ideology in Detective Fiction.* New Haven, Conn.: Yale University Press, 1982.

Pynchon, Thomas. *The Crying of Lot 49.* New York: Bantam, 1967.

Rowen, Norma. "The Detective in Search of the Lost Tongue of Adam: Paul Auster's *City of Glass*." *Critique* 32.4 (1991): 224–233.

Russell, Alison. "Deconstructing *The New York Trilogy:* Paul Auster's Anti-Detective Fiction." *Critique* 31.2 (1990): 71–84.

Spanos, William V. "The Detective and the Boundary: Some Notes on the Post-modern Literary Imagination." *boundary 2* 1.1 (1972): 147–168.

Stowe, William W. "From Semiotics to Hermeneutics: Modes of Detection in Doyle and Chandler." *The Poetics of Murder.* Pp. 366–384.

Tani, Stefano. *The Doomed Detective: The Contribution of the Detective Novel to Postmodern American and Italian Fiction.* Chicago: University of Chicago Press, 1984.

Auster's Sublime Closure: *The Locked Room*

Stephen Bernstein

In *The Locked Room,* as in the other novels of Paul Auster's *New York Trilogy,* the path the reader follows diverges considerably from what might be expected in conventional detective fiction. This is due to what are, by this stage in the trilogy, predictable recourses to narratorial unreliability, epistemological uncertainty, and existential contingency. As these strategies come into play in the trilogy's final volume, the trail leads neither toward nor away from a corpse, but instead into postmodern meditations on subjectivity, sexuality, sublimity, and silence. By engaging with the text's thematization of these concepts, we can begin to understand both *The Locked Room*'s location within the trilogy and the possibilities of closure which that place might be expected to confer.

It will be the purpose of this essay to discuss what Auster finally says "goodbye to" in the novel, why "[t]he entire story comes down to what happened at the end" (149). But since the figures for these ideas slip repeatedly into a realm of unspeakability, Auster's novels confer upon criticism some of the same limitations their protagonists realize for themselves. *The Locked Room* is finally Auster's powerful refusal to accede to the traditional category of closure, a refusal that makes repeated appeals to the sublime in order to frame its unimaginable task.

In order to examine Auster's text, a synopsis is useful. The novel's narrator is contacted by Sophie Fanshawe, whose husband has mysteriously disappeared. A friend of the narrator's in youth, Fanshawe has long since been out of touch with him. On the assumption that Fanshawe is dead, the narrator agrees to become his literary executor, getting novels, plays, and poetry into print and creating Fanshawe's posthumous reputation as an important, serious writer. The narrator is at this point notified by letter that Fanshawe is still alive but wishes to remain missing. For various reasons the narrator attempts to write Fanshawe's biography;

as a result he begins to lose his grip on reality. He gives up the study, and is subsequently summoned to the threshold of the room in which, it turns out, Fanshawe, still alive, is hiding. A conversation (through "double" doors) ensues in which Fanshawe claims to have taken a fatal dose of slow poison hours earlier. The doors are never opened; the two men never see one another. On his way home the narrator reads a notebook Fanshawe has left for him that, not surprisingly, fails to clear up the fundamental mysteries of Fanshawe's existence.

As nearly every critic of Auster notes, doubling is central to his fiction. Just as routinely it is the pivotal problem of *The Locked Room,* operating in a number of ways. The novel's nameless narrator establishes the semi-nameless Fanshawe as his alter ego from the novel's first paragraph:

> It seems to me now that Fanshawe was always there. He is the place where everything begins for me, and without him I would hardly know who I am. We met before we could talk, babies crawling through the grass in diapers, and by the time we were seven we had pricked our fingers with pins and made ourselves blood brothers for life. Whenever I think of my childhood now, I see Fanshawe. He was the one who was with me, the one who shared my thoughts, the one I saw whenever I looked up from myself. (7)

In its quiet way this opening is nothing less than a thematic tour de force: everything that will be of importance as the novel continues is already germinally present. The "seems" of the first sentence posits the tenuous nature of countless assertions in the novel; simultaneously Fanshawe's omnipresent relationship to consciousness is maintained. Fanshawe is further established as a "place," a prolepsis for the string of locked rooms, real and metaphorical, that will follow. The relationship of the two characters precedes language, a vital conception for the narrator's frequent questioning of linguistic presence, while the fingerpricking and mixing of blood signal not only the "brotherhood" of the doubles but also an incipient homoeroticism that will obtain in the novel's many sexual episodes. The irony of such a passage should be clear, of course: Auster offers up a textbook example of the opening paragraph's narrative plenitude, then goes on to call narrative structure into question through the arch-narrative of the detective quest. Though this problem will eventually engage us, for now it is important to establish the nature of the doubles' relationship in the novel.

Traditional cues toward doubling become common as the narrative proceeds; the narrator and Fanshawe become "one another's twin ghosts" (Saltzman 67). Fanshawe's mother relates that she "would sometimes confuse [them] from a distance," while a former lover of Fanshawe's meets the narrator with "an initial double take" (one of the novel's frequent puns), having mistaken him for Fanshawe (101, 143). Such examples could be multiplied indefinitely, but this is probably unnecessary given the context the trilogy provides. The more important issue is to see how the novel's doubling helps to motivate its plot, and how that plot, in turn, impinges on the doubling.

The problems *The Locked Room*'s narrator faces all center on Fanshawe's ghostly intervention into his life. As Fanshawe's literary executor he takes a certain amount of credit for Fanshawe's success ("it was probably necessary for me to equate Fanshawe's success with my own" [56–57]); he also eventually senses the horrifying pun on this appointment, that Fanshawe had "chosen me as his executioner" (113). The discrepancy between the two tasks thrusts the narrator into his detective project, the writing of Fanshawe's biography, which is only a "cover story" for his own investigation into the meaning of Fanshawe's disappearance. "It had become a private matter for me," he relates, "something no longer connected to writing. . . . All the facts I would uncover as I dug into his past . . . were the very things I would use to find out where he was" (112). Ironically it is in his absence that Fanshawe acts most directly on the narrator's life — he becomes the invisible force of inevitability, one very much like fate, guiding the narrator's movements and mental stability.

The existentialism lurking in the minds of many Auster characters conflicts with this last situation. The novel's narrator speaks almost obsessively of life's meaninglessness: "each life is no more than the sum of contingent facts, a chronicle of chance intersections, of flukes, of random events that divulge nothing but their own lack of purpose" (35); "[e]very life is inexplicable" (80); "[l]ives make no sense" (85). Posed against this almost nihilistic bravado is the unavoidable fact that the narrator's life is being steered by Fanshawe. The letter proving that Fanshawe is still alive directs the narrator to "say nothing to Sophie. Make her divorce me, and then marry her as soon as you can. . . . The child needs a father, and you're the only one I can count on" (66). Not surprisingly these events all come to pass within the next five pages. Though the narrator significantly claims that in proposing to Sophie he "was acting out of character," he goes on to admit "I couldn't help myself" (69). Later, when the narrator goes to France to try to learn more about Fanshawe's past, he discovers that while in the employ of a movie producer Fanshawe was offered acting work that he turned down. Within paragraphs the narrator notes that "no one was watching me anymore" and pronounces that "[t]he charade was over" (142). His rejection follows Fanshawe's, again demonstrating the invisible grasp Fanshawe exercises over the narrator's choices. Though Arthur Saltzman claims that the narrator is quick to "write himself into Fanshawe's place" (67), it is the exact opposite situation that appears to be the case. The novel takes place, we see, in Tony Tanner's "city of words," where the dream of an "unpatterned, unconditioned life" exists in provocative tension with "an abiding American dread that someone else is patterning your life, that there are all sorts of plots afoot to rob you of your autonomy of thought and action, that conditioning is ubiquitous" (15).

Sophie is actually quicker to see this than the narrator. On the eve of his departure for France she insists that he must forbear "bringing [Fanshawe] to life" (136), a resuscitation presumably taking place within the narrator's skin. By retracing Fanshawe's steps he begins to undergo a comparable breakdown in subjectivity. "Don't you see what's happening?" Sophie asks (137), but the narrator, who has acknowledged that as literary executor he is "no more than an invisible instrument" for Fanshawe (44), will only much later admit to having been "blinded by the book that had been written for me" (179). With his double as his scriptor the narrator actually loses the capacity for choice, for the manipulation of contingency, which he so boldly claims to have. "You are my friend, and my one hope is that you will always be who you are. With me it's another story," Fanshawe narratologically asserts in his early letter; in the next paragraph the narrator reports the sentence as "remain who you are" (67). What Fanshawe offers (however insincerely) as aspirational conjecture, the narrator understands as imperative. Such careless or misdirected reading is again foregrounded in the closing chapter, when the narrator says to Fanshawe "I thought you wanted to see me. That's what you said in your letter," to which Fanshawe replies "I said that I wanted to talk to you. There's a difference" (167). The narrator refers to the distinction as hair splitting, but this is merely a further dramatization of his difficulties with both linguistic specificity and interpretive accuracy.

If Fanshawe's writings — his manuscripts and letters — become a metawriting that scripts the course of the narrator's existence, then the narrator's early conception of Sophie's unhappiness ("No one wants to be part of a fiction, and even less so if that fiction is real" [47]) obtains just as clearly for himself. His homicidal urge ("I wanted to kill Fanshawe. I wanted Fanshawe to be dead, and I was going to do it. I was going to track him down and kill him" [109]) becomes thoroughly explicable as an attempt to thwart the fatalism he only hazily detects controlling his existence. Shortly before he gives voice to his murderous impulses, the narrator has claimed that "sexual desire can also be the desire to kill" (108). In fact, it is in the elision of sexual desire with a variety of other impulses in the novel that the problems of the narrator's relationship with — and to — Fanshawe are manifested most clearly.

From the mutual fingerpricking of childhood the narrator and Fanshawe go on to share several varieties of eroticized experience. As children they ask the narrator's mother "if it was possible for men to get married" (29); the boys want to live together "in a big house in the country" (*à la* Flower and Stone in *The Music of Chance*). This scene is certainly legible as merely the naive ramblings of the six-year-old mind, but later developments cast such a nonsexual interpretation into doubt. It is during their teens that the two boys go to a New York City brothel, "and it was there that we lost our virginity" (32). The locution employed here could, again, be read as implying nothing of a homoerotic bond, but the narrator's remark on the following page, that listening to Fanshawe and the prostitute "I could only think about one thing: that my dick was about to go into the same place that Fanshawe's was now" (33), makes the implication seem undeniable. "Things might have gone well for me if I hadn't been distracted by Fanshawe's shoes," he claims, " . . . but it was a long struggle, and even at the end I felt no real pleasure" (33).

Fanshawe's interference with the achievement of closure is notable here. On one level the intense homoeroticism causes near impotence in the narrator; at the same time the scene becomes a metaphor for the problematic of closure that will haunt the narrator as he continues to follow in Fanshawe's tracks. "[T]his is where the story should end," the narrator claims when Fanshawe's novels become a success (62), but the narrative goes on to belie such easy closure (admittedly seen as a "fairy tale" by the narrator [62]) with assertions that "it turns out that this is only the beginning," (62), "[s]tories without endings can do nothing but go on forever" (63), and (more than halfway through the novel) "[t]he worst of it began then" (111). New, botched beginnings fill the latter portion of the text, and even the final chapter finds the narrator meditating "that the story wasn't over" (160).

Following classic novelistic tradition, the narrator hopefully views marriage as closure. As he proposes to Sophie, "The uncertainty of the situation was impossible to live with, and I felt that I had to resolve things right then and there" (69). But Sophie, of course, is actually still married to Fanshawe at this point, is still his traditional "better half," and the narrator has earlier reported feeling "that Fanshawe was speaking through her" (19). The marriage, not to mention the couple's already well-advanced sexual relationship, works here as another sexual linking of the narrator with Fanshawe. "[H]e was inside me day and night," the narrator reports of Fanshawe shortly after the marriage takes place. Again the implications are multiple.

This theme reaches its most extreme stage as the narrator attempts to follow Fanshawe along yet a third vaginal trail, one that vaults the previously established sexual subtext to an overtly oedipal level. On a visit to study some of Fanshawe's letters the narrator finds himself in bed with still another Mrs. Fanshawe, Fanshawe's mother Jane. She emphasizes the doubling relationship ("You're the father of my grandson. . . . You're married to my son's wife" [101]), demonstrating at the same time a wish to substitute the narrator for the absent Fanshawe. "He wasn't half the boy you were," she says, and the stage is set for a moment of Faulknerian sexual truth. The narrator's version of Jane Fanshawe's logic is that "fucking me would be like fucking Fanshawe — like fucking her own son — and in the darkness of this sin, she would have him again — but only in order to destroy him. A terrible revenge" (101–102). Here the elision of sex and cruelty, indeed destruction, is what leads into the previously cited statements by the narrator concerning his desire to kill Fanshawe. "I had entered my own darkness," he observes, "and it was there that I learned the one thing that is more terrible than anything else: that sexual desire can also be the desire to kill, that a moment comes when it is possible for a man to choose death over life" (108). In this most literal and graphic attempt to trace Fanshawe's origins, the narrator accomplishes several things. Not only does he stand in for Fanshawe in Jane's fantasy of incestuous punishment, but he also transforms mother into son for his own purposes. "[G]rinding away at this woman as though I wanted to pulverize her," the narrator realizes that "she was no more than a shadow, and that I was using her to attack Fanshawe himself" (108, 109). But even as mother becomes son and phallus dagger, the narrator recovers his own adolescence when he happened to see Mrs. Fanshawe sunbathing topless in her back yard. The image becomes "the quick of late-night fantasies" (106), so that the narrator's masturbatory fantasy life is also intricately linked to Fanshawe.

Fanshawe has gone missing after telling Sophie "he was going to New Jersey for the afternoon to see his mother" (11). The sexual relationship between the narrator and Jane Fanshawe is thus yet another example of doubling, though a more shadowy one than those cited earlier. If Fanshawe disappears (putatively) while visiting his mother, the narrator does the same thing, since his intercourse with Jane is what immediately precedes his noting that "[t]he worst of it began then" (111). When Sophie complains to him, "You're going to vanish, and I'll never see you again" (137), she is merely noting the parallel, one which the narrator less consciously remarks in Paris when he finds that Fanshawe "was gone — and I was gone along with him" (149). The mutual disappearance follows yet another series of sexual episodes, episodes that by this point have degenerated into drunken debauchery. In Paris the narrator feels his "grip loosening" (139), the beginning of a descent into near amnesia, memories that "come back . . . in fragments when they come at all, bits and pieces that refuse to add up" (148). In *City of Glass* Quinn had eventually "arrived in a neverland of fragments" (113); now the narrator of *The Locked Room* makes a similar journey, in a narrative where *Neverland*

and *Blackouts* are both titles of Fanshawe's novels. Even in near dementia, then, the narrator's scripted life continues. Significantly, the fragments he recalls are sexual:

> I see myself prowling the rue Saint-Denis at night, picking out pros-
> titutes to sleep with, my head burning with the thought of bodies, an
> endless jumble of naked breasts, naked thighs, naked buttocks. I see
> my cock being sucked, I see myself on a bed with two girls kissing each
> other, I see an enormous black woman spreading her legs on a bidet
> and washing her cunt. (148–149)

By this point in the narrative the enormous black woman would appear to be a rather awkward gesture by the narrator to figure the immensity of the personal darkness he has entered. As before, Fanshawe's trail is one the narrator follows first with his penis, then (in the form of *The Locked Room*) with his pen. If sexuality precedes language in this way, then once more the narrator's attraction to Fanshawe is implied as we recall from the novel's opening paragraph that the two "met before we could talk" (7).

Shortly before his final sexual libertinism, the narrator sees that the terms of his investigation seem to have been altered. Looking around a house in the French countryside where Fanshawe had stayed years earlier, he remarks that

> Fanshawe was there, and no matter how hard I tried not to think about
> him, I couldn't escape. . . . Now that I had stopped looking for him, he
> was more present to me than ever before. The whole process had been
> reversed. . . . I felt as though I was the one who had been found. Instead
> of looking for Fanshawe, I had actually been running away from him.
> (147)

This inversion of detection finds a parallel later in the novel when Fanshawe describes how he got rid of Quinn, the detective Sophie had hired shortly after his disappearance. When asked how he got Quinn off his trail, Fanshawe replies, "I turned everything around. He thought he was following me, but in fact I was following him" (169). Though it works nicely as a metafictive description of the trilogy's organization, this statement is more usefully seen as a corroboration of the circular nature of the detective quest. And the considerably gothic atmosphere of Auster's novels also allows the two descriptions to fit into that genre's "homosexual panic," as Eve K. Sedgwick describes it in *Between Men*.

It is in the "paranoid gothic" of James Hogg's *Private Memoirs and Confessions of a Justified Sinner* that Sedgwick sees this strategy at work. Like

Auster's novel, Hogg's features a chase that becomes circular — two male characters (doubles as well) are constantly at one another's backs; the novel becomes one of several Sedgwick analyzes "about one or more males who not only is persecuted by, but considers himself transparent to and often under the compulsion of, another male" (91). But as Sedgwick points out, "the fact that it is about what we would today call 'homosexual panic' means that the paranoid Gothic is specifically not about homosexuals or the homosexual; instead, heterosexuality is by definition its subject" (116). The same might be said for Auster's novel; it is, after all, an ironically conventional love story as well, with a boy-meets-girl, boy-loses-girl, boy-gets-girl-back structure (perhaps — this matter is taken up below). What the narrator loses Sophie to, however, whether temporarily or permanently, is his attraction to Fanshawe, an attraction he acts out in consistently overstated scenes of heterosexual aggression.

But the novel's thematics are not limited to an investigation of a bipolar alternation between homo- and heterosexual drives. What we can take away most usefully from this aspect of the novel are two things: the fact that the narrator's narrative of homoerotic attraction to Fanshawe never achieves closure, and the fact that the homoerotic itself, as Sedgwick notes, "had, throughout the Judaeo-Christian tradition, been famous among those who knew about it at all precisely for having no name — 'unspeakable,' 'unmentionable,' 'not to be named among Christian men' " (94). This very move toward unspeakability actually combines with the problematics of closure to intensify the novel's focus on what initially seems to be an ancillary consideration, but which is actually one constantly threatening to become central to the narrative's concerns, the sublime. The darkness alluded to above toward the end of the narrator's Parisian exploits is mentioned on several other occasions. This is also an aspect of Auster's self-admitted debt to Hawthorne: his appropriation of the name Fanshawe not only clarifies the intertext, but the word includes in its last syllable the first syllable of both Hawthorne and Auster.[1] It is not my intention here to examine Auster's forays into American romanticism, but rather to point toward the nature of the darkness that he in part absorbs from Hawthorne, that nineteenth-century purveyor of "blackness" (Melville 2060).

Thus, in accordance with the gothic and romantic heritages he excavates so avidly, Auster's darkness is actually a subcategory of a more encompassing sublime in his novels. Indeed, an analysis of the role of the sublime in *The Locked Room* is essential for rounding out the contours of the novel's meditations on identity and writing. If the locked room mystery "is at least as old as the Gothic tale," and if the locked room is "among the strongest devices of the Gothic sublime" (Madoff, 49–50), then Auster's usage of locked rooms should lead us toward a developed understanding of the meaning of the sublime in his work. The number of real or metaphoric locked rooms in the novel is immense; as Saltzman notes, "graves and boxes figure prominently in the biographical details the narrator uncovers" (68). Small rooms, dark houses, secret cores to personality, sheltered lives, all these connote the problem of isolation the novel develops. The narrator's most important discovery as a result of his trip to France is "one impoverished image: the door of a locked room. . . . Fanshawe alone in that room. . . . This room, I now discovered, was located inside my skull" (147).

The locked room, and the isolation implicit within, centers on the sublime, as several passages in the novel amply demonstrate. The first and most important image of a grave is presented in an early chapter in which the narrator recalls scenes from his childhood with Fanshawe. In the final anecdote the two (now in their late teens) drive to a cemetery in February and Fanshawe climbs down into an open grave where he pretends to be dead. "It is still completely vivid to me: looking down at Fanshawe as he looked up at the sky, his eyes blinking furiously as the snow fell onto his face," the narrator recalls (39). He then goes on to deepen the meaning of the episode by comparing it to a period when the boys were "four or five" and Fanshawe would interrupt their games to go sit in a large appliance box. As the narrator reports, "It was his secret place, he told me, and when he sat inside and closed it up around him, he could go wherever he wanted to go, could be wherever he wanted to be. But if another person ever entered his box, then its magic would be lost for good. I believed this story" (39).

The central darkness is the most persistent trait in these parallel images. Fanshawe's compulsion toward a death-like solitude is a drive established in childhood; we are shown various manifestations of the same fundamental gesture. As the narrator describes the cemetery scene again, he relates that "I stood there waiting for Fanshawe to come up, trying to imagine what he was thinking, for a brief moment trying to see what he was seeing. Then I turned my head up to the darkening winter sky—and everything was a chaos of snow, rushing down on top of me" (40). One of the novel's first figurations of the sublime, the scene establishes the difficulty of ecstatic thought: as the narrator tries to enter the mind of the other he is overwhelmed by chaos and his own sense of live burial. The psychological movement is comparable to both of the key eighteenth-century theories of the sublime. As in the Burkean model the narrator's consciousness is in contact with "*general* privations" both great and terrible: "*Vacuity, Darkness, Solitude, and Silence*" (Burke, *A Philosophical Enquiry* 71), and the result is a feeling of terror—the narrator is, after all, standing at the edge of the grave. At the same time the passage is reminiscent of Kant and his description of a sublime that "cannot be contained in any sensuous form, but rather concerns ideas of reason, which, although no adequate presentation of them is possible, may be excited and called into the mind by that very inadequacy itself which does admit of sensuous presentation" (92). The narrator's inability to enter Fanshawe's thoughts — a constant preoccupation throughout the novel — thus gives rise to a sublime that originates in the mind but feeds on the terrifying details of the scene in the graveyard.

Fanshawe's entry into the open grave occurs the same day his father dies, a detail that allows us to match this scene at the end of chapter 2 with a statement made in chapter 1: "I tried to remember the last time I had seen him. . . . My mind wandered for several minutes and then stopped short, fixing on the day his father died" (9). The scene in the graveyard thus attains even greater thematic power in the narrative by virtue of its status as a sort of premature closure, the end of the previous relationship between the two youths. The death of the father and all the relaxation of authority it implies also serves to empower Fanshawe toward his future assumption of authorship and authority.

The narrator's later project — ensuring Fanshawe's nonexistence by authoring his death in the authorized biography — is simply a more metaphoric burial plot than the one from adolescence, and it too will drag the narrator to the brink of the sublime. Arriving in Paris to conduct further (biographical) investigations, the narrator notes that

> [t]he sky was more present than in New York, its whims more fragile. I found myself drawn to it, and for the first day or two I watched it constantly — sitting in my hotel room and studying the clouds, waiting for something to happen. These were northern clouds, the dream clouds that are always changing, massing up into huge gray mountains, discharging brief showers, dissipating, gathering again, rolling across the sun, refracting the light in ways that always seem different. The Paris sky has its own laws, and they function independently of the city below. If the buildings appear solid, anchored in the earth, indestructible, the sky is vast and amorphous, subject to constant turmoil. (139)

The opposition here of the sky and the world of people, the turmoil of the heavens and the solidity of the city, is a useful one for the development of an imagery of the sublime in the narrative. It is only a few lines below this description that the narrator states "I felt my grip loosening" (139); the amorphous cloud world thus begins to descend into the mind of the subject. Once more, as the narrator attempts to encompass the contents of Fanshawe's mind, he is thrust into psychological confusion. This time, however, the confusion is so complete that even near the end of the Paris chapter the narrator will speak of giving in to "the vertigo of pure chance" (155). The mountain imagery contained within the description of the Paris sky unites with the narrator's progressive mental imbalance to the degree that he ends up once more teetering at the brink of the void, just as years earlier and less figuratively, Fanshawe has played around construction sites, "clambering up ladders and scaffolds, balancing on planks over an abyss of machinery, sandbags, and mud" (31).

The abyss over which Fanshawe walks comes to mind not only during the narrator's increasing flirtation with self-destruction. The mention of "machinery" also has resonance in a passage concerning the flurry of activity accompanying the publication of Fanshawe's novels; the narrator reports feeling "a kind of delirium . . . like an engineer, pushing buttons and pulling levers," and so on (56). If this is metaphorically the same machinery over which Fanshawe has delicately balanced, the pair of descriptions works nicely as yet another of the trilogy's meditations on the interrelationships of subjectivity and textual production. It demonstrates as well, however, the narrator's early notation (not adequately self-recognized) of the self-diminishing nature of the project he has taken on, a reduction that he does not become fully aware of until the end of the Paris section.

Like its homoerotic subtext, the novel's sublime occasions finally converge on images of darkness. The opacity beyond death, in fact, is perhaps the single most sublime consideration in the novel, as the narrator tries to reason out the relationship between death and closure in several passages. Taking a page from Walter Benjamin, who held that "not only a man's knowledge or wisdom, but above all his real life — and this is the stuff that stories are made of — first assumes transmissable form at the moment of his death" (94), the narrator affirms that "it would seem impossible to say anything about a man until he is dead. Not only is death the one true arbiter of happiness . . . it is the only measurement by which we can judge life itself" (89). By imagining Fanshawe dead, killed by the letter, the narrator hopes at last to comprehend, to encompass, the contents of Fanshawe's consciousness. Fanshawe, who at one point has lived in a house lent him by the Dedmons (123), who speaks of himself as "living like a dead man" (173), certainly provides the perfect subject for such a project; as Saltzman notes, Fanshawe's is a "relentless, ritualistic privacy so severe as to be indistinguishable from death itself" (68). But since the narrator knows that Fanshawe is still alive, all that the biography, the life, can develop toward is another unsettling sublimity: "Stories without endings can do nothing but go on forever, and to be caught in one means that you must die before your part in it is played out" (63).

This unsettling postmortem sublimity is not unique in American postmodernism. Don DeLillo's *White Noise* similarly develops an interrelationship between plotting and death. In that novel the protagonist, Jack

Gladney, comments that "[a]ll plots tend to move deathward. This is the nature of plots. Political plots, terrorist plots, lovers' plots, narrative plots, plots that are part of children's games. We edge nearer death every time we plot" (26). Like Auster's narrator, then, Gladney accepts that death is the only adequate narrative closure, and much of *White Noise*'s first-person narrative energy is devoted to avoidance of what this confluence of plots implies. DeLillo, too, thus ends up figuring forth a set of sublime images: not simply the "airborne toxic event" that dwarfs the other concerns of the novel's characters, but the white noise of the title as well, which is explicitly discussed in deathly terms:

> "What if death is nothing but sound?"
> "Electrical noise."
> "You hear it forever. Sound all around. How awful."
> "Uniform, white." (198)

Uniform whiteness, uniform darkness, colors real or metaphoric — the distinctions become unimportant when it is clear that all sublime figuration merely stands in for that which cannot be spoken, the post-closural language of death.

Thus we are drawn back to the key metafictive pronouncement of *The Locked Room*'s penultimate chapter. Speaking specifically of the Paris sequence, but by extension addressing the entire *New York Trilogy*, the narrator comments that

> [t]he entire story comes down to what happened at the end, and without that end inside me now, I could not have started this book. The same holds true for the two books that come before it, *City of Glass* and *Ghosts*. These three stories are finally the same story, but each one represents a different stage in my awareness of what it is about. (149)

But what has happened at the end? At the conclusion of the chapter in which this statement appears the narrator is beaten senseless and decides to return to Sophie and New York; at the end of the novel he is standing on a train platform, having finished reading Fanshawe's notebook. In a very real sense the novel has no ending, but rather defers ending just as the trilogy's two previous volumes have. The last paragraph of *City of Glass* finds its narrator saying of Quinn that "it is impossible for me to say where he is now" (202), while *Ghosts* "concludes" with the comment that "from this moment on, we know nothing" (96).

With *The Locked Room* another "stage" of these earlier narratives, we should take care to note that there is very little conclusive language about the narrator's return to Sophie; rather he reads Fanshawe's notebook on the train platform, tearing up and throwing away the pages as he reads them. "I came to the last page just as the train was pulling out," he says (179), but this puts him neither on the train nor on his way back home. Closure, "living happily ever after" with his wife and sons, is only vaguely alluded to, despite the narrator's claim that having "won [Sophie] back . . . is the only thing that matters" (159). A later assertion that "where Sophie is concerned, I tend to believe that nothing is hidden" (162) hints through its tense that the narrator and Sophie remain together, but the novel continues with the episode about which he has "never bothered to tell Sophie the truth" (160). Considering the narrator's statement that "darkness is what surrounds me whenever I think of what happened . . . writing about it is the one chance I have to escape. But I doubt this will happen, not even if I manage to tell the truth" (63), a great dubiousness still obtains in the novel's final chapter. Though the comment comes relatively early in the novel (and the novel does, in various places, drama- tize the fact that time passes as it is being written[2]), it nevertheless broad- casts a hopelessness that persists to the final page. The statements are part of the same paragraph that contains the previously cited dire medita- tions about "stories without endings," so the implications for *The Locked Room* and *The New York Trilogy* seem clear. As Alison Russell points out, then, "Since the self in the text must die when the story ends, the rewrit- ing of the detective story in [the trilogy] is also a deferment of death for the author" (80). At the end of *The Locked Room* there would seem to be no more possibility of deferment, but in actuality this is precisely how the novel closes.

Auster's intertextual debt to Samuel Beckett is as great as that he has to the American Renaissance. Thus the closure of *The Locked Room* is like nothing more than that of Beckett's *The Unnamable*, the final volume of his seminal postmodern trilogy. "I can't go on, I'll go on," claims Beck- ett's nameless narrator (414), a narrator who has already significantly taken credit for the authorship of the previous two novels in his trilogy. "[H]ow can one be sure, in such darkness?" the Unnamable asks con- cerning his solitude (292), and again we find the parallel with Auster's narrator. What comes to mind as well is the conclusion of Beckett's *Com- pany*, which speaks of "[t]he fable of one with you in the dark. The fable of one fabling of one with you in the dark. And how better in the end labour lost and silence. And as you always were. Alone" (63). This is the dead — and deadly — end that Auster's postmodern narrator arrives at as he stands at the railroad terminus. Though it is true that from here he returns to Sophie and a seemingly conventional family closure, I am concerned with the way that the novel defers that ending by focusing more intensely on (and giving pride of ultimate place to) the other, earlier one.

As this problem of closure has been broached through analysis of Auster's sublime, it may be useful to remember some terms of the debate over the postmodern sublime. We can begin with the important discussion by Lyotard, who revives a Kantian sublime, "a conflict between the faculties of a subject, the faculty to conceive of something and the faculty to 'present' something" ("Answering," 77). For Lyotard the modern presents "the fact that the unpresentable exists" (78), while the postmodern "puts forward the unpresentable in presentation itself" (81). Such a formulation would appear to offer excellent descriptive possibilities for Auster's sublime and its obsession with the impossibility of naming the posthumous, the unpresentable.

Countering Lyotard, however, are the contentions of Fredric Jameson, who argues for a postmodern "hysterical sublime" based on the disappearance of the world behind the "glossy skin" of the simulacrum ("Postmodernism," 77). Rejecting Burke's figuration of divinity behind the sublime along with Heidegger's later gesture toward a diminished nature, Jameson posits instead "the whole new decentered global network of the third stage of capitalism itself," and the quixotic hope of trying "to think the impossible totality of the contemporary world system" ("Postmodernism," 80). Since Lyotard mentions that "we have the Idea of the world (the totality of what is), but we do not have the capacity to show an example of it" (*Postmodern Condition* 78), there is clearly some consonance between the two theorists. That world is for Jameson, however, specifically the world of late capitalism and multinational corporate entities. Jameson's formulation offers considerable explanatory power for DeLillo's sublime; however, it poses some difficulty in the interpretation of Auster's work.

In a discussion of Pynchon, Marc Redfield suggests that Jameson's version of a postmodern sublime demonstrates that "[t]o discover truth in the sublime is to read the sublime sublimely," going on to note that "it would be part of the problem . . . to imagine that the terms *sublime* and *postmodern* refer to entities or events ontologically stable enough to support such a narrative" (153). In this sense Lyotard's is perhaps the better account, since it does not finally hinge on the sort of historical narrative upon which Jameson, as a Marxist, must rely. Lyotard may characterize "the postmodern condition" through recourse to the "breaking up of the grand Narratives" (*Postmodern* 15), while Jameson must try to rewrite the gesture by asserting that "Lyotard seems unwilling . . . to posit, not the disappearance of the great master-narratives, but their passage underground" ("Foreword," xii). But Lyotard has foreseen (and forestalls) such a critique, it appears to me, in his recognition that Marxism ultimately requires some form of "narrative legitimation" (*Postmodern* 36).

If this lends greater credence to Lyotard's concept of the "unpresentable" it helps us in our approach to Auster. The difficulty with a Jamesonian approach is in the blankness of the historical frame in Auster's trilogy. Though it is possible to date all three of the novels in the trilogy, and though *The Locked Room* in particular offers numerous cues to the exact dates of events, we find here neither the "glossy skin" nor the terrified figuration of multinational capitalism. The narrative's time period extends from the late forties to the early eighties, with its closest focus on the years from 1976 to 1982. But analysis of the Carter and Reagan administrations, of "malaise" and false boom, do not get us very far in a reading of Auster. Even if we posit a "political unconscious" to the novel, and see in its version of a Kantian sublime a denial of the concept's historical specificity, that is, if we see in the absence of the actual tools of the writer (no one in the trilogy seems to own a word processor, and in *City of Glass* "Paul Auster" writes with a fountain pen! [143]) a denial of the "machines of reproduction rather than of production" which Jameson assigns to postmodern industrialism ("Postmodernism" 79), then it is still unclear how far we have gotten in understanding what Auster accomplishes with the sublime. *The Locked Room* resorts to the sublime in its figuration of subjectivity, sexuality, and narrative; all movement toward closure in the novel ends up in the sublime maelstrom. Lyotard's Kantian insistence on the unpresentable in relation to a historicized breakdown of faith in narrative, then, appears the more useful definition.

What *The Locked Room*'s narrator needs desperately is the ability to fashion a sentence — that smallest grammatical unit of narrative — which apperceives the contents of the locked room, the sublime site beyond closure. Thus statements about language in the novel are central to this final aspect of detective questing; as Alison Russel points out, any of the trilogy's novels is a "recursive linguistic investigation of the nature, function, and meaning of language" (71). The narrator likens the possibility of declining his role as literary executor to issuing "a death sentence" (44), an enunciation he chooses not to make. But the pun is an important one since in evading the death sentence at this early stage of the narrative he actually motivates the remainder of his quest, his search for a way to write the sentence of death that will interrogate and inter Fanshawe. Though Fanshawe has reached a point, as a writer, when "one senses a new availability of words inside him, as though the distance between seeing and writing had been narrowed, the two acts now almost identical, part of a single, unbroken gesture" (124), the narrator not only fails to perform such an elision in his own writing, but increasingly finds himself drawn "to experience language as a collection of sounds . . . forced to the surface of words where meanings vanish" (140). By the inconclusive dead end of the last chapter various aspects of the sublimity/death/language matrix coalesce, and the narrator claims that when anything can happen — that is the precise moment when words begin to fail. To the degree that Fanshawe became inevitable, that was the degree to which he was no longer there. I learned to accept this. I learned to live with him in the same way I lived with the thought of my own death, and he functioned as a trope for death inside me. (161)

By seeing Fanshawe as a trope for Atropos, the narrator glosses over the problem of closing on the sublime, performing a metaphoric act of substitution instead. Earlier, speaking of the "traditional language of love. . . . Metaphors of heat, of burning, of barriers melting down," the narrator has claimed that though the terms may sound "overblown," "in the end I believe they are accurate" (58). This statement of faith, this "I believe" that allows metaphor to become substantially factual, paves the way for Fanshawe to stand in, more precisely, for death. The opening claim, then, that "Fanshawe was always there. . . . [T]he place where everything begins" (7), becomes an *et in Arcadia ego* and a preliminary definition of the novel's problem of closure. The irony of death as precedent to existence parallels the ironic dilemma of naming a sublimely unnameable ending.

The Locked Room's ironic narrative compulsion is described most clearly when the narrator speaks of the entire trilogy by saying "I have been struggling to say goodbye to something for a long time now, and this struggle is all that really matters. The story is not in the words; it's in the struggle" (149). Not only does the claim bring to mind the similar formulation at the beginning of *City of Glass* that "whether or not it means something is not for the story to tell" (7), but it also aligns Auster's project with a modernist predecessor such as Conrad's *Heart of Darkness*. It is in that narrative, as Peter Brooks demonstrates, that "the process [of narration] is potentially infinite, any closure or termination merely provisional. . . . Meaning will never lie in the summing-up but only in transmission: in the passing-on of the 'horror,' the taint of knowledge gained" (260). Auster's narrator then, like Conrad's Marlow, becomes one more inheritor of the curse of Coleridge's Ancient Mariner, for whom

Since then, at an uncertain hour,
That agony returns:
And till my ghastly tale is told,
This heart within me burns.
    (413)

A character who has been won at dice by life-in-death, the Ancient Mariner displays more than a passing resemblance to Auster's narrator; Fanshawe, meanwhile, aligns himself with Conrad's Kurtz by saying, "That whole time in New York, I was filled with murderous thoughts. . . . I came close to a kind of horror there" (172); within Fanshawe, not surprisingly, the narrator perceives "a great darkness" (31).

But Fanshawe is also an intertextual reincarnation of Lord Jim: "he remained one of us" (31), the narrator claims, echoing the last sentence of Conrad's "Author's Note," "He was 'one of us' " (ix). The narrator of *The Locked Room* admits of Fanshawe that "there were times when he shocked me by his willingness to jump" (31); Jim's story hinges on his jump from the Patna where he feels that "[i]t was as if I had jumped into a well — into an everlasting deep hole" (111). This Conradian parallel, like that with the narratorial status of *Heart of Darkness*, allows the narrator to assume the role of Marlow, the raconteur of "inconclusive experiences" (*Heart of Darkness* 6). But in *Lord Jim* the difficulty of closure again presents itself. Marlow knows that Jim is dead, but his last empirical memory is the stunning image of Jim standing on the shore of Patusan:

> For me that white figure in the stillness of the coast and sea seemed to stand at the heart of a vast enigma. The twilight was ebbing fast from the sky above his head, the strip of sand had sunk already under his feet, he himself appeared no bigger than a child — then only a speck, a tiny white speck, that seemed to catch all the light left in a darkened world. . . . And, suddenly, I lost him. . . . (336; ellipses Conrad's)

This is not so distant from *The Locked Room*'s narrator's last memory of Fanshawe in the open grave; the sublime occlusion of perception, the incommensurability of representation to observation, is the governing aesthetic of both descriptions.

These comparisons to Conrad bring us full circle in our consideration of *The Locked Room*. Following the novel's emphases on doubling, homoeroticism, and sublimity, and understanding the problems of closure that inform all of these facets, it finally seems impossible to go farther into the problem. Concluding a study of Auster's problematic of closure, then, is predictably difficult, but the present essay cannot end on a train platform. Instead I would suggest that we look again to what *The New York Trilogy* might hope to accomplish through its postmodern genre revisionism. What the traditional novel most wanted through closure, D. A. Miller has suggested, was "to disappear, to get rid of its own excessive energies and deficient figures by an act of nomination that, once performed, would relieve them of a reason for being" (50). The formulation is a fine one through which to view the ending of *The Locked Room:* the novel's thematization of disappearance, of frustrated nomination ("Not Fanshawe — ever again," Fanshawe shouts during the final meeting [167]), and of sublimely chaotic energies works well as a strategy that relentlessly

revises the terms of classical narrative, just as the classical narrative closure of marriage and family is nearly pushed off the page before the
actual ending of the novel.

But the problems *The Locked Room* introduces also point strongly toward a postmodern narrative dead end. Though Auster, of course, continues to write, *The New York Trilogy* itself collapses into its own sublime
namelessness, vanishing into the same "dead of night" during which
Quinn's telephone rings at the beginning of *City of Glass* (7). Thus detective fiction's predictable linearity becomes a darkened moebius strip of
deferal, with sublime darkness subsuming all.

Notes

1. See Saltzman (68), for a good account of the novel's relationship to Hawthorne.

2. On page 7 the narrator dates Sophie's first contact with him as "[s]even years
ago this November"; their subsequent meeting is 25 November 1976 (70), so the
composition of the narrative begins in 1983. Chapter 6 is written "close to six
years after the fact" of the narrator's liaison with Jane Fanshawe (107), which is
dated June 1978 (93). In the final chapter the narrator speaks of "the vantage
point of this moment (May 1984)" (159), so one might conjecture that the narrator "writes" *The Locked Room* from pre-November 1983 through May of 1984, the
narrator's final encounter with Fanshawe occurring 1 April 1982 (161). Sun &
Moon Press first brought out the novel in 1986.

Works Cited

Auster, Paul. *City of Glass*. Los Angeles: Sun & Moon Press, 1985.

——. *Ghosts*. Los Angeles: Sun & Moon Press, 1986.

——. *The Locked Room*. Los Angeles: Sun & Moon Press, 1986.

Beckett, Samuel. *Company*. New York: Grove Press, 1980.

——. *The Unnamable: Three Novels*. New York: Grove Press, 1965. Pp. 289–414.

Benjamin, Walter. "The Storyteller." In Hannah Arendt, ed., *Illuminations: Essays
and Reflections*. Trans. Harry Zohn. New York: Schocken, 1969. Pp. 83–109.

Brooks, Peter. *Reading for the Plot: Design and Intention in Narrative*. New York:
Vintage, 1985.

Burke, Edmund. *A Philosophical Enquiry into the Origin of our Ideas of the Sublime and
Beautiful*. Ed. James T. Boulton. London: Routledge, 1958.

Coleridge, Samuel Taylor. "The Rime of the Ancient Mariner." In David Perkins,
ed., *English Romantic Writers*. New York: Harcourt, 1967. Pp. 404–413.

Conrad, Joseph. *Heart of Darkness. Three Short Novels*. New York: Bantam, 1960.
Pp. 1–94.

——. *Lord Jim*. New York: Doubleday, 1920.

DeLillo, Don. *White Noise*. New York: Penguin, 1986.

Jameson, Fredric. "Foreword." In Jean-François Lyotard, *The Postmodern Condition*. Pp. vii–xxi.

——. "Postmodernism, or The Cultural Logic of Late Capitalism." *New Left
Review* 146 (1984): 53–92.

Kant, Immanuel. *The Critique of Judgement.* Trans. James Creed Meredith. Oxford: Clarendon, 1952.

Lyotard, Jean-François. "Answering the Question: What Is Postmodernism?" Trans. Régis Durand. In Lyotard, *The Postmodern Condition,* 71–82.

———. *The Postmodern Condition: A Report on Knowledge.* Trans. Geoff Bennington and Brian Massumi. Minneapolis: University of Minnesota Press, 1984.

Madoff, Mark. "Inside, Outside, and the Gothic Locked-Room Mystery." In *Gothic Fictions: Prohibition/Transgression.* Ed. Kenneth W. Graham. AMS Ars Poetica: No. 5. New York: AMS Press, 1989.

Melville, Herman. "Hawthorne and His Mosses." In Ronald Gottesman et al., eds., *The Norton Anthology of American Literature.* Vol. 1. New York: Norton, 1979. Pp. 2056–2070.

Miller, D. A. *Narrative and Its Discontents: Problems of Closure in the Traditional Novel.* Princeton, N.J.: Princeton University Press, 1981.

Redfield, Marc W. "Pynchon's Postmodern Sublime." *PMLA* 104 (1989): 152–162.

Russell, Alison. "Deconstructing *The New York Trilogy:* Paul Auster's Anti-Detective Fiction." *Critique* 31 (1990): 71–84.

Saltzman, Arthur. *Designs of Darkness in Contemporary American Fiction.* Philadelphia: University of Pennsylvania Press, 1990.

Sedgwick, Eve Kosofsky. *Between Men: English Literature and Male Homosocial Desire.* New York: Columbia University Press, 1985.

Tanner, Tony. *City of Words: American Fiction 1950–1970.* New York: Harper and Row, 1971.

"Looking for Signs in the Air": Urban Space and the Postmodern in *In the Country of Last Things*

Tim Woods

"Space is for us an existential and cultural dominant." So concludes Fredric Jameson, having described postmodernism's dependence on a "supplement of spatiality" that results from its depletion of history and consequent exaggeration of the present (365). Indeed, recent years have seen an increasing interest in the politics of place, the cultural function of geography, and the reassertion of the importance of space in any cultural study. The territory of these arguments is marked out in diverse areas in the work of people like Michel Foucault, Gaston Bachelard, David Harvey, Edward Soja, Doreen Massey, Fredric Jameson, Pierre Bourdieu, and Michel de Certeau. However, the most significant development of this "spatial turn" in recent theory is Henri Lefebvre's *The Production of Space* (1991), in which he rigorously argues that space is the key component in the analysis of economic production. As a consequence, one can no longer practice a historical analysis without taking account of the politics of spatialization embedded within the production process. Geography, place, space, locale, location — such terms form one of the lexicons gaining ascendancy within cultural analysis.

Lefebvre explores the "production of space," maintaining that space is produced and reproduced, thus representing the site and outcome of social, political, and economic struggles. Arguing that new modes of production exist in concomitant relation to new conditions of space, Lefebvre deconstructs the illusions of the naturalness and transparency of space and erects a typology of spatialities. The postmodern novel's deliberate foregrounding of the discourses of the sensual and the analytic, of private memory and public representation, of personal "lived" experience and "official" public constructions, parallels this "new geography" by showing how spatial constructions are created and used as markers of human memory and of social values in a world of rapid flux and change.

Lefebvre's conception of space as something that is "felt" as much as "known" or analyzed, leads to the emergence of two sorts of space. One is the empirical rational space or place perceived as a void to be filled up. The other is what might be termed "affective space," a space that is charged with emotional and mythical meanings, community symbolism, and historical significances. Space does not have an autonomous, objectively separate existence from subjects. Rather, as Henri Lefebvre has argued in *The Production of Space*, space is *produced* by the material forms of production. Consequently, Lefebvre conceives of the city as "a space of differences." His crucial distinction lies between a social space constituted by the activity of everyday life and an abstract space laid down by the actions of the state and the economic institutions of capital. The reproduction of social relations of capitalism is therefore accomplished as a constant struggle between these different modes of reproducing space.

It is increasingly being noted that Paul Auster's fiction frequently touches upon the postmodern preoccupations of subjectivity, sexuality, sublimity, and silence. However, *In the Country of Last Things* foregrounds Auster's engagement with an additional postmodernist "S" word — spatiality. As the novel gradually overlays discourses about spatial control and control by space, the complex complicity of these apparently different concerns emerges. Much of Auster's fiction pivots on spatial loci, on the actions of individuals within locked rooms, isolated garrets, enclosed spaces, circumscribed areas, and the effects of closure and openness on human consciousness: how a change in society's modes of production changes social conceptions of space and how, in turn, space constructs, and is constructed by, individual consciousness. A good deal of Auster's "Book of Memory" in *The Invention of Solitude,* for example, meditates upon the effects of being cut off and isolated from the world by one's spatial circumstances, like the recurrent image of Jonah being trapped within the belly of a whale (for example, see *The Invention of Solitude*, 89, 99–100, 124–126, 131, 157–159, 162–164). *In the Country of Last Things* explores, in particular, the urban space in a putative apocalyptic future, and the manner in which it is occupied, inhabited, and experienced both phenomenologically and emotionally, by individuals and communities. Through the personal letter of the narrator-protagonist Anna Blume, reporting her bewildering and disorientating experiences in the city while searching for her lost brother, *In the Country of Last Things* constantly confronts one with the intersection of private and public spaces, as her urban experience allows public space to become the stage for private experiences, and private spaces to be unfolded onto public spaces.

David Harvey's discussion of space as a characteristic of postmodernism points out how Michel Foucault conceives of space as the site of social constriction and occasionally the site of processes of liberatory potential: "The body exists in space and must either submit to authority (through, for example, incarceration or surveillance in an organised space) or carve out particular spaces of resistance and freedom — 'heterotopias' — from an otherwise repressive world" (213). Harvey goes on to describe how Michel de Certeau argues, contrary to the Foucauldian concept of a "technological system of a coherent and totalizing space," that this is substituted daily by a " 'pedestrian rhetoric' of trajectories that have 'a mythical structure' understood as 'a story jerry-built out of elements taken from common sayings, an allusive and fragmentary story whose gaps mesh with the social practices it symbolises' " (214). De Certeau, like Auster, is not unconcerned with the way in which order is transmuted into a repressive technology, but rather seeks to excavate those surreptitious forms created by the marginal, dispersed, tactical, and makeshift creativity of groups or individuals already caught in the nets of "discipline." "Spaces" are more easily liberated than Foucault imagines. Paradoxically, the challenge to the domination of space becomes the invention of new spaces. Within the despotic social and political climate of the city, Anna Blume's letter demonstrates — as political resistors have continually shown during the twentieth century — that the most radical and expansive political gesture against the totalitarian attempt to dominate spatiality is the challenge provided by the creative and imaginative space of the human body. In this respect, Paul Auster's novel is a spatial cartography that explores the manner in which human history is subject to various structures and forms of power that traverse the body and the world, break it down, shape it, and rearrange it — yet always fail to conquer it.

Auster's essay concerning Charles Reznikoff's representation of the city, "The Decisive Moment," might be instructive here: "It seems no accident that most of Reznikoff's poems are rooted in the city. For only in the modern city can the one who sees remain unseen, take his stand in space and yet remain transparent" (*Art of Hunger* 39). Auster's novel, like Reznikoff's poetry, is engaged with the "strange and transitory beauties of the urban landscape" (40). Anna Blume's experience of coming to terms with an otherness, in exile in a foreign land, is exactly reminiscent of Auster's description of Reznikoff's work: "It is exile, and a way of coming to terms with exile that somehow, for better or worse, manages to leave the condition of exile intact. Reznikoff was not only an outsider by temperament, nurturing those aspects of himself that would tend to maintain his sense of isolation, he was also born into a state of *otherness,* and as a Jew, as the son of immigrant Jews in America, whatever idea of community he had was always ethnic rather than national" (42). Anna Blume discovers herself to be a constant outsider, looking in on this life in the city, which she always appears to treat as a temporary nightmare until she can find her brother. Perhaps not accidentally, Blume also crucially announces her Jewish identity during her meeting with the rabbi in the National Library. Displaced into the turmoil of the city, as someone who "had grown up in another place" (*In the Country of Last Things* 106), Anna Blume's ontological, epistemological, and ethnic positions coalesce in her Judaic roots. Amongst Auster's important extended reflections on Judaic roots and culture, is this quotation from Marina Tsvetaeva in *The Invention of Solitude:* "In this most Christian of worlds / All poets are Jews" (95). This persistent exiled consciousness of the writer and the Jew is reiterated by the rabbi, who impresses upon Blume a most "startling" comment: "Every Jew, he said, believes that he belongs to the last generation of Jews. We are always at the end, always standing on the brink of the last moment, and why should we expect things to be any different now?" (*Country* 112). Having lived as if she is the only person left in the world, Blume's meetings with the rabbi reestablish some glimmer of her former self-identity, as she gradually experiences the protective order of the patriarch:

> It was strange what had come over me in the presence of this man, but the more I talked to him, the more I sounded like a child. Perhaps he reminded me of how things had been when I was very young, back in the dark ages when I still believed in what fathers and teachers said to me. I can't say for sure, but the fact was that I felt on solid ground with him, and I knew that he was someone I could trust. (96)

Although the rabbi's allusions to persecutions of the Jewish population in the city echo less savory periods of European history, it is precisely the communal aspect of the rabbi and his disciples that steady Blume at this point of near collapse. The absent father is a persistent theme in Auster's writing, but here is a familiar, solid patriarchal foundation and ethnic security she never experienced in the ever-shifting social sands outside the library, where a sense of *communal* space is at best a vestige shored up by desperation, and at worst nonexistent.

Since we cannot live outside representations of space, and there is no clear dividing line between an authentic *place* and one that may have been constructed along the way, Anna Blume tends to be always negotiating various locales in the city, continuously working to make sense of and articulate both place and event. People are shown to be never simply fixed within a locale, but are active, space-producing *bricoleurs*. Living in complex, contradictory places, one differentiates the pull of events and places. We feel the pull of specific constructions of space or place, and in many ways, are involved in reproducing them on a daily basis; but we can nevertheless alter a vision of strict interpellation with the recognition that discourses are negotiated.

Michel de Certeau has written about the way in which the city is constituted by the "raw material" of "walkers, *Wandersmanner*, whose bodies follow the cursives and strokes of an urban 'text' they write without reading" (124). Auster's sense of the city is similar: many passages are given over to the patterns traced through the city by Blume's walks. Preeminently, walking assumes the imperative of self-preservation: "One step and then another step and then another: that is the golden rule" (*Country* 24). However, just as Reznikoff's poetry was built upon the fundamental experience of *walking* through a city, gauging the topographical and emotional by traversing the landscape on foot, so Anna Blume derives her intimate knowledge of the city from her perambulatory experiences: "The streets of the city are everywhere, and no two streets are the same. I put one foot in front of the other, and then the other foot in front of the first, and then hope I can do it again. Nothing more than that" (*Country* 2). Gradually Blume's journeys assume an epistemological importance, walking being analogous to traveling from one thought to another. Auster's texts constantly fold into one another, and in "The Book of Memory," Auster stresses his conception of the mind's "wanderings" as a walking through a city:

> just as one step will inevitably lead one to the next step, so it is that one thought inevitably follows from the previous thought . . . and so on, and in this way, if we were to try to make an image of this process in our minds, a network of paths begins to be drawn, as in the image of the human bloodstream (heart, arteries, veins, capillaries), or as in the image of a map (of city streets, for example, preferably a large city, or even of roads, as in the gas station maps of roads that stretch, bisect, and meander across a continent), so that what we are really doing when we walk through the city is thinking, and thinking in such a way that our thoughts compose a journey, and this journey is no more or less than the steps we have taken. (*The Invention of Solitude* 122)

Journeys are equivalent to mental movements, and walking becomes an actualization of cognition itself. In his poem "White Spaces" Auster seeks "to think of motion not merely as a function of the body but as an extension of the mind" (*Disappearances* 104). He continues on this subject of space, physical movement and mental thought:

> I remain in the room in which I am writing this. I put one foot in front of the other. I put one word in front of the other, and for each step I take I add another word, as if for each word to be spoken there was another space to be crossed, a distance to be filled by my body as it moves through this space. It is a journey through space, even if I get nowhere, even if I end up in the same place I started. It is a journey through space, as if into many cities and out of them, as if across deserts, as if to the edge of some imaginary ocean, where each thought drowns in the relentless waves of the real. (107)

Within a single room, the writer can experience "the infinite possibilities of a limited space" (*The Invention of Solitude* 89). Words shape and extend mental and physical spaces. In Auster's novel, the spaces of the city, Blume's mind, and the textuality implode into a space of representation.

What emerges in the novel *In the Country of Last Things* is akin to Lefebvre's argument concerning the dialectical interaction between the space of representation and representational spaces. How is the relation between place and being to be understood? As separate spheres? As interdependencies? As shaped entirely by the forcefulness of the absolute ego? As shaped entirely by the materiality of place? Place as a specific demarcation of space is crucial to the establishment of social order. As Anna Blume gradually discovers, to challenge what that place might be is to challenge something fundamental in the social order.

The city is constantly described as being in a state of perpetual contingency, impermanence, ephemerality, and transience by Anna Blume: "Slowly and steadily, the city seems to be consuming itself, even as it remains" (*Country* 21–22). When Blume first arrives, it is like "entering an invisible world, a place where only blind people lived" (18). There is no clear sense of how the city has arrived at such a state of decrepitude or collapse, why it is cordoned off, or why it is a no-go zone. It appears in an indefinite future and as an indefinite space, marked by the typicality of New York City and also the indeterminacy of all contemporary urban constructions.[1] It is merely a *space*, a condition in which the author explores, observes, and represents certain states of social behavior. As such a *zone*, it has similarities with Brian McHale's sense that postmodern fiction constructs spaces that allow for experiments, opening up new ontological existences "in a kind of between-worlds space — a zone" (*Postmodern Fiction* 43–58). The city is just such a place and non-place, in which people are completely indifferent to reality, knowing no logic or negotiation or causality or contradiction, wholly given over as they are to the instinctual play of the desires and the search for survival. The novel's apocalyptic title suggests a world that is disappearing, and there is an incomprehensibility about this knowledge, seemingly lying beyond the limits of the imagination: "I don't expect you to understand. You have seen none of this, and even if you tried, you could not imagine it. A house is there one day, and the next day it is gone" (*Country* 1). The city's organic cycle is repeatedly perplexing and confusing:

> For nothing is really itself anymore. There are pieces of this and pieces of that, but none of it fits together. . . . At a certain point, things disintegrate into muck, or dust, or scraps, and what you have is something new, some particle or agglomeration of matter that cannot be identified. It is a clump, a mote, a fragment of the world that has no place: a cipher of it-ness. As an object hunter, you must rescue things before they reach this state of absolute decay. . . . Everything falls apart, but not every part of every thing, at least not at the same time. The job is to zero in on these little islands of intactness, to imagine them joined to other such islands, and those islands to still others, and thus to create new archipelagoes of matter. (35–36)

Life is a process of constructing order out of chaos, an idea that much preoccupies Stillman senior in *City of Glass* in *The New York Trilogy,* with his collection of oddments from the streets of Manhattan. Yet what interests Blume is that a change in one's material circumstances in life in turn alters the value accorded to refuse and rubbish. One person's waste is another person's treasure. In this constant cycle of decomposition and recomposition, the city is represented as a "metonymic site, a zone of spatial contiguity, interdependence, and circulation" (*Postmodern Fiction* 190). Garbage collectors need to look at the world in a new fashion, to think metonymically, where the part forms a new yet different whole. The destruction, collapse and resurrection of identity are crucial factors in the transience of the city, where this new metonymical arrangement causes alternative spatial arrangements to emerge.

Amidst this physical decay, the city inverts one's conventional ideas about life: "It turns your thoughts inside out. It makes you want to live, and at the same time it tries to take your life away from you. There is no escape from this. Either you do or you don't. And if you do, you can't be sure of doing it the next time. And if you don't, you never will again" (*Country* 2). Life in the city is one of black-and-white situations; yet paradoxically, as a result of this stark choice, subjectivity is put under severe pressure — agency is almost a defunct concept. The city is something that has to be carefully negotiated, since it seeks to invade one's very being. Isabel's advice to Blume at one point warns: "Never think about anything, she said. Just melt into the street and pretend that your body doesn't exist. No musings; no sadness or happiness; no anything but the street, all empty inside, concentrating only on the next step you are about to take"

(57). In this chameleon-like eradication of any sense of physical, emotional, or mental self, the reader is constantly reminded about how physical space structures social consciousness and activity. "It would have taken a strong imagination to see what was really there, and if anything is in short supply in the city, it's imagination" (61). All people play roles: Isabel and Blume seek to "create the illusion that Ferdinand was a Leaper" (75); Boris Stepanovich invents varying "personal histories" for himself that "were part of an almost conscious plan to concoct a more pleasant world for himself—a world that could shift according to his whims, that was not subject to the same laws and bleak necessities that dragged down all the rest of us" (147); and Samuel Farr's reappearance to pose as a doctor and confessor figure at Woburn House also acts as a self-protective mechanism of distancing the quotidian misery of the city ("It's better not having to be myself . . . If I didn't have that other person to hide behind — the one who wears the white coat and sympathetic look on his face — I don't think I could stand it" [168]). Constantly acting for her own self-preservation, Blume is similarly forced to change her appearance, "to make feminine things about me less apparent" (60). In order to protect herself, she has to eradicate herself, to feign otherness, to feign masculinity: "It looked so ugly that I didn't recognize myself anymore. It was as though I had been turned into someone else. What's happened to me? I thought. Where am I?" (59–60). Desexed, Blume is also displaced. This alteration of her gender identity is a direct consequence of (and necessity in) her new social space in the city, as she seeks to blend in with her environment. Yet Blume's own contradictory conclusion is that one cannot completely identify oneself with the fabric of the city or afford to succumb to the habitual life of the city: "The essential thing is not to become inured. For habits are deadly" (6). Habit, as Beckett once wrote, is a great deadener, and here it is literally a killer: "Even if it is for the hundredth time, you must encounter each thing as if you have never known it before. No matter how many times, it must always be the first time. This is next to impossible, I realize, but it is an absolute rule" (6). One must constantly practice a "defamiliarization" of life's experiences, preventing oneself from becoming too accustomed to a routine or a familiar place, since this lulls one into a false sense of security.

The city raises phenomenological cognition to the absolute stakes of life and death: "Your eyes must be constantly open, looking up, looking down, looking ahead, looking behind, on watch for other bodies, on your guard against the unforeseeable" (5). Later, when Blume loses her cart, the drastic consequences that a loss of vigilance has upon livelihood are evident: "A moment or two when your attention flags, a single second when you forget to be vigilant, and then everything gets lost, all your work is suddenly wiped out" (82). Blume is obsessive about the problems concerning falling down, reiterating the warning on several occasions: "You must be careful. . . . Otherwise, you will stumble as you walk, and I need not enumerate the dangers of falling" (21). Consequently, Anna Blume subjects her environment of the city to microscopic scrutiny and finds herself rooted, inbuilt, and constructed by that place. The city is not geographically divorced from the self, but is rather constitutive of the self: geography, topography, and subjectivity are intricately interrelated.

Yet how is such a social space connected to language? Is it a precondition of language or merely a formulation of it? In *The Production of Space*, Lefebvre asks "[t]o what extent may a space be read or decoded? Such a produced space can be read and as such, implies a process of signification. And although there may be no general code of space, inherent to all languages or in language, there appear to have existed specific codes, established at specific historical periods and varying in their effects" (17). What Auster does is to work at the as-yet concealed relations between space and language. The city could be construed as a "logarithm" that contains the structure and texture of all individual urban experiences. The city space in Auster's work acts as both a scene of textual events and a text for individual interpretation. Gradually the city emerges as a text in which, in order to survive, "you must learn how to read the signs" (*Country* 6). Yet even this eternal vigilance is not an adequate and secure mode of existence, since "[b]it by bit, the city robs you of certainty. There can never be any fixed path, and you can survive only if nothing is necessary to you. Without warning, you must be able to change, to drop what you are doing, to reverse. In the end, there is nothing that is not the case" (6). The negation of Wittgenstein's famous phrase of positivist philosophy, from the *Tractatus Logico-Philosophicus*, suggests that the world is a set of unpredictable possibilities rather than a set of finite existents, and that the subject acts in a foundationless, uncertain, and constantly disruptive environment. Blume continues:

> In the city, the best approach is to believe only what your own eyes tell you. But not even that is unfallible. For few things are ever what they seem to be, especially here, with so much to absorb at every step, with so many things that defy understanding. Whatever you see has the potential to wound you, to make you less than you are, as if merely by seeing a thing some part of yourself were taken away from you. (18–19)

Even the phenomenal appearances of things are not reliable, as they defy cognitive apprehension and possess the potential to destroy one's integrity. In this tangled web of comprehension, the conventional Western metaphysical reliance upon the metaphor of sight for truth is undercut, and seeing is *not* believing. The result is that Blume feels that although she can only function as an observer, remaining detached and aloof rather than engaging with the city (where so much remains hidden, secretive, below the surface), this knowledge will always remain partial and inadequate: "There is no way to explain it. I can only record, I cannot pretend to understand. . . . The facts fly in the face of probability" (22). Any sense of totality of representation or comprehension is constantly undercut, as Blume recognizes that the selective nature of words and the artifice of boundaries prevents totalization: "I've been trying to fit everything in, trying to get to the end before it's too late, but I see now how badly I've deceived myself. Words do not allow such things. The closer you come to the end, the more there is to say. The end is only imaginary, a destination you invent to keep yourself going, but a point comes when you realize you will never get there" (183). Such contingency makes even daily weather predictions, for example, so vital if life is lived outside, resistant to any logical and precise interpretation or syntactic sense:

> It would be one thing if the weather could be predicted with any degree of accuracy. Then one could make plans, know when to avoid the streets, prepare for changes in advance. But everything happens too fast here, the shifts are too abrupt, what is true one minute is no longer true the next. I have wasted much time looking for signs in the air. . . . But nothing has ever helped me. To correlate this with that, to make a connection between an afternoon cloud and an evening wind — such things lead only to madness. You spin around in the vortex of your calculations and then, just at the moment you are convinced it will rain, the sun goes on shining for an entire day. (25–26)

Looking for signs in the air is like building castles in the air — idle fancy, speculative, and groundless. In the maze-like experience of the city, the questions that are asked and the answers that are given appear inappropriate to each other, presenting a confusion of semantic and phenomenological horizons. The goal posts are constantly shifting, causing one to lose one's bearings. The space of the city is also persistently shifting, which in turn causes signs to become unstable:

> In spite of what you would suppose, the facts are not reversible. Just because you are able to get in, that does not mean you will be able to get out. Entrances do not become exits, and there is nothing to guarantee that the door you walked through a moment ago will still be there when you turn around to look for it again. That is how it works in the city. Every time you think you know the answer to a question, you discover that the question makes no sense. (85)

Contrary to Wittgenstein's proposition in the *Tractatus* that "[t]he facts in logical space are the world" (5), what is apparently logical constantly turns out not to be the case. Like living inside a kaleidoscope, each turn of the head presents a different set of circumstances and perspectives: nothing remains the same.

Here is the full consciousness of the implications of modern totalitarianism. Totalitarianism appears to be the organization of the bewildered masses who react to their personal incomprehension, the manipulation of their economic weakness, and their spiritual insecurity. Life is organized in the state by accident or whim, such that Anna believes that "[o]ur lives are no more than the sum of manifold contingencies, and no matter how diverse they may be in their details, they all share an essential randomness in their design: this then that, and because of that, this" (*Country* 143–144). Consequently, reality itself is called into question; and thus the basis on which ideas might be verified are themselves unreliable. In the face of this, Auster explores the means by which individuals can challenge or resist such control in this nightmarish existence where received ontologies are disrupted. People develop modes of dealing with the horror, anxiety, and tension that confronts them on a daily basis. Anna Blume records the protocol for speaking about food and how it is necessary for "you to allow your mind to leap into the words coming from the mouths of the others. If the words can consume you, you will be able to forget your present hunger and enter what people call the 'arena of sustaining nimbus.' There are even those who say there is nutritional value in these food talks—given the proper concentration and an equal desire to believe in the words among those taking part" (10). Acutely conscious of the materiality of language, Blume constantly worries away at the issue of representation, and how one's environment shapes writing and narratives. As Isabel slowly dies in Blume's company, Blume reflects upon this interrelationship: "I tremble when I think how closely everything is connected. If Isabel had not lost her voice, none of these words would exist. Because she had no more words, these other words have come out of me. I want you to remember that. If not for Isabel, there would be nothing now. I never would have begun" (79). Narratives and their evocative power are crucial to these characters who are divorced and cut off from their collective pasts. Some use narratives to evoke the good times of previous days, recreating the city as it was: "All this belongs to the language of ghosts. There are many other possible kinds of talks in this language. Most of them begin when one person says to another: I wish. What they wish for might be anything at all, as long as it is something that cannot happen" (10). While Anna Blume confesses her one-time penchant for the power of stories in her childhood, she now recognizes that "the language of ghosts" erects false and nostalgic pictures and is misleading and harmful. Firmly practicing Brecht's dictum that one must not look back to the good old days, but face the bad new ones, Anna Blume refuses to be seduced into playing this narrative game: "Now I am all common sense and hard calculation. I don't want to be like the others. I see what their imaginings do to them, and I will not let it happen to me" (11). Her refusal is a protective mechanism, determinedly fending off the death that inevitably follows the erection of this metaphysical illusion of happiness and peace through narratives of longing (11).

In Auster's focus on Francis Ponge (*The Invention of Solitude* 137–138), Edmund Jabes (*Art of Hunger* 99–106), Louis Wolfson (*Art of Hunger* 26–34), and Paul Celan (*Art of Hunger* 82–94), he is clearly fascinated by their common interest in the complexities of reference, of the relationship between word and thing, and the manner in which they handle words "as if they had the density of objects, . . . a substantiality that enables them to become a part of the world" (*Art of Hunger* 89). This interest in the materiality of language finds significant expression in the novel. There is Otto Frick's linguistic difficulty, but for whom words "were physical objects, literal stones cluttering his mouth" (*Country* 133). His palindromic play with A-N-N-A and his own name, and his intimate grasp of language as a substance, which makes him "sensitive to the internal properties of words themselves: their sounds as divorced from their meanings, their symmetries and contradictions" (133), endows Frick with a peculiar although intangible strength. In "The Book of Memory" Auster suggests that such wordplay acts as a form of "magic," and concludes that playing with words is "not so much a search for truth as a search for the world as it happens in language" (*The Invention of Solitude* 159–162).

Similarly, Boris Stepanovich's wheelings and dealings on behalf of the Woburn House community is another example of how the world can be altered or felt differently through manipulating the material substance of language at work in referentiality. Owing to his conscious sense of "language as an instrument" (*Country* 146), Boris devises a rhetorical prowess in his speeches, "always looping back and forth between hard sounds and soft, allowing the words to rise and fall as they poured out in a dense, intricately fashioned barrage of syllables" (151). His ability to attach narratives to objects raises them to symbols of value in a market where there is little demand for precious antiques, since "from Boris Stepanovich, you were not just getting a vase, you were getting an entire world to go along with it" (151). With this clear sense of separation between signifier and signified in language, and the concomitant opportunity to control words for profitable ends, narratives and language are frequently described as something about which to be suspicious, since truth and history are quickly muddled: "I have since learned not to take the things I am told too seriously. It's not that people make a point of lying to you, it's just that where the past is concerned, the truth tends to get obscured rather quickly. Legends crop up within a matter of hours, tall tales circulate, and the facts are soon buried under a mountain of outlandish theories" (18). Facts cannot escape fictions, as Blume repeatedly struggles with language to express this inexpressible experience and place, and she constantly finds her narrative straying from a linear progression as it becomes dominated by the sheer existential need to get the information down:

> I know that I sometimes stray from the point, but unless I write down things as they occur to me, I feel I will lose them for good. . . . Each day brings the same struggle, the same blankness, the same desire to forget and then not to forget. When it begins, it is never anywhere but here, never anywhere but at this limit that the pencil begins to write. The story starts and stops, goes forward and then loses itself, and between each word, what silences, what words escape and vanish, never to be seen again. (38)

Blume's narrative is a series of broken recollections as literal blanknesses and gaps creep into the (non)progression of the events, and the temporal sequence slowly recedes in importance as the novel continues.

There are strong similarities between this novel and Auster's description and meditation upon what occurs in Knut Hamsun's *The Art of Hunger:* the wandering and hunger, maintaining oneself on the edge of death, and the strange effects of disembodiment that this produces within one's consciousness. Auster is particularly intrigued by the experience of living at the edge of one's physical and emotional endurance, of ridding oneself of the weight of the body, of freeing the mind from its corporeal shell, and the concomitant experience of a transcendent mental activity. He argues that in Hamsun's book, "[h]istorical time is obliterated in favor of inner duration. With only an arbitrary beginning and an arbitrary ending, the novel faithfully records all the vagaries of the narrator's mind, following each thought from its mysterious inception through all its meanderings, until it dissipates and the next thought begins. What happens is allowed to happen" (*Art of Hunger* 10). Anna Blume's mental vagaries are the course of *In the Country of Last Things,* and they are not controlled by anything other than the logic of thought and sensation. The erasure of history and information about the city is repeated over and over in Anna Blume's narrative:

> There is so much I want to tell you. Then I begin to say something, and I suddenly realize how little I understand. Facts and figures, I mean,

precise information about how we live here in the city. That was going to be William's job. The newspaper sent him here to get the story, and every week there was going to be another report. Historical background, human interest articles, the whole business. . . . I have no idea how the city keeps itself going . . . I can't give you the answers, and I have never met anyone who could. (28)

Her experience of the city occurs in a space without a history: her life is a spatial rather than temporal experience.

In the face of this, *In the Country of Last Things* can be read as a novel about making sense of the postmodern urban environment, a process described by Jameson in terms appropriated from Kevin Lynch as "cognitive mapping" (*Postmodernism, or the Cultural Logic of Late Capitalism* 51–51, 415–417). Blume's inability to overcome the urban alienation in the city overwhelms her, as she desperately tries to enact that process Jameson describes as "the practical reconquest of a sense of place and the construction or reconstruction of an articulated ensemble which can be retained in memory and which the individual subject can map and remap along the moments of mobile, alternative trajectories" (51). For Jameson, the inability to map the urban space is part of a larger problem, the inability to position oneself within the new decentralized communication networks of capitalism. Blume's attempts at such mapping are continually stymied, and her potential to act is consequently vitiated at every turn. Hence, memory becomes increasingly important to Blume, as she constantly finds herself reacting to the effects of mentally constructing the past. Linked as it is to the "language of ghosts," which constantly seduces one into a reconstructed nostalgic period of security and stability, memory as the Wordsworthian store of refreshing images collected and used to sustain one in the future, proves to be equally fallacious for Anna Blume. Instead, memory produces only a blur, since "things themselves passed too quickly. . . . It was always gone, even before I had it" (*Country* 88). The disappearance of things causes a selective forgetfulness in the general public which "creates difficulties, insuperable barriers against understanding" (*Country* 88). This disintegration of memory coincides with the destruction of language, and whole aspects of the past cease to exist:

It is a slow but ineluctable process of erasure. Words tend to last a bit longer than things, but eventually they fade too, along with the pictures they once evoked. Entire categories of objects disappear . . . words become only sounds, a random collection of glottals and fricatives, a storm of whirling phonemes . . . As more and more of these foreign-sounding words crop up around you, conversations become rather strenuous. In effect, each person is speaking his own private language, and as the instances of shared understanding diminish, it becomes increasingly difficult to communicate with anyone. (89)

The gradual obsolescence of language and the entropy of reference causes isolation and the collapse of social interaction. The disappearance of the material realm destroys the realm of representation, and this in turn destroys collective understanding and comprehension. History is slowly erased as a consequence of the erasure of the material existence of objects. Any attempt to resurrect these "lost," "absent" objects or words becomes a form of social insurrection. As one character advises Blume when she asks about the availability of airplanes, "You could get into trouble for spreading that kind of nonsense. The government doesn't like it when people make up stories. It's bad for morale" (87). Hence, memory and history are ultimately part of an imaginative and representative space that is strictly controlled, surveyed, and supervised by the hegemonic power. Narratives, stories and fictions, are treated implicitly as lies and as anti-authoritarian, which need to be firmly edited or suppressed. Narratives are perceived to act as political levers that can pry open alternative spaces, gaps, niches in dominant ideologies. As such, an active "memory" becomes a potent political tool: remembering the past, narrating it, preserves alternative versions of the present circumstances. Blume constantly confronts mechanisms that seek to replace private spaces with public spaces, private narratives and representations with public versions. Yet all the while, she correspondingly finds public narratives and representations collapsing into solipsistic "private languages," which militates against any totalizing orders or ideologies.

Auster's "The Book of Memory" in *The Invention of Solitude* is in part a sustained meditation on the function and action of the architecture of memory. Auster constructs this metaphor of the shape of memory literally, as a defined space:

Memory as a place, as a building, as a sequence of columns, cornices, porticoes. The body inside the mind, as if we were moving around in there, going from one place to the next, and the sound of our footsteps as we walk, moving from one place to the next. (82)

This passage contains several of the preoccupations of *In the Country of Last Things* — memory, place, walking, the relation of body to mind, texts as spaces. This matrix of ideas is further linked to history in his statement: "Memory: the space in which a thing happens for a second time" (*Invention of Solitude* 83). Memory is here conceived of as a space in which history repeats itself. For this reason, memory has the potential to be a crucial source of political resistance and autonomy. As Auster notes from his reading, Saint Augustine has observed that memory is a part of the self that paradoxically lies outside the body (88–89); and as such, it functions as a part of the self that challenges the machinery of social control.

Desperate times require desperate remedies, and with the disappearance of a *raison d'être,* religious fervor seems to permeate the social fabric to its core, with the establishment of a variety of fanatical groups that institutionalize a *raison de mourir* as a ritualistic action. The narrative details several of these organizations, such as the "Runners," "Leapers," and members of "Assassination Clubs." Death is transformed into an aesthetic action, in which beauty and the "grand spectacle" dominate as ritualized forms of self-transcendence: "The Last Leap is something everyone can understand, and it corresponds to everyone's inner longings: to die in a flash, to obliterate yourself in one brief and glorious moment. I sometimes think that death is the one thing we have any feeling for. It is our art form, the only way we can express ourselves" (*Country* 13). With the premium placed upon leaving this miserable existence, even death enters into the market economy. Profits are reaped from Euthanasia Clinics, where one can buy one's death on a graded scale of luxury, and where the desire to lead the good life ironically becomes the prelude to death. Paradoxically, joining an Assassination Club where you pay to be killed at some unspecified time, as an alternative mode of death, seems to heighten life: "The effect of all this, it seems to me, is to make one more vigilant. Death is no longer an abstraction, but a real possibility that haunts each moment of life. Rather than submit passively to the inevitable, those marked for assassination tend to become more alert, more vigorous in their movements, more filled with a sense of life — as though transformed by some new understanding of things" (15). In an intriguing fashion, death, rather than functioning as a form of narrative closure, actually spices up the narrative and urges a new opening to life. Such a space of economic deprivation and daily hopelessness causes an inversion of "normal" human values, making the assassin a valuable social asset and death something one longs for, spending a great deal of money and effort upon, rather than seeking to avoid at all costs. Resulting from these sorts of inversions and paradoxes, Blume finds that a strange space emerges within the city, which one is unable to define and comprehend: a space that defies conventional actions; a space that incapacitates all habitual thought:

> Life as we know it has ended, and yet no one is able to grasp what has taken its place. Those of us who were brought up somewhere else, or who are old enough to remember a world different from this one, find it an enormous struggle just to keep up from one day to the next. I am not talking only of hardships. Faced with the most ordinary occur-

rence, you no longer know how to act, and because you cannot act, you find yourself unable to think. The brain is in a muddle. All around you one change follows another, each day produces a new upheaval, the old assumptions are so much air and emptiness. That is the dilemma. On the one hand, to accomplish this seems to entail killing off all those things that once made you think of yourself as human. Do you see what I am trying to say? *In order to live, you must make yourself die.* (*Country* 20; italics mine)

The constant push and pull of death on life always tests Blume's sense of self. This sublimation of self occurs repeatedly, and at one crucial point combines a sense of loss felt in the absence of the freedom of sexual expression, and the intense power that emerges in Blume when she is on the verge of murdering Ferdinand, Isabel's crippled and taunting husband. Blume mentions the way in which her body is subjected to sexual pressures as much as physical dangers. During these moments of reflection, she is aware that her mind and body are subjected to "an ache inside you, a horrendous, clamoring ache, and unless you do something about it, there will never be an end to it" (62). In the chaos of her mind every night, she feels battered by her daily existence: "my brain would be in such turmoil, heaving up images of the day I had just spent, taunting me with a pandemonium of streets and bodies" (62). Her release from this is lonely masturbation, a "sad little game," making believe "as if there were two of me and we were in each other's arms" (62). Rather than providing comfort, this merely reinforces her sense of isolation and loneliness, and Ferdinand's "barrage of insinuations and ugly cracks" (63) only adds to her sense of personal degradation. On the night of Ferdinand's attempt at rape, however, sex and murder coalesce, the one acting as a substitute for the other. At the moment that Ferdinand assaults her, Blume places her fingers around his neck in feigned embrace:

Then I began to squeeze, and a sharp little gagging sound came out of his throat. In that first instant after I began to apply the pressure, I felt an immense happiness, a surging, uncontrollable sense of rapture. It was as though I had crossed some inner threshold, and all at once the world became different, a place of unimaginable simplicity. I shut my eyes, and then it began to feel as though I were flying through an enormous night of blackness and stars. As long as I held on to Ferdinand's throat, I was free. I was beyond the pull of the earth, beyond the night, beyond any thought of myself. (65)

"Killing him for the pure pleasure of it" (65), Blume realizes with horror and disgust the sheer power and incredible absence of self brought on by her action. The sexual *frisson* excited by the power to kill is made clear in the metaphors of loss of control, surge, and rapture. The climax is described as freedom, flight, purity, and a release of subjective consciousness from enchainment. The power of taking life becomes equivalent to releasing her own life from the daily torture of her miserable existence. Here is an instance where sexual desire and the desire to kill are linked in a clear bid for release from physical limitations, a concept well-glossed by the narrator in *The Locked Room:* "I had entered my own darkness, and it was there that I learned the one thing that is more terrible than anything else: that sexual desire can also be the desire to kill, that a moment comes when it is possible for a man to choose death over life" (108). Blume retreats from this realization and reasserts her integrity through her resistance to the bestial and immoral behavior inculcated in and exerted upon people by the social structures of the city's exigencies and pressures.

Auster frequently uses death as an image of release and of transcendence: "I suddenly felt I was dead, as dead as Ferdinand in his blue suit, as dead as the people who were burning into smoke at the edges of the city. I became calmer than I had been in a long time, almost happy in fact . . . for several months after that I did not feel like myself anymore. I continued to live and breathe, to move from one place to another, but I could not escape the thought that I was dead, that nothing could ever bring me to life again" (*Country* 74–75). Auster has always been fascinated in his fiction with the experience of loneliness and isolation, of being detached from one's social environment, and the disembodied psychological effect this produces in the individual. This occurs most specifically in *City of Glass* where Stillman junior has suffered linguistic and mental dysfunction from isolation, and the detective-narrator Quinn ends up isolating himself to carry out his observations; in *Moon Palace,* where Marco Fogg finds himself living in isolated poverty in his apartment and then in Central Park, during which he tries "to separate myself from my body . . . In order to rise above my circumstances, I had to convince myself that I was no longer real, and the result was that all reality began to waver for me. Things that were not there would suddenly appear before my eyes, then vanish" (29–30); and more forthrightly, in *The Invention of Solitude,* where Auster powerfully relates his emotional loneliness after his father's death, and the breakup of his marriage. *In the Country of Last Things* widens the screen and amplifies these previously small episodes into the overriding narrative experience: the separation of an individual from conventional social intercourse and the effects that this deprivation and isolation have upon Anna Blume. Magnifying the most obscure and apparently paltry emotions, ideas, and feelings, the novel homes in on society's basic organization, observing the ways in which social structures change, the ways thoughts alter, and the change in social priorities and perspectives:

> Let everything fall away, and then let's see what there is. Perhaps that is the most interesting question of all: to see what happens when there is nothing, and whether or not we will survive that too.
>
> The consequences can be rather curious, and they often go against your expectations. Utter despair can exist side by side with the most dazzling invention; entropy and efflorescence merge. (29)

One is left with a clear description of social determination at work, and a clear demolition of any remnants of human essentialism.

The manner in which the city enforces the abolition of the self in order to survive is reminiscent of Marx's analysis of the workings of capitalism, where the demands of the system of commodity exchange impose a subtle eradication of subjectivity upon the individual consumer. With this metaphorical association, it is no surprise to find that this city is also a space of rampant individualistic competition. Pitting one against another in the outright cut-and-thrust of material acquisition rather than encouraging some form of communal development makes Victoria's project all the more unusual for its existence, despite the "swamp of contradictions" (142) that makes up the politics of welfare at Woburn House. Having been reduced to such abject poverty and desperation as scavengers, people are gullible and easily prey to confidence tricks: "Many of them are duped out of their money before the end of their first day. Some people pay for apartments that don't exist, others are lured into giving commissions for jobs that never materialize, still others lay out their savings to buy food that turns out to be painted cardboard" (7). The city works by a single ethical code — everything is a free-for-all: corruption, extortion, and racketeering function as the sole economic mechanisms. Government, as far as it functions, works best in the city when placed under some form of threat: "Dead bodies and shit — when it comes to removing health hazards, our administrators are positively Roman in their organization, a model of clear thinking and efficiency" (30).

However, as the fabric of society collapses and the social infrastructure disappears, society's ills and problems are exacerbated. Since people are constantly walking, footwear is vital. Blume outlines how people's efforts to keep dry are constantly foiled, and there are innumerable problems of ill health attendant upon this failure (23–24). The disrepair of sidewalks causes additional problems for people wishing to keep themselves dry and their vital shoes in decent condition (25). With predictions about the weather being so crucial to daily life, it comes as no surprise that there are fanatical organizations of belief about this aspect of existence as well.

Blume tells us about the Smilers, a sect that believes they can control the weather by personal feeling; and the Crawlers, who feel that the weather will only improve if we abase ourselves beneath the sky. In an imaginative representation, Auster demonstrates how social conditions determine the superstructural beliefs in a society.

Yet the novel goes on to demonstrate how dominant and hegemonic definitions of social space (and time) are perpetually under challenge and always open to modification. In this respect, *In the Country of Last Things* explores the interface between society and the social construction of time and space. The location of place becomes inextricably linked with its position within time: the exploration of situation is also an exploration of temporality. Location is understood as dependent on history or chronology, insofar as the classification of experience is indivisible from what came before and what knowledges were previously sanctioned. This exploration of place and time also embraces the exploration of what constitutes a subject, or how place and temporality constitute subjectivity. As we have seen, ontological interrogations persistently shape *In the Country of Last Things* as Auster reconfigures the relationship between spatial and temporal categories. The notion of subjective identity shifts throughout the text, oscillating between a fairly fixed and locatable entity and a much more fluid and slippery sense of subjectivity. Anna Blume's voice is shaped by her entangled relations with her "lived experience" and the dictates of the boundaries, placements, divisions, and lines of the city's abstract space. This intersection of spaces results in large measure from the cut-and-thrust competition in the marketplace of the city, since it is the market that is especially capable of mediating private desire and public activity.

What finally emerges from Auster's *In the Country of Last Things* is how fragmentation, ruptures, and discontinuities, far from being construed as liabilities and weaknesses, can be transformed into political strengths and opportunities for social resistance. Consequently, this network of pedestrian trajectories and "perambulatory processes" produces an "errancy that multiplies and assembles the city [as] a vast social experience in site deprivation," a series of intersections and interweavings in which "a universe of places haunted by a non-site or by dreamed sites" emerges (de Certeau, "Practices of Space," 139). Place and displacement are bound together, and de Certeau's "insertion strategies" allow for this dialectical movement.

Place, and what escapes articulation and emplacement, become the principal focus. Auster is concerned with unsanctioned histories, those not directly oppressed but occluded. He works between and among endorsed categories of knowledge, and in so doing, he jostles the sequencing of location. Instead of presenting direct causal links or chains for

Blume's narratives, the emphasis is placed on establishing loose sets of relations, capillary actions and movements, spilling out among and between different fields. Consequently, Auster is not interested in distancing himself from his locale in order to study it: universalizing the local is perceived as an obscurantist and dangerous thing. Rather than collapsing the local, he opens it up. He looks at the way the local has been constructed, what event is being reproduced in what place and how Blume's subjective experience of the local is circumscribed by the processes of location. The novel is a series of cognitive exercises, attempting to investigate the ongoing production of the world, its structural apparatuses, and how these function to shape one's perception of the world. In this manner, Auster's exploration of place is also a description of the epistemological maneuvers whereby categories of knowledge are established and fixed. Knowledge does not arise in direct correlation to the abolition of the subject's specificity. On the contrary, *In the Country of Last Things* demonstrates that knowledge is deeply complicit with the location of the subject, the "geography of the articulation," the space of the production of discourse.

Note

1. Auster has stated that he had a firm sense of historical realities when writing the novel, carrying around in his head the phrase " 'Anna Blume walks through the twentieth century' " when writing (306). See "Interview with Larry McCaffery and Sinda Gregory," in *The Art of Hunger* (269–312).

Works Cited

Auster, Paul. *The Art of Hunger: Essays, Prefaces, Interviews*. Los Angeles: Sun & Moon Press, 1992.
——. *City of Glass*. Los Angeles: Sun & Moon Press, 1985.
——. *Disappearances: Selected Poems*. Woodstock, N.Y.: The Overlook Press, 1988.
——. *In the Country of Last Things*. New York: Viking, 1987.
——. "Interview with Larry McCaffery and Sinda Gregory." In *The Art of Hunger: Essays, Prefaces, Interviews*. Los Angeles: Sun & Moon Press, 1992. Pp. 269–312.
——. *The Invention of Solitude*. New York: Penguin, 1988.
——. *The Locked Room*. Los Angeles: Sun & Moon Press, 1986.
——. *Moon Palace*. New York: Viking, 1989.
de Certeau, Michel. "Practices of Space." In M. Blonsky, ed., *On Signs: A Semiotics Reader*. Oxford: Blackwell, 1985. Pp. 122–145.
Harvey, David. *The Conditions of Postmodernity*. Oxford: Blackwell, 1989.
Jameson, Fredric. *Postmodernism, or the Cultural Logic of Late Capitalism*. London: Verso, 1991.
Lefebvre, Henri. *The Production of Space*. Trans. Donald Nicholson-Smith. Oxford: Blackwell, 1991. (Trans. of *La Production de l'espace*. France: Anthropos, 1974.)

McHale, Brian. *Constructing Postmodernism*. London and New York: Routledge, 1992.

———. *Postmodern Fiction*. Basingstoke: Macmillan, 1987.

Wittgenstein, Ludwig. *Tractatus Logico-Philosophicus*. Trans. D. F. Pears and B. F. McGuinness. London: Routledge and Kegan Paul, 1961.

Inside *Moon Palace*

Steven Weisenburger

> In the 1960s it was obvious, to the point of appearing to be "natural order," that language was with the people. Not so. The people it turned out were infinitely more unsettled than originally supposed. They were sick of the body, and many of them longed for the public body, for age, wisdom, and strong authority. The disgust with the political process and the wish for simple clarity also reflected a distrust of the Outside, a rejection of the metaphysical and a new desire for the comforting routine of the interior.
> —Andrei Codrescu, *The Disappearance of the Outside*

This epigraph is lifted from Andrei Codrescu's 1989 essay, "The North American Combine: Moloch and Eros," first published in *Columbia* magazine. Columbia University is also the alma mater of Marco Stanley Fogg, narrator of Paul Auster's *Moon Palace,* a 1989 novel saturated with references to 1492 and Cristoforo Columbo, to the systematic westwarding domination of the Outside after Columbus, and to the crisis of that progressive, modern, imperialistic ethos during the sixties — Codrescu's topic as well. In his essay Codrescu critiques the many sixties radicals who naively believed they could recuperate a "natural" and presumably regenerative "free speech" whose daisies, chucked against Moloch, would jam the gears of state power like organic monkeywrenches. Yet these pseudo-revolutionary desires, typically phrased in a discourse of polymorphous physicality, often masked a deeper abjection of the body and, moreover, a desire for restraint and even absolute control within "the public body" of the totalitarian state. Thus an age that pushed into the "final frontier" of space was paradoxically marked by a thoroughgoing suspicion of the Other, the Outside. The age burrowed Inside, Codrescu argues, naively disregarding how various "Outside" plots of mastery and violence criss-crossed its own discourses. Once inside, it only replayed old dramas of authority.

Paul Auster's fifth novel, *Moon Palace,* partly figures that cultural crisis in the terms of inheritance and genealogy. It was a canny move. In fictions of imperialist culture genealogical figuration has always been a dominant means for imagining the transmission and maintenance of power; and the quest for "proper" genealogy has been — from *Tom Jones* through *Absalom, Absalom!* — a quest for the origins of propriety and property. Auster's postmodern play with such figures turns an otherwise nostalgically retrospective novel into a revisionary critique. *Moon Palace* thus figures an American sixties that seems ontologically *similar* and yet importantly *different* from the one we (collectively) knew. Everywhere it is geographically and historically referenced; but these references also drive the narration Inside, into landscapes of metaphysical obsession that Andrei Codrescu also described in 1989. Now, I know of no relation, no "influence" or intellectual genealogy, that places the parallel texts of Codrescu and Auster in a line of descent. Their contemporaneous publication seems quite coincidental, yet that is itself worth remarking because chance and coincidence name the counterforces working against inheritance and genealogy in Auster's novel, and may even begin to define ways out of the degenerating interiors that Codrescu critiques.

As though it were an extended narrative meditation on Codrescu's argument, *Moon Palace* unfolds through a series of quests for natural language, fathers, authority, and history, always occurring within claustrophobic interiors. These spaces — in apartments, bedrooms, and caves — are sites for what Codrescu aptly defines as a "comforting routine," a degenerative obsession for origins and power that is dimly backlit, throughout *Moon Palace,* by oblique references to the historical 1960s: the occupation of administration offices at Columbia, the Apollo moon landing, and the Kent State massacre are key instances. Such moments unfold just beyond Fogg's threshold, or on television screens suspended in fogs of barroom smoke, in either case seemingly without embodiment, much less a connection to Fogg's intellectual preoccupations.

The novel insists otherwise. M. S. Fogg defines himself as a glitch "in the national machine," a text (or MS, as he notes [7]) whose actions are "living proof that the system had failed, that the smug, unfed land of plenty was falling apart" (61). The deteriorating social body thus finds its analogy in Fogg's body, as well as in the body of his story, itself a conventionally chronological quest-narrative whose recurring figure is the bodily self sliding irrevocably, like the story itself, toward the Zero: towards bankruptcy, starvation, and death; toward "the end." Yet Fogg's degenerative descents are also always checked and redirected by moments of coincidence, by glitches demonstrated in the text of the novel through characters' recognitions of the errant potentials in representational texts themselves. Such recognitions of errant coincidence are staged against the recuperation of Fogg's genealogy. For Marco himself this process of discovery unfolds through accidents so farfetched, so apparently contrived, that Gary Indiana (for example) uses them to flog Auster for writing a dryly "theoretical" and "mechanical" plot. It *is* mechanical, in the reading proposed here, but for purposes that need to be differently reckoned, though from the same details of the story its reviewers thrashed.

What is that story? In brief, it opens with Marco's relating the story of his mother's untimely death (she's run over by an errant bus), his adolescence spent with an eccentric uncle, and the death of Uncle Victor that leaves young Marco seemingly without family: these events set the stage for a series of extraordinary coincidences and accidents that unfold the long-standing mystery of the boy's paternity. First, though, Marco pays for his education at Columbia by gradually spending his mother's legacy and by selling off some 1,492 books inherited from Uncle Victor. After graduating in 1969 he's forced out of his claustrophobic apartment and into vagrancy, whereupon in a near visionary state induced by malnourishment he watches Neil Armstrong's moon walk, foretold (he reflects) at the end of "Passage to India," Whitman's ode to Columbus and Manifest Destiny. Rescued from starvation and disease that autumn, Fogg recovers and finds a lover in a Chinese woman named Kitty Wu, also an orphan. He answers a newspaper ad that leads to his becoming the companion for a wealthy eccentric, blinded by old age. This man's identity, as "Thomas Effing," then turns out to be a fifty-four-year ruse, as Marco discovers in transcribing the man's orally narrated autobiography, embedded as a story-within-the-story.

In 1916, as artist Julian Barber, Effing experiences a series of misfortunes while on a painting expedition in the Utah desert. Accident gives him the opportunity to abandon a frigid wife and contrive both a new self as well as a new fortune during the Jazz Age stock market boom. Subsequently, though, Effing realizes that before departing for Utah he had conceived a child with his wife Elizabeth, which child the woman's brother had reared after her lapse into insanity during childbirth. On Effing's death Marco contracts this heir, an obese professor of history named Solomon Barber, who turns out (in the novel's most extreme coincidence) to have been Emily Fogg's teacher and one-time lover, therefore Marco's father. This recognition comes almost simultaneously with Marco's own frustrated attempts at paternity (Kitty, over his vigorous objections, gets an abortion), but it is not the novel's end. Visiting Emily Fogg's grave with his newfound father, Marco accidentally tips Solomon Barber into an open grave, which fall eventually kills him, an absurdly oedipal twist that sends Marco westward, into the lunar, southwestern landscape where Effing's identity switch occurred, a site of seemingly limitless Gatsby-like potential. Effing's cave, however, has been recently inundated by the waters of Lake Powell. Thus failing that quest, and robbed of all but some four hundred dollars, Fogg resumes his linear, westwarding trajectory and walks from Lake Powell to the Pacific shore just south of Los Angeles at Laguna Beach. There the novel ends, a "full moon, round and yellow as a burning stone" shining over his shoulder (307) while he gazes on the Pacific Ocean, itself the watery trench formed by a cataclysmic tearing free of the moon sometime in geological prehistory. The reconstruction of Fogg's genealogy, now further inscribed under the aegis of geologic or cosmic temporality, stands complete.

Marco begins his tale in New York with "no evidence" of paternity and thus "a blank" (4) where his genealogy should be. He ends it at Los Angeles, having filled that gap through a quest for paternal origins, a quest that Marco never really intended but that readers (acting similar to Marco) rather systematically and authoritatively reconstruct. We do so, I want to argue, for quite powerful reasons of genre. The result, just as one might reconstruct genealogy in a Faulkner novel, may be graphed as follows:

Reconstruction of M. S. Fogg's Genealogy.

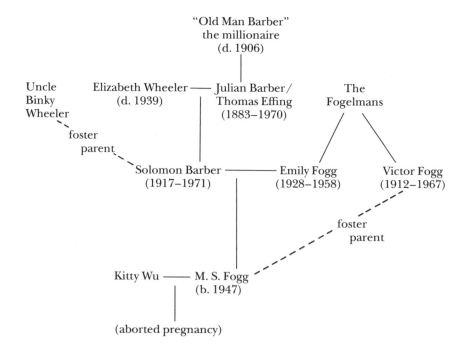

One point of reproducing Marco's heritage like this is to stress its profoundly in-grown effects. This genealogy simply fails to exfoliate in any "natural" way; it never grows "outside" the highly formalized obsessions of the family it represents. Instead the genealogy collapses inward on Marco and thus approaches a near erasure, or zeroing-out, in the abortion Kitty demands over his objections. Marco's genealogy formally inscribes the insanity, absence, and abortiveness of its maternal side, as compared to the alienated, unstable, and obsessive (yet equally successful) features of his recovered paternal side. Its putative beginning, in the nineteenth-century wealth of Effing's robber-baron father, "old man" Barber (146); then the successive degradation of that wealth through three generations, until Marco loses the last of it to unknown highway thieves somewhere in southern Utah, in 1971; and the *logic* of this, indeed its progression *from* the lunacy traced on Marco's maternal side *to* the rationality of his father, Sol: in all such details one recognizes a narrative so obviously symbolical, so anti-realistic (to borrow John Kuehl's terminology), it's a wonder that critics like Indiana (or Kornblatt, and others; for only Sven Birkerts's intelligent review of the novel broke through to understanding) would all so slavishly flog the narrative for violating realistic conventions. Clearly, one aim of Auster's technique is to push those conventions over the top, into a kind of metafictional, postmodern counter-practice.

Among the naturalizing conventions of narrative, none is more basic than "the genealogical imperative." Years ago Robert Nisbet described how the complex of causal propositions — the *proteron hysteron* sequences subtending narrative itself — achieve their clearest figuration in genealogy. The belief, as Nisbet puts it, "that events give birth to events" (352), or that in narrating a genealogy one merely uncovers causalities in natural events rather than artificially imposing them, commits realistic writing to a potent set of secondary assumptions. Chief among these is the assumption of an "inside" force or dynamic of event sequences, which it is the narrator's "natural" function to represent (359). Another is the assumption of some inherent determinism of which the novelistic diegesis, in all the formalist complexity of its plot orderings, stands as the privileged model.

Patricia Tobin has further analyzed the ways that these assumptions also serve to legitimize state authority by equating "the temporal form of the classical novel — the conceptualized frame within which its acts and images find their placement — with the dynastic line that unites the diverse generations" (6–7). Perhaps more than any other convention the genealogical metaphor thus limits a narrative fiction to the mimesis of a supposedly homogenous time and to the principal alibi for that linear, developmental temporality, "the subject" or hero. Most recently, Elizabeth Ermarth stresses these epistemological affiliations (22–24). She works from Kristeva's 1979 essay, "Women's Time," and equates the disposition toward linear and teleological temporality with a linguistic disposition to propose and summarize (rather than to play and multiply). In its totalizing demands it thus recalls the "obsessional time" of psychoanalysis; it figures a zeal for mastery over temporal process that is itself "the true structure of the slave" to official power (40–41). To Ermarth, these relations of temporal structures to ideology are deeply embedded in Western culture.

In modernist fictions, such as *The Rainbow* or *Go Down, Moses,* genealogy subtends a range of assumptions about origins, degraded modern society, and traces of man's primitive potency in the "blood." Faulkner and Lawrence valorize that power in differently inflected but ideologically similar (reactionary) myths. By contrast the postmodernist fiction, such as *J R* or *Gravity's Rainbow,* deploys a range of discontinuous and chance events to subvert genealogical, "historical" time. Edward Bast's inwardly collapsing family tree, like the diminution of an originary, Puritan self in Slothrop ("last of his line, and how far fallen," notes Pynchon), are principal figures reconstructed by any reading of these two novels. Yet in both novels such monuments to genealogy and dynastic history teeter above the increasingly quake-fractured ground of postmodern events. Undermined by the entropic and negentropic rhythms of Gaddis's narrative or by the stochastic flux into which Pynchon's postmodern subject (Slothrop) disappears, causal history tumbles aside. Conventional, causal history is too fragile, too limited, to fully *do* contemporary work. It cannot function as a reality principle for postmodern theatres of action. The more open the perceptive universe is to fluctuation and coincident innovation, the less *useful* are metaphors of genealogy and progressive growth.

Moon Palace opens with references to a dramatic expansion of that perceptible universe in the Apollo moon shot. Moreover, it quickly begins to plot the characters' loss of a continuous and coherent genealogy as the occasion for degenerative obsessions. Always staged *inside*—in Fogg's apartment or Effing's house—it is also figured as a stepwise, seemingly absolute consumption or divestiture. Attending Columbia, Fogg runs through his inheritance, as well as his uncle's 1,492 books, and gradually divests himself of things and conveniences. Knowing that "the process could not go on forever" (27), Marco recognizes that "the mind cannot win over matter" (29) but presses on in any case, nearly consuming his body through starvation. In contrast Sol Barber literally eats "his way to the brink of oblivion" (242) after his disastrously discovered intercourse with Emily Fogg, which loss of a beloved has (he erroneously thinks) cut short any hope for genealogical extension. His eventual death is also phrased as a long, slow rallentando into the grave whose financial cost, ironically, further diminishes the inheritance of a son and heir he never knew he fathered. Analogously, Barber/Effing authors a new identity without any conception of Elizabeth's conception. Then, painting from the threshold of his Utah cavern, in 1916, Effing runs through his tubes of pigment as well as his available canvasses and consumes the available scenery itself, "as though he could feel the landscape vanishing before his eyes" (171). These are Marco's words, as conventional a "foreshadowing" of the old man's actual blindness as readers could want, but understood here as the 20-20 hindsight commanded by determinist temporality. Yet Effing's calculated diminution of his fortunes and his vitality toward the zero-point of death has a further twist: he accurately predicts the date of his demise, on May 12, 1970. (After Kent State, American soldiers were "Pulling Out of Cambodia," notes the *New York Times;* and Marco's team, the Chicago Cubs, grabbed a 4-to-3 eleventh inning victory over the Braves on Ernie Banks' 500th home run: more coincidental tidbits from the annals of time.) Yet any such predictive, millenialist inscriptions of "the End," the informing apocalyptic desire of modernist temporality, is exactly what Auster's narration always counters. In the midst of the first, long drift toward starvation in 1969, Marco already glimpses the possibility of his own release from determinist time. "Causality was no longer the hidden demiurge that ruled the universe," he recalls thinking, for "down was up, the last was first, the end was the beginning" (62). That echo of Eliot, though, is a calculated deception. The narrative never proposes a metaphysical leap out of time.

What then is the alternate mode of temporality that *Moon Palace* imputes to events? In the desert, having exhausted his food supplies, paints, and canvas, Barber/Effing recognizes that a phase of his existence has concluded "with the force and speed of a book slamming shut." He feels it also as the conclusion of a sentence; a death sentence, in fact. Precisely at this moment, however, "his life suddenly veered in a new direction" (181). The Greshams, a band of outlaws, shows up to reclaim the booty on which Effing has been surviving in his cave. He kills them, and twenty thousand dollars of stolen money found in their saddlebags places him at the doorstep of a new existence, "trying to imagine what he would do next" (182). This instance strikingly implicates the structures of imaginative discourse, especially narrative discourse, in the fashioning of temporality: what seemed foreclosed and predetermined, a *sentence,* veers randomly off on unforeseen trajectories. Over and over again this is the rhythm of events in *Moon Palace.* Each time characters approach a "dead end" or "period" (289) concluding any particular "sentence," then chance and contingency take over. Thus even as Marco slowly starves in Central Park, the charitable gifts of total strangers alter his daily course and it seems to him as though each miraculous gift is "always the last miracle. And because it was the last, I was continuously being thrown back to the beginning" (59). This amounts to saying that any conception of events as "plot" (with beginning, middle, and end), must be ceaselessly reinvented on the basis of contingent potentials. On this view the "sentence" or "period" is supplanted by the "phase."

There are strong analogies for such a reading in current science. Ilya Prigogine and Isabelle Stengers, for example, discuss how the lineal trajectories of classical dynamics have given way to new models of "dissipative" processes defined by phasal rhythms. In their descriptions, the "end" of any process requires neither theories of finality nor closure (as with entropy), but instead those of "translation" or phasal "fluctuation." Now, in a complex, multilevel environment of life processes beyond prediction or "control" in any classical sense, the "end" of one phase must be conceived as the probabilistic fluctuation of forces leading — but only *stochastically* leading — into the "beginning" of still another phase. These ceaseless, sustaining, negentropic fluctuations do indeed bring "order out of chaos," in Prigogine and Stengers's phrase; yet they also resist mechanical description and depend entirely on stochastic formulae for any modeling of them. The element of chance, then, emerges (if we must) as *the* definitive law in the rhythm of nature, particularly in the ceaseless production of novel states.

Such concepts sharpen the edge of Marco's statement, in the first paragraph of *Moon Palace*, about how he "eventually" came to see "chance as a form of readiness, a way of saving myself through the minds of others" (1). Going inside *Moon Palace* means readying oneself for such chances. It also means being undeceived about the ethics of such chances. After all, the prospects for self-renewal "through the minds of others" would seem to involve conventional standards of immanence or compassion with presumably stable subjects, an ethos where humanistic intentionality remains intact. Marco, for example, is saved from starvation because of the dogged efforts of Kitty Wu and Zimmer, an old friend. But this is not always the case. Barber's several shifts of phase in the desert are enabled by brutal violence: first, the prior murder of the cave-dwelling hermit whose stockpiled foods allow Effing to survive and paint; then Barber's murder of the outlaws whose fortune in money and bonds enables his full assumption of a new identity, as "Effing." Traditional hierarchies of value have nothing, necessarily, to do with such chance transitions. In a still greater extension of these problems, Auster puts historiographic representation on the same uncertain ground by disclosing that Sol Barber's nationally acclaimed scholarly "histories" are the phantasmic products of his own lack of, or quest for, a father, itself a phasal process whose markers are his three books. Each is received as another hallmark of determinist historical thought, another explanatory narrative of America's westwarding destiny. Each was composed, however, over the abysses of that originary lack. Temporality thus took shape as "history" for Sol under the aegis of his Apollonian name; but ironically, too, this process climaxed for him during phases of proliferating coincidences and deeply felt crises (bankruptcies) of phallogocentric power.

Moon Palace submits representational art to the same critique, and its principal instances are taken from American landscape painting. So in a long, rambling discourse to Marco, at the virtual center of the novel, Effing criticizes the nineteenth-century realists, Thomas Moran and Albert Bierstadt in particular, for their complicity with structures of domination and control:

> Manifest Destiny! They mapped it out, they made pictures of it, they digested it into the great American profit machine. Those were the last bits of the continent, the blank spaces no one had explored. Now here it was, laid out on a pretty piece of canvas for everyone to see. The golden spike driven right through our hearts! (149)

This seems a rhetoric of romantic revolutionism, but Effing insists not ("I didn't hold with any of that romantic bullshit") and instead stakes his claim to difference from these painters on the basis of painterly versus linear technique: "The line didn't interest me. Mechanical abstraction, the canvas as the world, intellectual art — I saw it as a dead end" (150). In fact Effing regards the modernists who hung about Stieglitz's gallery at 209 Fifth Avenue — John Marin, Charles Demuth, Man Ray — as merely the unwitting inheritors of nineteenth-century realism, an extension of that dead-end path.

By contrast, Effing's exemplary artist is the obscure nineteenth-century painter Ralph Albert Blakelock (1847–1919). Indeed, so vital is Blakelock to this novel, and particularly Blakelock's 1885 canvas "Moonlight," that any reading of Auster will have to take account of the Blakelock image as a standard of aesthetic, moral, and ideological values in this novel. Its plotting in the narrative needs careful reading. Marco sees "Moonlight" at Effing's behest, putting himself before it in the Brooklyn Museum after being urged "to enter the landscape before you. See if you can't begin to enter the mind of the artist who painted the landscape" (135). Effing's enjoinder presumes on aesthetic texts as intersections of "inside" and "outside" as well as on a vigorous response to them, one goal of which is to reconstruct intention. But Marco himself realizes the difficulty of reading the traces of intentionality on the canvas, mainly because he also pays heed to the contingencies of "noise" — figured as the voices of other museum goers that "imposed themselves" in the gallery, despite Marco's attempts to "shut them out" (136). Persisting, in fact, he eventually recognizes in "Moonlight" a "landscape of inwardness and calm" so opposite to the rantings of his "mad employer" (137) that he must put Effing out of mind as well. In short he must also unwittingly (for he doesn't yet know the full facts of his heritage), as well as coincidentally (because of the noisiness around him) deny the imperatives of his grandfather. In doing so Marco denies the genealogical imperative in a broader sense.

What follows in *Moon Palace* is a reading of "Moonlight" that Auster originally published (with slight variations) in a 1987 issue of *Art News*. For our purposes the significant aspect of it is Auster's reading of the canvas as an antirepresentational text, one whose mimetic details (the disk-like moon centered over a lake, a stream dividing the landscape in two, the left bank and its Indian teepee, the right with a large tree and solitary horseman) are significantly undone by Blakelock's painterly brushstrokes and, still more important, by his apparently lunatic disregard for realistic color: an underwash of green pigment shows "beneath the cracked glazes" (138) and suffuses the moonstruck figures in a weirdly serene hue. Marco (like Auster, in the magazine piece) therefore recognizes that any reading of the canvas must involve "wild, symbolic judgments," as well as Blakelock's intention of "painting an American idyll" (138), a "memorial" for "a vanished world" of cross-cultural contacts between Native American and Eurocentric culture. What most troubles Marco (and, apparently, Auster) is the loss of a unique chance to claim a contingent but symbolically rich ground for innovative cultural contact, a chance seen as having been destroyed under the wheels of an obsessively lineal narrative of progress and destiny.

If this is the ideological center of *Moon Palace* — and I believe its placement in the text says so, just as Blakelock's moon appears in "the precise mathematical center" (137) of his canvas — then there are further consequences for reading. One of them is that with few exceptions Blakelock himself has existed as an absence or unrecognized chance, his place on the genealogy of American art acknowledged only in "a few articles here and there, a couple of old catalogues, nothing much" (140), as Marco notes. In this claim he is historically right. Excepting the Whitney and Stuurman catalogues, or Vernon Young's fine essay, there's little of any note on Blakelock. In fact, like Young and Stuurman, Auster derived most of his details about the painter's life from Lloyd Goodrich's introduction to the 1947 Whitney exhibition, and if one is interested in the provenance or intellectual inheritance of "historical" facts then the Blakelock vignette in *Moon Palace* makes an interesting study.

One strategy of Auster is to have Effing particularize the details about Blakelock where Goodrich offered only generalities. For example, where the Whitney catalogue of 1947 describes Blakelock as "small and slightly built" with "shy yet keen eyes — the face of a dreamer" (Whitney Museum, *Ralph Albert Blakelock* 9), in Effing's "recollection" the man is "like a midget. Eighty, ninety pounds if he was lucky," and with a "sunken, far-off look in his eyes, the eyes of a madman" (*Moon Palace* 131). Far more important, though, is the modal shift these "facts" describe. In the Goodrich account Blakelock's is the "face of a dreamer," which is consonant with the narration of his biography in a tragic mode, indeed as "one of the most tragic artist's lives ever recorded" (Whitney Museum, *Blakelock* 41). But Effing's reinscription — "the eyes of a madman" — occurs in a mode of irony, and the disruptive force of that irony has important consequences for one's reading of *Moon Palace*. For example, Goodrich makes relatively little of Blakelock's contact with Native Americans and his eventual adoption — during the onset of his madness — of Indian garb. According to a letter from the artist's wife, quoted by Goodrich, around 1885 (the time he painted "Moonlight") Blakelock "had a very fantastic way of dressing. He had a beard and wore his hair long. He made *for himself* all sorts of sashes and belts of richly colored embroidery, to these he attached long strings of beads and trinkets of all sorts. He also carried an old dagger which he made no effort to conceal. . . . I am sure he wore it only because he thought it artistic" (Whitney Museum, *Blakelock* 31; italics mine). Her account stresses the costume as an act of nineteenth-century Bohemian self-styling, with only a partial debt to the Native Americans he had evidently befriended (Whitney Museum, *Blakelock* 12). In Effing's account, however, the artist's relations with Native Americans take on a central role and his insane costuming becomes a clear inheritance from Blakelock's Indian sojourn: "when he finally cracked," says Effing, Blakelock "put on an Indian costume some chief had given him twenty years before and started walking through the streets of god-damned New Jersey dressed like that. Feathers sticking out of his head, beads, sashes, long hair, a dagger around his waist, the whole kit and boodle. Poor little bugger" (132).

With its obvious reflections on the counter-cultural self-stylings of sixties radicals, this reinscription of Blakelock's biography links both the artist and his aesthetic to American history in crucial ways. Blakelock is, in the first place, the lunatic offspring of American art, omitted from most available histories and scarcely ever recalled in authorized genealogies of aesthetic influence. In the second place, in Auster's novel his life story stresses the subversion of representational values within that official genealogy. For in canonical genealogy value is represented, most obviously, in terms of inheritance: specifically by way of properties or monetary sums. Yet long after he was locked up, Goodrich explains, the impoverished Blakelock had painted his own money, and just a few years before his death Blakelock handed over to art collector William Cresmer a "roll of bills . . . paintings of the size, shape and color of paper currency . . . but actually landscapes painted to resemble it. One of them bears the figure $1,000,000" (Whitney Museum, *Blakelock* 38). In what becomes the clearest reinscription of Blakelock's biography, Auster places these events *before* the artist's incarceration, and puts them in more clearly subversive terms: "As if that wasn't bad enough, he [Blakelock] got it into his head to start making his own money. Hand-painted thousand-dollar bills with his own picture on them — right in the middle, like the portrait of some founding father. One day he walks into the bank, hands one of those bills to the teller, and asks him to change it. . . . It wasn't long before they decided to cart him off for good" (132). In this account, Blakelock's lunacy is documented by the attempt to become his own "founding father" in putting the picture of himself "right in the middle" of the counterfeited bills, all of which we recognize as Auster's fictional embellishment (in Goodrich, the bills had landscapes instead of faces painted on them). What makes this moment different from the attempt of any canonical American subject — from Ben Franklin through Jay Gatsby — to become a self-made man, his own "founding father"? Is it, perhaps, that in Auster's view that self is always already a patchwork or "intertext" of stylings, or degraded parodies of other, often over-romanticized subjects? If so, then doesn't Auster's figure of Ralph Albert Blakelock further the irony in the naively nativistic self-fashionings of sixties radicals, whose claims of authentic selfhood only managed to lead them (according to this view) even more decisively, like Blakelock, into the asylum or "Moon Palace" of their own lunacies?

Such interrogations of *Moon Palace* would stress its revisionary critique of sixties radicalism but mistakenly sidestep the issue of money: the cash nexus of American artistic production and consumption. By all accounts (see Begley's 1992 essay, for example, or the McCaffery-Gregory interview of 1992) Auster's own career was for years defined by financial hardships punctuated, like that of Marco Fogg, by a timely but seemingly coincidental inheritance. On this view the presence of Ralph Albert Blakelock dead center in *Moon Palace,* dressed as an Indian brave and attempting to exchange those bills, his own image painted dead center on them, becomes doubly significant. He's an artist gone lunatic, Effing claims, because of stresses brought on by eight starving children and unscrupulous art dealers, people like Effing's father, whose name (Barber) Effing is given the extraordinary *chance* to renounce. But what is finally involved in such a wholesale renunciation of paternal authority, genealogical determinations, and the cash nexus? Auster's reading of Blakelock's "Moonlight" provides answers. It focuses, notably, on the *gaps* of a realistic representation. Marco says that the moons in Blakelock's paintings always resemble "holes in the canvas, apertures of whiteness looking out onto another world" (141). Not windows, in the conventional mimetic sense, they are understood as the gaps or "apertures" specific to any medium; in *Moon Palace* they are figured as highly contingent insufficiencies or errancies in any representational apparatus. Their potential function, once one has gotten Inside, is to paradoxically open onto the unrecognized and novel world Outside, a world of "alteriors" charged with new social and ideological powers.

This reading of the Blakelock scenes in *Moon Palace* also spins us back to prior moments when the novel has been concerned with representational discourse. At one point, responding to another of Effing's enjoinders — this time that he supply the blind old man with a verbal picture of the sights around them — Marco considers the immensity of such a task. There are for instance "the accidents and losses" of temporality itself, the mutability of natural being, in which "inanimate things were disintegrating [and] all living things were dying"; but most of all there is the absolutely unstable ground of things seen from the standpoint of physical phenomena: "the unceasing explosions of matter, the collisions, the chaos boiling under the surface of all things" (122). At first Marco errs on the side of overdetermination. In "a mad scramble to leave nothing out" he builds wild Whitmanian catalogues and piles "too many words on top of each other, and rather than reveal the thing before us, they were in fact obscuring it." Marco soon recognizes that, if his purpose is to "help him [Effing] see for himself," then "the more air I left around a thing, the happier the results" (123). He learns to exult in the gaps. Rejecting Emerson's idealist doctrine, in *Nature,* that "words are signs of natural facts," Marco revels in the errancy of representational discourse rather than in its finality. There, amidst the acausal spaces between words and things, in the gaps that a determinist or genealogical metaphysics would seek to banish, are chances for innovation. As I see it, more than just the postmodernity of Auster's novel rests on such recognitions. *Moon Palace* represents the sixties as an age deeply complicitous with the very discourses that it sought to escape, even as alternate modes of symbolization lie scattered in the coincidences and fissures of the times. This recognition makes it a novel of remarkable political power.

A further recognition of this argument in *Moon Palace* occurs when we realize how the Chinese restaurant for which the novel is titled exists, practically, as a gap or absence. Marco eats three meals there, we're told; yet the restaurant exists mainly as a name, without descriptive passages or traits of any kind. "Moon Palace" remains, literally, just its sign, first glimpsed from Marco's dingy little room during the political upheavals of the 1960s. Being inside *Moon Palace* means, then, inhabiting this representational gap or errancy. It means rejecting our "wish for simple clarity" in the dissimulated authority of dynastic power and its narratives. It means recovering, through the contingencies in texts, "apertures" leading to that complex Outside of which Andrei Codrescu has written.

Works Cited

Auster, Paul. "Interview with Larry McCaffery and Sinda Gregory," in *The Art of Hunger: Essays, Prefaces, Interviews.* Los Angeles: Sun & Moon Press, 1992. Pp. 269–312.
———. *The Invention of Solitude.* 1982. New York: Penguin, 1989.
———. " 'Moonlight' in the Brooklyn Museum." *Art News* 86.7 (September 1987): 104–105.
———. *Moon Palace.* New York: Viking, 1989.
Begley, Adam. "Case of the Brooklyn Symbolist." *New York Times Magazine,* 30 August 1992, pp. 41, 52–54.
Birkerts, Sven. Review of *Moon Palace. The New Republic* 27 (March 1989): 36.
Codrescu, Andrei. *The Disappearance of the Outside.* Reading, Mass.: Addison-Wesley, 1990.
Dangerfield, Elliot. "Ralph Albert Blakelock." *Art in America* 51.4 (August 1963): 83–85.
D'Otrange-Mastai, D. L. "Ralph Blakelock, American Visionary." *Connoisseur* 151 (1962): 272.
Ermarth, Elizabeth Deeds. *Sequel to History: Postmodernism and the Crisis of Representational Time.* Princeton, N.J.: Princeton University Press, 1992.
Gebhard, David, and Phyllis Stuurman. *The Enigma of Ralph Albert Blakelock, 1847–1919.* Santa Barbara, Calif.: The Art Galleries, University of California-Santa Barbara, 1969.
Indiana, Gary. "Pompous Circumstance: Paul Auster Indulges Himself." *Village Voice* 4 April 1989, p. 45.
Klein, Ellen Lee. "Ralph Albert Blakelock." *Arts Magazine* 62.4 (December 1987): 102.
Kornblatt, Joyce Reiser. "The Remarkable Journey of Marco Stanley Fogg." Review of *Moon Palace, New York Times Book Review,* 19 March 1989, pp. 8–9.
Kristeva, Julia. "Women's Time" [1979]. Trans. Alice Jardine and Harry Blake. *Signs* 7.1 (1981): 31–53.
Kuehl, John. *Alternate Worlds: A Study of Antirealistic American Fiction.* New York: New York University Press, 1989.
Nisbet, Robert. "Genealogy, Growth, and Other Metaphors." *New Literary History* 1.3 (1970): 351–364.
Prigogine, Ilya, and Isabelle Stengers. *Order out of Chaos: Man's New Dialogue with Nature.* 1979. New York: Bantam, 1984.
Tobin, Patricia D. *Time and the Novel: The Genealogical Imperative.* Princeton, N.J.: Princeton University Press, 1978.
Whitney Museum of American Art. *Ralph Albert Blakelock: Centenary Exhibition.* Intro. Lloyd Goodrich. New York: Whitney Museum, 1947.
Young, Vernon. " 'Out of the Deepening Shadows': The Art of Ralph Albert Blakelock." *The Arts* 32.4 (October 1957): 24–29.

The Music of Chance: Aleatorical (Dis)harmonies Within "The City of the World"

Tim Woods

In a poignant moment of gradually dawning consciousness in Paul Auster's novel *Ghosts* in *The New York Trilogy,* the quasi-detective figure Blue begins to reflect upon the circumstances in which he finds himself:

> The picture is far more complicated than Blue ever imagined. For almost a year now, he has thought of himself as essentially free. . . . Now, after the incident with the masked man and the further obstacles that have ensued, Blue no longer knows what to think. It seems perfectly plausible to him that he is also being watched, observed in the same way that he has been observing Black. If that is the case, then he has never been free. From the very start he has been the man in the middle, thwarted in front and hemmed in on the rear. (55–56)

Characteristic of his abiding interest in the way our narratives ground our perspective, and constitute dialectical relationships of power, this passage demonstrates Paul Auster's preoccupation with the fictions of power and the power of fictions. In many of his novels, Auster's focus falls on the single or isolated individual's efforts to realize a degree of independence and freedom. The struggles against the restrictions of individual freedoms often result in specific epistemological and ontological anxieties, frequently precipitating crises of confidence in what separates reality from appearance for the various protagonists. The intricate relationships of text, narrative, and authority are explored in *The New York Trilogy,* resulting in the perplexing relationship between Quinn and Stillman in *City of Glass,* and the tangled power perspectives of Blue in *Ghosts.* Auster also explores the manner in which language invades and structures sound and silence in his poems in *Disappearances,* the working out of the tense and difficult father-son relationship in *The Invention of Solitude,* the embattled and complex triangular relationship of Effing, Fogg, and Kitty in *Moon Palace,* and the futurist critique of a totalitarian society in *In the Country of Last Things.* In all these texts, Auster has concentrated on the function of power, especially on its constitutive and oppressive effects.

Ghosts continues with Blue recognizing that some form of action is called for to rectify his position of insecurity, and through an image of the master-slave relationship, he envisages himself

> like a slave stumbling onto a vision of his own freedom. He imagines himself somewhere else, far away from here, walking through the woods and swinging an axe over his shoulder. Alone and free, his own man at last. He would build his life from the bottom up, an exile, a pioneer, a pilgrim in the new world. But this is as far as he gets. For no sooner does he begin to walk through these woods in the middle of nowhere than he feels Black is there too, hiding behind some tree, stalking invisibly through some thicket, waiting for Blue to lie down and close his eyes before sneaking up on him and slitting his throat. It goes on and on, Blue thinks. If he doesn't take care of Black now, there will never be any end to it. This is what the ancients called fate, and every hero must submit to it. There is no choice, and if there is anything to be done, it is only the one thing that leaves no choice. (222)

This is an allegorical passage suggestive of Thoreau's spontaneous encounter with nature recorded in *Walden.*[1] In Auster's parodic allusion, the threat of hidden physical violence lurking to waylay the heroic pioneering figure in the wilderness, and the realization that Blue is locked into some inescapable relationship of struggle with Black, forces a speculation on the cause of events. Blue's paradox is that if he has any chance at all, it is that he must accept fate and his determined course of events; and if he has no choice, it is because he is subject to fate. This submission of agency, the recourse to fate and the implied unalterable succession of events, opens another theme that preoccupies the writing of Auster: self-determination, inevitability, agency, and chance. The metaphor of the heroic pioneer seeking a pure space for freedom and independence, where someone can control every chance, is also an attempt to master death. Yet the subject is never autonomous. The "escape" from the unmasterable becomes an undermining of the centered self, an upsetting of the self-determining subject, an exile from oneself. The proximity of death is forever with us, and causes us to live in a state of perpetual separation from ourselves. Black becomes the unmasterable double that makes Blue a "self"-doubting Thomas. He recognizes the abyss of his own undoing. Blue has to kill his double; this is his heroic submission to fate.

It is also the manner in which Blue acts out his fictional archetype as a "hero." Yet what is his fate, and how does one know that, other than by an enunciation, which is itself a human product?

The Music of Chance is no exception to this interest in the effects and operations of power, and the nature of cause and effect. Furthermore, as the passage from *Ghosts* suggests, these ideas are bound up with a meditation on the American ideology of progress and expansion, especially as it was figured and represented in the settlement of the American wilderness. As with the novel *Moon Palace,* Auster's exploration and critique of power and the desire for freedom continues to form part of a critique of the ideology of American capitalism based on Puritan expansionism. His exploration of myths and archetypes attached to the American dream centers specifically on the thematic of freedom, a central pole of the Constitution of the United States. The problem of whether one's life is determined, or whether one is in control of one's life, is an echo that resonates throughout *The Music of Chance.* The principal protagonist, Nashe, is constantly pondering whether he either is or is not in control of things any longer; and his conclusions frequently turn out to be merely illusions on his part, since things clearly slip from his grasp only too easily.

The issue of self-determination and freedom against a predetermined set of ends — whether one has the freedom to control one's own actions or not — is a subject that recurs in a number of different guises throughout *The Music of Chance,* and consequently, the principal figures are kept in a state of indecision and uncertainty about their ontological status. It is an anxiety that haunts Auster's fiction time and again, from the anxiety-ridden statements of the female narrator of *In the Country of Last Things,* to the speculative and interrogative fictional strategies of *The New York Trilogy,* to the coincidental associations within *Moon Palace.* In the final analysis, chance or accident is regarded as an unknowable and impenetrable possibility of pattern, although always obscurely evading specific definition and tangible isolation.

This essay will focus on this interrelated matrix of agency, freedom, and power, as Auster explores their relationship within the context of late twentieth-century capitalist America. It will suggest that Auster's interest is in the way the subject continually finds itself the victim of fictions, a willed unity hiding a variety of paradoxical and contradictory desires, ideas, opinions, and ideologies. The definitions of self and world emerge as the result of a struggle for conceptual mastery, against or within various formations of power, and this becomes an attempt to defer the moment of death, the ultimate fate. In so doing, *The Music of Chance* dramatizes the current feeling of living through a "legitimation crisis." The text oscillates between the notion that mental and conceptual representations passively reflect the structure of an ultimately fixed and unaltering reality of essences, and alternatively, the recognition that existence is largely an aesthetic act, and that one can become the author of one's own life, become one's own supreme fiction.

The Matrix of Chance

The title of *The Music of Chance* suggests an oxymoronic state of affairs, wherein there is a harmony of discontinuities, a set of uncontrollable parameters that nevertheless provide a fine pattern of togetherness and interconnectedness. This paradoxical "ordered disorderedness" signals the text's central concern with the implications of chance, and the extent to which an arrangement of events is predetermined or not. As the novel opens, self-identity and the location of subjectivity hinge on the sequence and origins of events or actions: "It all came down to a question of sequence, the order of events" (1). Yet the opening pages of the novel emerge as a collage of chance events: his father winning a huge amount of money (his legacy to Nashe) by playing "the stock market in his spare time" (3); the chance finding of Nashe by his father's lawyer; the "sudden, unpremeditated decision" (6) when Nashe misses the correct ramp on the freeway for Boston, which makes him drive south for two weeks and which opens up "a dizzying prospect — to imagine all that freedom, to understand how little it mattered what choice he made" (6). Having been grabbed by the travel bug, Nashe seeks a new existence by exorcising the old one: he "kills" himself by putting the bullet of life through his head, which "triggers the birth of new worlds" (10). He forges a new life as he melts the old, cutting off his past through an orgy of aimless travel and topographical shiftlessness. This existence of casual and indeterminate drifting breeds a "new life of freedom and irresponsibility" (11). Chance disrupts the logic of causality, and there are now no reasons for Nashe to do one thing or another: chance opens up the possibility of anything, or indeterminacy. This new mode of existence establishes specific changes in Nashe's spatial and temporal orientations, as a certain release from fixity occurs:

> Speed was of the essence, the joy of sitting in the car and hurtling himself through space. . . . Nothing around him lasted for more than a moment, and as one moment followed another, it was as though he alone continued to exist. He was a fixed point in a whirl of changes, a body poised in utter stillness as the world rushed through him and disappeared (11).

This has an uncanny resemblance to certain descriptions of the modernist existence: the hierarchy of space over time; the transitory and solitary nature of existence, almost solipsistic and psychedelic; the subject as the "still point" in a modernist vortex, gyre, or chaos of existence, in which life is only manifested *through* him. Nashe enters into an existence that liberates him from his material and physical circumstances. Endless travel provides the means to experience a freedom from the exigencies and demands of a life determined by the pressures of a daily job and a collapsing marriage. Through cutting loose "on the road," Nashe can defy conventional temporal demands as well as spatial demands, limited only by the technical requirements of the car and the physical capacities of his body. He can escape the transcendent demands made by impersonal forces and fulfill all his personal cravings. The music in Nashe's car has the effect of

> turning the visible world into a reflection of his own thoughts . . . he had only to enter the car to feel that he was coming loose from his body, that once he put his foot down on the gas and started driving, the music would carry him into a realm of weightlessness. (12)

This disembodiment, a release of self-consciousness, is also a shift from the material world into the immaterial world, or the space of incorporeality. In his sense of social failure as a father and a husband, Nashe seeks an ontological suspension, what one reviewer has described as an "orbital nullity" (Bell, "Poker and Nothingness," 15–16).

Nashe also desires to achieve a sense of independent agency: "to feel that he had taken his life into his own hands" (*Music* 12–13). In a "situation . . . beyond repair" (4), a life that has already been determined beyond his control, "he saw the stranger [Pozzi] as a reprieve, as a last chance to do something for himself before it was too late" (1). While Nashe desires to chart a determined course through his life, he nevertheless finds events continually occurring as a result of "one of those random, accidental encounters that seem to materialize out of thin air — a twig that breaks off in the wind and suddenly lands at your feet" (1). Even his meeting with his old friend Fiona Wells in Berkeley, "like most things that had happened to him that year, it came about purely by chance" (14). The entire plot is shaped by a chance event.

Despite these recognitions, Nashe constantly attempts to rationalize chance, to dig up the archaeology of random events, to fit illogical interruptions back into the schema of logical progressions. Like Rousseau's dream in the *Confessions,* which he reads one night, Nashe seeks to create a certainty from chance: after opening oneself up to the vagaries of accident, and not liking what chance determines, he narrows the odds until chance is virtually eliminated, in "naked self-deception" (53). Such a hedging of bets is what staves off the threat that possibly the world is not within his control, and that the concept of human agency is a self-induced illusion; or worse, that subjectivity and agency are a sort of Althusserian ideological fallacy imposed by some form of hegemonic group[2] (see my later discussion of Stone's City of the World and the Four Realms of Togetherness [*Music* 79], as analogous to the columns of Althusser's conception of Ideological State Apparatuses and ideological control). The novel appears to suggest that through one of the cruel ironies of modern existence, by following the appeal of chance and accident, Nashe ineluctably ends up in a totally determined and controlled system.

As a subject who desires a sense of self-determination, Nashe frequently objectifies his situations and the future possibilities of his actions in a remarkably detached and collected manner:

> The strange thing was not that he was able to imagine this possibility but that he could do so with such indifference and detachment, with so little inner pain. It was as if he finally had no part in what was about to happen to him. And if he was no longer involved in his own fate, where was he, then, and what had become of him? (59)

As usual for Auster, the collapse of agency incurs an ontological uncertainty and crisis, as a desperate Nashe tries to fix his temporal and spatial location. Yet Nashe's predilection for such analytical thought typifies his rationalist character. Even on the brink of possible calamity in his life, the disappearance of all his money and with it, his potential for freedom, he objectifies the nature of autonomy and dependence in the clinical reduction of his freedom and capacities, to ten one-thousand-dollar notes: "There was something clean and abstract about doing it this way, he found, a sense of mathematical wonder in seeing his world reduced to ten small pieces of paper" (92). Yet despite Nashe's scrupulous analyticism, he becomes engaged in a picaresque adventure, in which his search for self-definition occurs in a world of unstable subjectivity, insecure social values, and a complete lack of clearcut and definite logical progressions. If Nashe learns anything as a result of his experiences with Pozzi, it is that there are no epistemological certainties; and furthermore, that perhaps in an existentialist mode, the only ontological certainty is death.

For *The Music of Chance* presents us with a narrative that invites a rationalist and realist interpretation, but which increasingly takes on a surrealist content. The narrative moves from freedom (for example, Nashe's discussion with Fiona Wells, the United States as the embodiment of freedom, and the open traveling across the states on "freeways"), to a lack of movement and complete isolation and enforced fixity: utter imprisonment. The novel proceeds by certainties giving way to doubts, appearances crumbling into illusions, determined courses being undermined by chance events. Perhaps the single most tantalizing issue of chance occurs in the poker match, and the extent to which the loss in the poker game was due to bad luck (chance), or to Flower and Stone cheating (agency). Like the poker player, the reader looks for patterns in the novel, only to find that the patterns are hesitantly presented, and tentatively gestured toward. Like the poker player, the important thing is to remain inscrutable, and the text operates by minimizing clues to what is occurring. With these preoccupations, Auster's novel deals with the perennial postmodern anxiety of neurosis and paranoia about the extent to which everything is plotless or totally plotted: whether one lives in a world of hermetic containment in complete meaning, or in a world of undifferentiation and pure randomness.

The City of the World

The novel falls roughly into two fairly distinct parts, and they hinge upon the poker game between Pozzi, Flower, and Stone. The first part of the text deals with Nashe's restlessness, and his preparation, after meeting Pozzi, for the poker match. The second part of the narrative considers the ramifications of losing the game, getting into debt to the millionaires, and then working off that debt by erecting a wall in the estate's meadow. It is here that the text locates its central interest: in the behavior, actions, and emotions of two men in isolation, a perennial treatment by Auster, and the examination of what pressures and anxieties are born out of psychologically and physically insecure and unstable situations.

Nashe's initial reaction to losing the poker game, and having to make good the debt by working for Flower and Stone, is the relief at no longer having to make decisions: "It was almost a relief to have the decision taken out of his hands, to know that he had finally stopped running. The wall would not be a punishment so much as a cure, a one-way journey back to earth" (110). Nashe's path is now determined for him, mapped out, firmly routed and rooted. The "medicine" of the labor is considered to be a cure for his state of restless indifference and lack of fixed destinations, which motivated his relentless criss-crossing journeys across the continent. It will be a "one-way journey back to earth" after living in the "realm of weightlessness" (12). In a curious paradox, Nashe envisages this nothingness as a form of exorcising his past listless anonymity, a "weightlessness" that returns him to the solidity of being somebody. This crisis precipitates a recognition of direction. With their change in status from guests to debtors, Pozzi and Nashe "had been relegated to the category of non-persons" (113). Nevertheless, despite this non-identity, or *because* of it, Nashe now regards his new situation "as if it were precisely this sort of crisis that he had been searching for all along" (98).

This sense of relief is shortlived though, as it becomes clear that they are living in what amounts to a prison, without "an opportunity to escape" (119). In fact, far from being a "cure," Flower considers the entire wall-building exercise to be a means of inculcating some form of moral correction: "A punishment would have to be meted out . . . punishment that would have some educational value to it . . . that would teach the culprits a lesson" (105). Nashe and Pozzi have not actually broken the law, and so they are only "culprits" in the eyes of the two millionaires. But in what sense are they culpable?

A clue to this lies in Stone's intricate model of the City of the World, which Nashe and Pozzi are shown as the two millionaires conduct them around their mansion. Once in the meadow, Nashe senses that "[a]n atmosphere of suspicion and mistrust continued to hover around the place" (125). This is almost a direct echo of Nashe's earlier reactions upon first looking at the model of the City of the World, where "[a] threat of punishment seemed to hang in the air" (96), and his unsettled sense detects a "hint of violence, an atmosphere of cruelty and revenge" (87) lying within the intricacy of its design. This pervading aura of suppressed menace and threat is a critical link between American capital and the ethical imperatives of Puritanism, and by implication, between the wealthy American millionaires and their ideological constructions. The novel's debate about "free action" versus "controlled action" engages with an ideological anxiety in the stage of late capitalism, or in the United States in the late twentieth century. It is no coincidence (is it?) that Flower and Stone are venture capitalists, and that their own millions came from a game of chance (the lottery). The extent to which money controls and coerces is one of the more insidious issues at stake in the novel. When the two millionaires threaten to call the police to make good their loan after the poker game (107), Nashe is quick to realize that the authorities will cooperate with the power and status of wealth. Ironically, possessing money becomes the very stuff of freedom: it enables Nashe to quit his fireman's job and take off on the road around the states; and one of the reasons for his entering into the desperate gambling stakes with Pozzi was that his money was running low.

That high capital is wrapped up in the hypocritical blankets of Puritanism, which purportedly preaches freedom, self-determination, and independence, comes as no surprise when the effects of capitalism on Pozzi's and Nashe's life-style become evident. Caged and terrorized, threatened and exploited, the two men become the victims of an ideology entrenched in the very foundations of conservative American capital. It is the City of the World that appears to depict such a society based upon terror, vengeance, harsh treatment, and penal servitude:

> "Willie's city is more than just a toy," Flower said, "it's an artistic vision of mankind. In one way, it's an autobiography, but in another way, it's what you might call a utopia — a place where the past and future come together, where good finally triumphs over evil. If you look carefully, you'll see that many of the figures actually represent Willie himself. There, in the playground you see him as a child. Over there, you see him grinding lenses in his shop as a grown man. There, on the corner of that street, you see the two of us buying the lottery ticket. His wife and parents are buried in the cemetery over here, but there they are again, hovering as angels over that house. If you bend down, you'll see Willie's daughter holding his hand on the front steps. That's what you might call the private backdrop, the personal material, the inner component. But all these things are put in a larger context. They're merely an example, an illustration of one man's journey through the City of the World. Look at the Hall of Justice, the Library, the Bank, and the Prison. Willie calls them the Four Realms of Togetherness, and each one plays a vital role in maintaining the harmony of the city. If you look at the Prison, you'll see that all the prisoners are working happily at various tasks, that they all have smiles on their faces. That's because they're glad they've been punished for their crimes, and now they're learning how to recover the goodness within them through hard work. That's what I find so inspiring about Willie's city. It's an imaginary place, but it's also realistic. Evil still exists, but the powers who rule over the city have figured out how to transform that evil back into good. Wisdom reigns here, but the struggle is nevertheless constant, and great vigilance is required of all the citizens — each of whom carries the entire city within himself. William Stone is a great artist, gentlemen, . . ." (79–80)

A "murderous avenging God" (96) seems to inhabit the world, and as "an artistic vision of mankind," it appears to represent the imposition of the Protestant work ethic as being morally corrective. Each individual is a microcosm of the entire city, and vice-versa, and thus the social fabric cannot tolerate any deviations from the prescribed norms. The city as a sort of autobiography — a literal inscription of the Stone in the world — is also a prescriptive model of "moral engineering," in which goodness is "recovered" through hard work: everything points to civic responsibility. As an idealistic, utopian vision of the world, actions are instantaneous and simultaneous (there is no cause and effect). An eternal present operates, as various stages of Stone's life occur in a fusion of past and future as a denial of history. Stone's City of the World, in other words, becomes symbolic of a certain ideological world order, a pattern of social life based upon the absolute ideological control of its subjects. With overtones of Orwell's Oceania and its four Ministries in *1984*, the "Four Realms of Togetherness" approximate the political operations, functions, and effects of Louis Althusser's "Repressive and Ideological State Apparatuses." According to Althusser, ideological practices are reinforced and replicated in our society in the institutions that he names Ideological State Apparatuses (ISAs). These institutions (such as the educational system, the family, the law, the media, and the arts) are distinguished from the Repressive State Apparatus, which works by force (the police, the prison system, the army), in that they seek to guarantee consent and complicity with the existing and dominating mode of production in a society. These ISAs represent and reproduce the myths and beliefs crucial to the smooth working of people within the existing social formation ("Ideology and Ideological State Apparatuses," 15–22). As with Althusser, Stone's City of the World is based on a fundamentally functionalist model of ideology, which seeks to bind together the social structure and mold individuals to its demands. The principal function of the "Realms" is to "process" subjects in a manner that ensures their cooperation within the social fabric. Like Foucault's vision of the Panopticon, discipline produces individuals as both its subjects and agents ("The Eye of Power," 146–165). One is dealing with the architecture of control here, the columns of power that uphold knowledge and generate the potential for the formation of particular kinds of subjects. Discipline forces everyone into an authorized place within a functioning hierarchy—that place is prison in the event of any serious expression of a desire for freedom from the world of discipline. The society functions as the Protestant God that keeps all under constant observation, and the individual members of the God-society absorb this surveillance unto themselves for their own and others' sakes, in acts of self-policing. Auster's point appears to be that Stone's model proposes a much too rigidly deterministic social system in its conception, since in so doing, it irons out the complexities and contradictions of class consciousness, making an unproblematic and unmediated mechanical leap from the economic sphere to the psychologistic sphere. This model does not take account of the shift that Raymond Williams has argued is so crucial to analyses of the relationship between social structures and their cultural productions: "We have to revalue 'determination' towards the setting of limits and the exertion of pressure, and away from a predicted, prefigured and controlled content" ("Base and Superstructure," 34).

An allegorical and symbolic structure begins to emerge between the

City of the World and the erection of the wall in Flower and Stone's meadow. The labor becomes the exercise of a morally corrective power by a wealthy hegemonic Puritan capitalism, and as such, the signs of this being "punishment" rather than working off a debt become increasingly clear. William Stone, as "a great artist," in constructing a totalitarian utopia disguised as a harmonious society of popular cooperation, aestheticizes social and political control. Constructing the physical wall becomes a reconstruction of the model of the City of the World. The ideologies that are theorized and conceptualized in the model are reproduced practically in the meadow. This alliance of the City of the World and the wall in the meadow finds another analogy, in that the stones are those of an old Irish castle transported to the United States. The erection of the wall thus also signifies the nostalgia for the Old World, the yearning for the "possession" of a "true" history. The displaced history is "rebuilt" so that Old and New Worlds come together, another fantasy secured through the use of the millionaire's money. What the money actually creates is the *semblance* of antiquity; it is "postmodern" in that the ruins of the old castle appear to become something new even if possessing a non-usable function. To borrow Fredric Jameson's terms, the wall is postmodern because it is a pastiche of its origins (*Postmodernism* 21–25). Like the purchase of London Bridge and its careful re-erection in Arizona, this wall acts as the symbol of American cultural practice in the age of high capital. It is an aesthetic pastiche of "originality":

> Rather than try to reconstruct the castle, we're going to turn it into a work of art. To my mind, there's nothing more mysterious or beautiful than a wall. I can already see it: standing out there in the meadow, rising up like some enormous barrier against time. It will be a memorial to itself, gentlemen, a symphony of resurrected stones, and every day it will sing a dirge for the past we carry within us. (*Music* 86)

Although Flower pictures history as apparently "resurrected" in the wall, it is also paradoxically a "barrier against time," a resistance to the past. This "resurrection" is a "quotation" of the past, a fetishization of history: a historicism which, in the words of Walter Benjamin's XVI thesis in his "Theses on the Philosophy of History," "gives the 'eternal image' of the past" (264). It is a fine irony that the description of the plan for the erection of the wall appears immediately after the description of Flower's collection of "historical memorabilia" (*Music* 82) in glass cases. For Nashe, these artifacts are "a demented shrine to the spirit of nothingness" (84), and they appear to have the properties of Marx's classic description of commodities:[3] "they were impenetrable, because they refused to divulge anything about themselves. It had nothing to do with history. . . . The fascination was simply for the objects as material things" (84). The wall and the memorabilia represent history as a commodified set of articles which achieve the monumental "auratic" status of belonging "to a tradition, to age-old habits and customs" (84), wrenched free and isolated from their historical constellation.

Once out in the meadow, the text takes on an almost laboratory-like experimental feel, as Auster's focus on power and its operation as a means of social control takes on a near Foucauldian twist. For power is demonstrated in the now classically defined Foucauldian forms ("The Eye of Power," 146–165): through measures of surveillance, both overt in the figure of Murks, and more invisibly (vis-à-vis the inexplicable violence done to Pozzi on his "escape" from the meadow); through more overt forms of force like Murks's gun; and ultimately through almost invisible and intangible forces such as capital itself (Flower and Stone and the authority they can summon rest somewhere behind Murks). Power in the novel operates as an open, more or less coordinated cluster of relations. Despite Nashe's suspicions, power is not a plot. Rather, it functions through the domain of the social body, through the establishment of a web of unequal relationships, operating from below as well as from above. Power "invests" itself in the relationship of causality and/or chance, the institution of the game of chance. It results from a given matrix of force-relations at a given place and time.

Yet domination is not the essence of power here: a process of self-formation or auto-colonization occurs. In order for the two men to be considered to have fallen prey to fate or chance, they have to construct a rationality of causal effect. The problem for the reader, and for Nashe and Pozzi, is the extent to which what happens to the two men is the consequence of intentional trickery and enforced situations by Flower and Stone, or whether it is, quite simply, chance. The enslavement of Nashe and Pozzi appears to be an intentional action, yet without a specific subject, a result without a clear demonstrable cause. Nashe and Pozzi are unable to work out the consequences of their actions, or whether their actions actually have consequences or results. In other words, the directionality of people's actions is frequently obscured, and this leads to the construction of chance, or the notion of the aleatorical. Flower and Stone impose a task upon the two men and thereby seek to hold them to their promissory of labor for debt; but it also becomes a mode for religious vengeance, moral education, class exploitation, cultural construction, and ultimately penal reform. The discipline "manufactures" them as individuals: Nashe feels that he "grows" while working. Meanwhile, as discipline targets the body with the function of training it, perception itself becomes invisible. The sense of continual surveillance *in absentia,* causes coercion over both the "convicts" (Nashe and Pozzi) and the "jailer" (Murks). The exertion of erecting the wall acts as a continual reminder of the "terrible justice" (132) and that they are like "some convict sentenced to a term at hard labor" (127). What constitutes the two men within this site of discipline and punishment is that the meadow becomes the construction of a *space* that is supple, interchangeable, without segregation and without exterior. When Pozzi escapes the confines of this space, he enters a more brutal regime that is quite shocking, and suggests that there is no exterior to the world of the vengeance of the two millionaires. The exercise of power on the two men literally occurs on their bodies: its disciplining, the optimization of its capabilities, the extortion of its forces, the parallel increase of its usefulness and its docility, its integration into systems of efficient and economic controls—all occur as a direct result of the exigent demands of erecting the wall.

"Looking at how things really work"

Once life has been established and regulated within the daily schedule of erecting the wall in the meadow under the scrutiny of Murks, Nashe and Pozzi have plenty of time to rationalize how their lives reached this point. Pozzi thinks that "the whole situation was absurd" (127), almost surreal, while Nashe regards the wall as a form of atonement, "a chance to redeem himself in his own eyes . . . as a way to atone for his recklessness and self-pity" (127). This atonement ironically coincides with Stone's perception of the wall as a "Wailing Wall" (86). However, this is the perspective of men who feel that they lost their poker match fairly. But slowly Pozzi begins to consider the way in which he lost, and begins to suggest that Nashe was the cause of his bad play by breaking "the rhythm" (137) and causing his sense of poise to collapse. Nashe's mistake was to upset the balance of the universe by tampering with the City of the World and stealing one of its figurines:

> It's like committing a sin to do a thing like that, it's like violating a fundamental law. We had everything in harmony. We'd come to the point where everything was turning into music for us, and then you go upstairs and smash the instruments. You tampered with the universe, my friend, and once a man does that, he's got a price to pay. (138)

This music of chance metaphor occurs at the center of the text's exploration of power, and Pozzi's superstitiousness constructs a world where every action has a consequence. In Pozzi's metaphysical construction, the world is a delicate, ordered harmony, which needs to be maintained carefully in balance for the wheels to be kept turning beautifully. Pozzi attributes events to a metaphysical cause and falls into the problematic identified by Spinoza. Where an action is perceived, a cause is established, which is often times mistakenly attributed to a divine source because one cannot know the actual source. Ignorance erects metaphysical answers to questions.[4]

Nashe responds in his usual pragmatic, empirically critical manner, by questioning the metaphysical structure of Pozzi's thoughts:

> You want to believe in some hidden purpose. You're trying to persuade yourself there's a reason for what happens in the world. I don't care what you call it—God or luck or harmony—it all comes down to the same bullshit. It's a way of avoiding facts, of refusing *to look at how things really work.* (139; italics mine)

Nashe's position here is complex and somewhat contradictory, and, interestingly, it can be interpreted from two somewhat opposed philosophical positions. He might well be perceived to be advancing a Jamesian or Rortyian pragmaticism, urging a focus on empirical facts to derive the "true" interpretation of events. On the other hand, in a postmodernist gesture, Nashe could be refusing any such "grand narrative" to explain what he feels amounts to accidental events. Yet at the same time, Nashe reinscribes a narrative by also claiming an epistemological high ground, as he argues that his perception is clearer, less prone to distortion and that he gets to the root of things by looking "at how things really work." His cognitive action is purer, more forthright, and more veracious. The return of the medicinal metaphor ("With the proper medicine, any illness can be cured" [140]), resonates with Nashe's earlier sense of the wall-building as curative. He sets about a ritual burning of the figurines of Flower and Stone, performed almost as an exorcism for Pozzi, and argues, "You see? There's nothing to it. Once you know the magic formula, no obstacle is too great" (141). Nashe's pragmatic, hard-headed flouting of black magic, superstition, religious belief, or any metaphysics by this act seeks to rend the veil of illusion about humanity caught in the grip of fatalistic control. This does not mean that Nashe is not prone to adopting metaphysical solutions himself at times, but rather that he thinks that everything can be rationalized. Pozzi is an idealist who believes in metaphysical workings beyond the grasp of reason and human control, and that people are ultimately guided by destiny or fate. Nashe clings to a concrete materialism.

And yet, for all Nashe's claims to perceive the "truth" of things, it is Pozzi who most clearly perceives their real incarceration:

> It meant Murks felt he had a right to carry [the gun]—and that he had felt that from the very beginning. Freedom, therefore, had never been

an issue. Contracts, handshakes, goodwill — none of that had meant a thing. All along, Nashe and Pozzi had been working under the threat of violence. . . . And given the way things had been set up, there was no question that he was acting on orders from Flower and Stone. (144–145)

When Murks appears with the gun, it shocks Nashe to see his illusion about cooperative goodwill shattered, but confirms Pozzi's sense of the threat of violence. The revolver acts as yet one more bar in their prison, and "Nashe was the one who had tricked himself into a false reading of the facts" (145). This sudden reversal in Nashe's perception of power relations destabilizes his sense of self-confidence and his powers to rationalize events. The narrative works as a series of ups and downs: there are points of crucial consolidation of the sense of self and situation and control over circumstances, before these are violently subverted or overthrown, as new facts act to unveil illusions of relationship or context. The correct interpretation of "facts" functions as a key epistemological motif in the text. This is evident at the crucial moment when Nashe accuses Stone of using violence to erect the wall: " 'I'm not making threats,' Flower said. 'I'm just presenting you with the facts' " (107). Narratives constructed by a "reading of the facts" are never as clearcut as Nashe likes to think: reading facts can also be an avoidance of facts. There is, finally, no way "to look at how things really work," because all perceptions are framed by perspective, interpretation, and partial knowledge.

The issue of what constitutes "reality" has always been a factor in Auster's fiction. Frequently, the boundaries between fact and fiction are tested, as in *The New York Trilogy* and *Moon Palace,* where the distinction between narrator and fictional character is blurred. "Reality" does not cease to be an issue in *The Music of Chance* either, despite the novel's apparently straightforward realist disposition. Nashe often wonders about the nature of the "reality" around him, and increasingly wonders whether he exists in a world that is constructed by him or whether it somehow exists independently of him. At one point, Nashe experiences a momentary "abrupt and radical shift of his inner bearings, as if the world around him had suddenly lost its reality. It made him feel like a shadow, like someone who had fallen asleep with his eyes open" (65). Fixing one's bearings in this trance-like state becomes a matter of pure self-consciousness rather than an objective siting. When he does enter the world of Flower and Stone, he finds it an unsettling experience, a world of pure kitsch, a world of the cinema and B-movies: the doorbell rings the first bars of Beethoven's Fifth Symphony, and the two millionaires appear to be Laurel and Hardy–like figures. This apparently naive parody is continued by the stereotypical maid who appears in starched gray, in the colonial atmosphere of the lounge, and in the guileless innocence of a children's birthday party at the dinner where all four men eat burgers.

Increasingly, there are no stable points of reference for Nashe and Pozzi. The realm of ideas gives way to a physical state brought about by circumstances of exceptional mental and physical fatigue and stress. One might cite Auster's own description of Knut Hamsun's *Hunger* as Nashe and Pozzi struggle to keep hold of their lives:

> Mind and body have been weakened; the hero has lost control over both his thoughts and actions. And yet he persists in trying to control his destiny. This is the paradox, the game of circular logic that is played out through the pages of the book. It is an impossible situation for the hero. (*Art of Hunger* 12–13)

Nashe and Pozzi are caught in a similarly circular logic played out in the last half of the book. For they must labor to gain their freedom, and yet that freedom seems to recede every time they approach it, until they face death. Slowly but surely, the idea of ending their ordeal is put off in the interests of maintaining the constant possibility of the end. The world of freedom and chance events in the early part of the novel is translated into a world of restrictions and a fixed, determined course of action. The poker player thus becomes a metaphor for the postmodern world, where one constantly oscillates between determination and indeterminacy. Certainty gives way to doubt, while life becomes one of need and desire. As Auster says of *Hunger*— speaking of the epistemological paradox in which a subject frequently finds itself— "there can be no arbitrary imposition of order, and yet, more than ever, there is an obligation to achieve clarity" (*Art of Hunger* 18).[5] If Auster has written a road novel in *The Music of Chance* (Ford, "Citizens of Sinister City," 11), then it quickly becomes something else. It proposes that we read *as if* it is a conventional road narrative and then subverts those expectations on the way. Like surrealist art, it turns what is a realist and apparently insignificant narrative into something completely unexpected. The increasing interruptions of the episodes of menace and unexplained violence threaten to upset a narrative that works by explainable logic. Indeed, Nashe is a rationalist and is always seeking the rational explanation to events that occur in the meadow. However, he increasingly abandons himself, in the face of the inexplicable, to wilder and wilder speculations about the causes of events. As events persistently deny his attempts at explanation and understanding, so he realizes the need for different logics, other forms of understanding.

However, the narrative form is at odds with this "different logical" demand, since it presents a rationalist perspective about the actions and events. What one gets is the incompatibility of "lived experience" with "narrative form": experiences that belie or escape the forms in which they are perceived. Nashe finds that his answers do not adequately match the events that are occurring around him. Although Auster is once again dealing here with his favorite problem of cognitive mapping, it is a more internalized structure than in his previous works. By probing the relationships between language, reality, and narrative authority in *The New York Trilogy* and the appearance/illusion problematic in *In the Country of Last Things,* his explorations of the processes of representation occur at a more overtly discursive and philosophical level.

The Music of Chance provides an exploration of the manner in which reason, emancipation, and equality are equated. The text focuses on the legacy of the Enlightenment's use of reason's "political power" disseminated throughout the social field, saturating all aspects of it. As Foucault has extensively argued, there is no "outside" to this power. Even beyond the confines of the estate's net fence, the estate's power (or some unknown force apparently connected with it) is exerted brutally on Pozzi. Power appears to be all pervasive. The subjects, Nashe and Pozzi, as part of a carceral society that everywhere disciplines and trains its subjects for labor and conformity, find their bodies the site of that exercise and operation of power. Part of Nashe's problem is his attempt to shift from the surface-depth and causal models utilized in "modernist" understanding to those that function by a more "postmodern" understanding of discontinuous surfaces of discourse unconnected by causal linkages. In this respect, Auster isolates one of the unstable "oppositions" of modern philosophy's construction — the cogito/unthought. In a Catch-22, humans are determined by external forces; yet, while aware of this determination, they illusorily think that they are able to free themselves from it. Foucault has identified in this opposition the manner in which humanist thought attempts to recuperate the primacy and autonomy of the thinking subject *and* to master all that is other to it. The disciplinary techniques in *The Music of Chance,* used during the erection of the wall, include timetables, constant imposition and regulation of activity, surveillance measures to monitor performance, and guards; however, despite these determinations of power, the relationship of the three men in the meadow undergoes several adjustments, shifts, and alterations as they change from debtors to hired laborers, thereby demonstrating that all power relations involve the possibility of resistance through modifications of its grip.

The Music of Chance demonstrates that modern American society functions as a room in which the key has been lost. The constant sense of unreliable and uncertain narrative positions ushers in radical epistemological crises, which always threaten to "tip over" into ontological crises, what Brian McHale has described as "limit-modernism" (13). The abrupt ending of the novel, with its unspecified suggestion of a car crash and the possible death of Nashe, carries the narrative ambivalence to the very (in)conclusion of the text. Power emerges as the victor, having forced the two protagonists into situations where there is no way out (as well as no way of knowing the way in). This pessimistic construction ultimately appears to suggest that in the late 1980s, American society has been totally sewn up by the power of capital, leaving little or no room for reflexive maneuver or ideological critique. Blue's anxiety of the extent to which he has ever been free is replayed with deafening cynicism in Nashe's experiences. Even a gradually dawning consciousness suspects itself to be the pawn of anonymous determining forces. There appears to be no point from which a critical perspective of the system in which Nashe lives may be developed. American capitalist society is represented as a latter-day version of the Weberian "iron cage," the metaphor in which modern, rationalized capitalism determines with irresistible force the lives of all the individuals who are born into this system (Weber, *Protestant Ethic* 181). The "postmodern" twist is that the prison bars themselves have become invisible and intangible.

Notes

1. See Henry D. Thoreau, *Walden* and *Civil Disobedience* (Harmondsworth: Penguin, 1983), 135: "I went into the woods because I wished to live deliberately, to front only the essential facts of life, and see if I could not learn what it had to teach, and not, when I came to die, discover that I had not lived. . . . I wanted to live deep and suck out all the marrow of life, to live so sturdily and Spartan-like as to put to rout all that was not life, to cut a broad swath and shave close, to drive life into a corner, and reduce it to its lowest terms."

2. The *locus classicus* for this argument is to be found in Louis Althusser, "Ideology and Ideological State Apparatuses," in *Essays in Ideology* (London: Verso, 1984), 1–60.

3. Marx describes the fetishized commodity as "abounding in metaphysical subtleties and theological niceties" and possessing a "mystical character." He adds that the commodity is "nothing but the definite social relations between men themselves which assumes here, for them, the fantastic form of a relation between things. In order, therefore, to find an analogy we must take flight into the misty realm of religion." See Karl Marx, *Capital*, vol. 1 of 3 vols., trans. Ben Fowkes (Harmondsworth: Penguin, 1976), 163–177.

4. See Baruch Spinoza, *Ethics,* I, Proposition xxix, trans. Andrew Boyle (London: Dent, Everyman, 1986), 23–24. See also the discussion of the misattribution of cause and effect in Christopher Norris, *Spinoza and the Origins of Modern Critical Theory* (Oxford: Basil Blackwell, 1991), 37–39.

5. Auster quotes Samuel Beckett in his argument for an art that maintains respect for "othernesses" and formal differences: " 'What I am saying does not mean that there will henceforth be no form of art. It only means that there will be

a new form, and that this form will be of such a type that it admits the chaos and does not try to say that chaos is really something else. . . . To find a form that accommodates the mess, that is the task of the artist now' " (*Art of Hunger* 19).

Works Cited

Althusser, Louis. "Ideology and Ideological State Apparatuses." In *Essays in Ideology.* London: Verso, 1984. Pp. 1–60.

Auster, Paul. *The Art of Hunger: Essays, Prefaces, Interviews.* Los Angeles: Sun & Moon Press, 1992.

——. *City of Glass.* Los Angeles: Sun & Moon Press, 1985.

——. *Disappearances: Selected Poems.* Woodstock, N.Y.: The Overlook Press, 1988.

——. *In the Country of Last Things.* New York: Viking, 1987.

——. *The Invention of Solitude.* New York: Penguin, 1988.

——. *The Locked Room.* Los Angeles: Sun & Moon Press, 1986.

——. *Moon Palace.* New York: Viking, 1989.

——. *The Music of Chance.* New York: Viking, 1990.

Bell, Madison Smartt. "Poker and Nothingness." *New York Times Book Review* 90, 4 (November 1990): 15–16.

Benjamin, Walter. "Theses on the Philosophy of History." In Hannah Arendt, ed., *Illuminations.* Trans. Harry Zohn. London: Fontana, 1973. Pp. 255–266.

Ford, Mark. "Citizens of Sinister City." *Times Literary Supplement* 4589 (1991): 11.

Foucault, Michel. "The Eye of Power." In Colin Gordon, ed., *Power/Knowledge: Selected Interviews and Other Writings, 1972–1977.* Brighton: Harvester, 1980. Pp. 146–165.

Jameson, Fredric. *Postmodernism, or, the Cultural Logic of Late Capitalism.* London: Verso, 1991.

McHale, Brian. *Postmodernist Fiction.* London and New York: Methuen, 1987.

Marx, Karl. *Capital.* Vol. 1 of 3 vols. Trans. Ben Fowkes. Harmondsworth: Penguin, 1976.

Spinoza, Baruch. *Ethics.* Trans. Andrew Boyle. London: Dent, Everyman, 1986.

Thoreau, Henry D. *Walden and Civil Disobedience.* Harmondsworth: Penguin, 1983.

Weber, Max. *The Protestant Ethic and the Spirit of Capitalism.* Trans. Talcott Parsons. London: Allen and Unwin, 1930.

Williams, Raymond. "Base and Superstructure in Marxist Cultural Theory." In *Problems in Materialism and Culture.* London: Verso, 1980. Pp. 31–49.

Leviathan: Post Hoc Harmonies

Arthur Saltzman

The detective novel provides some of literature's most durable endowments. Its sureties constitute a method and a message: mystery condenses then lifts like the day's weather; seemingly encouraged by the very conventions of his context, the hero patiently debrides whatever wound to propriety summons him; cases wind up tight and smooth as spools. Gordian plots are only, are always, temporary distractions at worst, or prods to appetite, and thanks to logic's stacked deck, these regularly succumb to investigation. As the detective whittles raw circumstance into habitable sense, he is secure in the conviction that at the core all incidents and outrages conform to code — each "Eureka" is really "Elementary" after all. In short, orientation is the detective novel's promise, tractability its principle. Such is the foundation of our devotion as the Good assumes its ritual guise and Evil performs the stations of the double-cross. When it comes to practicing literary convention, novelists, characters, and readers are all insiders, all blissful in the rigging.

Paul Auster has made his reputation largely by invoking the detective formula in order to steer it into metaphysical tundra. His *New York Trilogy* observes the steady disintegration of the motives, means, and results of inquiry, in which "the presence of the unpredictable, the powers of contingency" ultimately estrange us from those crisp generic assurances (*Art of Hunger* 270–271). Although it is in many ways a more straightforward work than its predecessors, Auster's *Leviathan* clarifies and extends the predicament: every author is at once a detective and an artificer, and these callings are incompatible. Moreover, as we are advised in the course of the novel, "the real is always ahead of what we can imagine" (180). The irony is that *Leviathan* is ostensibly Auster's most realistic novel, yet it is here that the question of what constitutes reality is rendered more subtle instead of extinguished. Whatever document results from the novelist's efforts is essentially a record of incomplete transactions whose authority must be taken under advisement.

An apology and projective analysis of the life of one Benjamin Sachs, *Leviathan* is ostensibly the work of Peter Aaron, a writer whose career suspiciously reflects (or refracts) Paul Auster's own. Aaron learns that Sachs, who had years before served time in prison for his refusal to serve in Vietnam, has accidentally blown himself up in the course of a politically inspired and increasingly folkloric assault on the nation's numerous replicas of the Statue of Liberty. Aaron also explains that he has arrogated to himself the responsibility of telling his friend's story properly before the redoubtable agents of law enforcement establish their version. His refusal to cooperate fully with the investigation enables Aaron not only to "keep his death to myself" (3), and thereby guarantee that it remain within the novelist's province and prerogative, but also to respect Sachs's life by composing the man's memory.

However, the very quality of Sachs that has defied forensic assaults so far also inhibits Aaron's attempts to "book" him. On the one hand, Aaron is tantalized by the sense that "everything is connected to everything else" (57) and that he continually seems to be the cynosure of consequential events. Accordingly, he undertakes the task of narration by announcing that precision and compassion will be his calipers. On the other hand, he confesses that "a book is a mysterious object" (5) in terms of its function and fate alike, and the accumulation of detail further obscures what it is designed to clarify. Aaron culls, then calls himself to account; he is equally skeptical about what coheres and what does not. Neither the official objectivity of the FBI nor the relentless alertness of the paranoid is sufficient to enable him to "[divine] the monstrous / sum of particulars" (*Disappearances* 83). What does commitment to his friend or to his art—that "attitude of remorseless inner vigilance" (29) — mean in the context of riven confidence?

> I don't claim to have more than a partial understanding of who he was. I want to tell the truth about him, to set down these memories as honestly as I can, but I can't dismiss the possibility that I'm wrong, that the truth is quite different from what I imagine it to be. (25)

Even translated into Aaron's words and dissolved into the context of this novel, Sachs retains his obscurity:

> Every time I tried to think about him, my imagination failed me. It was as if Sachs had become a hole in the universe. He was no longer just my missing friend, he was a symptom of my ignorance about all things, an emblem of the unknowable itself. (164)

Sachs is consistently portrayed as an embodiment of the difficult balance between unpredictability and pattern that Aaron tries to emphasize in his record. Neither their fifteen-year acquaintance nor the experience of preparing *Leviathan* really alters Aaron's drunken illusion during their initial meeting that Sachs was several dizzying figures that could not be focused (24). Sachs is introduced as someone cloaked in contradiction and disarming multiplicity, yet who somehow manages to embody "a single, unbroken presence" (19). He is simultaneously—and these adjectives are applied on a single page of the novel—sweet-tempered and gentle, yet rigidly dogmatic and prone to fits of rage; jaunty and good-humored, yet intolerant and scornful; peevish and embattled, yet large-spirited and cunning (20). He is at once mischievous and bookish, fervent and dismissive about his own writing, worshipful and caddish toward the women in his life, voracious for sensation yet longing for rest and release.

Leviathan is riddled with Aaron's disclaimers and misgivings, so much so that the story of Benjamin Sachs quickly evolves into a book-long delineation of the inevitability of storification. For every insight there is an apology. "We never know anything about anyone," Sachs tells Aaron by way of accounting for the secret instabilities in his "ideal" marriage to Fanny. "It's hard enough keeping track of ourselves. Once it comes to other people, we don't have a clue" (107), he says, anticipating the difficulty of future collusions. Especially relevant to Aaron's predicament are Nicholson Baker's comments about trying to pin down the imperial shadows of departed colleagues in *U and I,* an exercise in which idolatry, effrontery, and futility intersect: "The dead can be helpful, needless to say, but we can only guess sloppily about how they would react to this emergent particle of time, which is all the time we have. And when we do guess, we are unfair to them" (9). Mobbed by shadows, Aaron bears witness like a chalice, enduring his subject's delicate stresses with all the fastidiousness and wariness devotion is prey to. Indeed, *Leviathan,* whose title Aaron appropriates from Sachs's own book-in-progress "to mark what will never exist" (159), does not conclude so much as capitulate to the fact that "the story would go on and on, secreting its poison inside me forever. The struggle was to accept that, to coexist with the forces of my own uncertainty" (271–272).

Randomness cannot be erased from the record. Both Sachs and Aaron inherit from Wallace Stevens's Crispin:

> Preferring text to gloss, he humbly served
> Grotesque apprenticeship to chance event,
> A clown, perhaps, but an aspiring clown.
> ("The Comedian as the Letter C," 4.90–92)

A series of chance events, including an interrupted seduction at a party, Sachs's subsequent near-fatal fall from a balcony, and his hitchhiking episode, which leads to his killing a murderous assailant and discovering that his victim's car contains bomb components and a huge amount of cash, conspire to drive Sachs underground. But he emerges from his withdrawal to visit Aaron one last time in order to fill him in on his disappearance and to bequeath his manuscript to a sympathetic editor. Thus Aaron and Sachs reenact the relationship between the narrator and the spectral Fanshawe in *The Locked Room,* as well as verify the impasse that disqualifies the notion of congenial transactions between Self and Other: "No one can cross the boundary into another—for the simple reason that no one can gain access into himself" (*Locked Room* 80–81). That access having been barred, or at least rendered problematic, Aaron literally edits Sachs—he "ghost writes" the Phantom of Liberty (Sachs's mediagenic signature) into a palatable, if not confirmable, complex of intentions and activities. The progressive disorientation of Sachs after his deadly roadside implication is intolerable, so he fixes upon a plan, tortuously orchestrated, of compensating the estranged widow; his insinuations into Lillian's and her young daughter's lives has the virtue of rigor if not simplicity. Similarly, Aaron's narrative regimen is designed not only to combat detachment but to project a history. If it is true that, as Auster asserts in the poem "Incendiary," "The world / is / whatever you leave to it" (*Disappearances* 63), the writer's legacy carries the taint of his presumptions. The novel at first purports to conceive of language as an elaborate rescue mission, in that Aaron plots to pluck Sachs from the belly of the State in order to set him down in the bastion of the prepared statement. *Leviathan* exemplifies a selective, sustainable interpretation— Claude Lévi-Strauss's inevitable "history-for":

> Insofar as history aspires to meaning, it is doomed to select regions, periods, groups of men and individuals in these groups and to make them stand out as discontinuous figures, against a continuity barely good enough to be used as a backdrop. A truly total history would cancel itself out—its product would be nought. . . . History is therefore never history, but history-for. (Quoted in Thompson, *Rubbish Theory* 64)

Under these conditions, Aaron's integrity is less a matter of reliability than of open-handedness, which includes the warning that he exposes his prejudices not to eliminate but to exercise them. It is fitting in this regard that Thoreau is one of Sachs's champions. Certainly his celebrated civil disobedience sets a rousing example for events in *Leviathan,* but so does his stylistic incorrigibility (*Extra vagance!*), which he announces as a kind of creed at the close of *Walden:* "If the condition of things which we were made for is not yet, what were any reality which we can substitute? We will not be shipwrecked on a vain reality" (326). Slavish depiction is slavery, after all, and the trappings of verisimilitude the most devilish of contrivances.

But like the serial bomber Sachs becomes, Aaron is a vulnerable insinuator of events, a subverter subverted; neither the man who leaves art behind for action nor the one who holds fast to verbal craft finally escapes the detonations he initiates. "Each syllable / is the work of sabotage," the poet confesses ("Unearth," *Disappearances* 19). Sachs's eccentricities and disappearing acts intensify his gravitational pull upon Aaron, and whatever his role in Sachs's life at any given point—professional acolyte, sexual rival, or spiritual accomplice—Aaron never escapes the man's orbit. As Auster puts it in "Fore-shadows," "I numb you in the reach / of brethren light" and ultimately "become / your necessary and most violent / heir" (*Disappearances* 54). This again recalls *The Locked Room,* particularly the moment when the narrator realizes that his success—indeed, his identity—is inextricably bound to Fanshawe's: "I had stumbled onto a cause, a thing that justified me and made me feel important, and the more fully I disappeared into my ambitions for Fanshawe, the more sharply I came into focus for myself" (57). We are moved to consider the possibility that, despite his stronger sense of worldly footing and dimension (Aaron has family, occupation, friends), the narrator of *Leviathan* has entered the same secretarial purgatory of *The New York Trilogy* and turned into another ghost writer commemorating, and becoming, a quarry, an absence.

Further mitigating Aaron's incentives is the self-defeating quality of salvage: *Leviathan* as cloister is claustrophobic; even hagiography is but another instance of incarceration. Like Maria Turner, the novel's provocative performance artist who believes in the revelatory power of aleatory techniques and focuses, and like Sachs himself, who takes life's contingencies as cues, Aaron has to accommodate the leakiness, contradiction, and dubious leads that beset his enterprise *within* that enterprise. To press another of Auster's titles into service here, the music of chance is paradoxically at once freer and denser than the routine scales of evident cause. It would be arrogant, Aaron reasons, to "convict" his subject by "sentencing" him decisively, for as his words "happen" they do not necessarily recapitulate any ulterior episode. "I hope to find a way of going along, of running parallel to everything else that is going along," explains Auster in "White Spaces," "and so begin to find a way of filling the silence without breaking it" (*Disappearances* 103). In other words, silence is not only a fundamental tactic of surveillance, it is the natural and frail state of things; it may also be, as Peter Stillman, the mad linguist of *City of Glass,* posited during his search for a pure language prior to Babel, the preferable one, whereby the writer's most defensible goal is to minimize his contamination. In the famous formulation of Samuel Beckett, "I could not have gone through the awful wretched mess of life without having left a stain upon the silence" (quoted in Bair, *Samuel Beckett* 640). Auster echoes this oddly mixed message of fortitude and regret:

> It comes down to this: that everything should count, that everything should be a part of it, even the things I do not or cannot understand. The desire, for example, to destroy everything I have written so far. Not from any revulsion at the inadequacy of these words (although that remains a distinct possibility), but rather from the need to remind myself, at each moment, that things do not have to happen this way, that there is always another way, neither better nor worse, in which things might take shape. I realize in the end that I am probably powerless to affect the outcome of even the least thing that happens, but nevertheless, and in spite of myself, as if in an act of blind faith, I want to assume full responsibility. ("White Spaces," *Disappearances* 110)

"Running parallel" is the aesthetic compromise between a failure of analysis and false totalization; like the movie cliché of the young woman at the station who rushes alongside her departing lover and stays with him until the train gathers speed or she runs out of platform, Auster's Aaron speaks, stands in, or "doubles" for Sachs as long as cogency holds. "These stories came straight from Sachs himself," Aaron offers by way of authenticating his novel-as-deposition. "They helped to define my sense of what he had been like before I met him, but as I repeat his comments now, I realize that they could have been entirely false" (34). The writer suspects the trappings of coordination for the very comforts they provide.

How, then, can one be responsible in a mysterious, unpredictable world? When Aaron declares that books inevitably begin in ignorance and persist in ambiguity (40), he is essentially paraphrasing Sachs's commitment to duplicity. For example, Sachs unabashedly mingles fact and fiction, polemic and farce, in his first novel, then mythologizes his childhood (specifically, a traumatic experience at the Statue of Liberty) to suit the requirements of his eccentric politics. He systematically lies to his wife about his having had relationships with other women — unless, of course, that admission is itself unreliable — then tosses off the confusion he creates by scorning the value of coherence. (Once again, Maria Turner, for whom accident is oracle and chance aphrodisiac, epitomizes the vertiginous quality of freedom and the repudiation of taking too seriously that salient something that magnetizes experience into a stable order.) We can sympathize with Aaron's disappointment in face of coincidences that may or may not be significant and short-circuited cause, but when he compares a conversation with Sachs to the "procession of dimly observed moments" of a baseball game seen on television with the sound off (125), he may well have found the proper metaphor for *Leviathan.*

In this way we find ourselves cast into the realm of what poet Joseph Duemer refers to as "useful doubt" — an agnostic resolve that refuses reductionism. "The temptations of perfection are constant, and must be resisted," by which logic conscience becomes a matter of entertaining the demands of world and imagination simultaneously without eclipsing either (Duemer 270). On another level, this is perceived in Auster's novel as a compromise between elegant repose (whose extreme manifestation is "a swoon to the depths of immobility" [95], as Aaron describes his lovemaking with his friend's wife) and restless forms — miscible selves, coincidental collisions, ambiguous intentions and outcomes. Aaron's survival, both as a component of the narrative and as its artificer, depends upon an acutely self-conscious version of negative capability, a representative example of which may be seen in his conclusion to a prolonged analysis of his affair with Fanny Sachs:

> If so, then Fanny's actions become nothing less than extraordinary, a pure and luminous gesture of self-sacrifice. Of all the interpretations I've considered over the years, this is the one I like best. That doesn't mean it's true, but as long as it could be true, it pleases me to think it is. After eleven years, it's the only answer that still makes any sense. (99)

We immediately recognize in this passage Aaron's subjective criteria not for the truth but for the story he will settle for: not verifiability so much as shapeliness, not authenticity so much as immunity to authentication and refutation alike. Doubt makes room to ruminate and maneuver.

The trick is to discover the opportunities that chance provides and transform them, through the fervency that the political activist and the novelist share, into a calling. When Sachs the outlaw pays a final visit to Aaron, they debate the relative merits of their respective instigations as arbitrary acts of conscience. To a considerable degree, Sachs can trace his career as the Phantom of Liberty back to the moment he first succumbed to gravity, as it were — that is, his drunken fall from the balcony. This proves to be a fortunate fall; more accurately, in that he appears to plunge into incendiary designs, it is a fall into fortune. Activism implies a greater degree of predication than this, and hence it is no wonder that Sachs reads agency, connection, and cause into his affairs, if only to confer meaning upon them. Surely his compulsive attentions to the disdainful Lillian and her daughter have the effect of increments of purgation for the tragic accidents that preceded them. Haunting Dimaggio's ex-wife and child in Berkeley (whom Maria Turner, his abandoned concern and intimate witness to his fall at the party, happens to know), plying them with measured payments out of the dead man's stash, and slowly insinuating himself into their trust constitute a system of repayment and responsibility for the hidden crime. More to the point, perhaps, they symbolize the attempt to surrender himself to a system and thereby stem the tide of contingency.

Lillian's sudden abandonment—the punishment she had intended for him all along? another example of her preemptive arbitrariness?—forces Sachs to seize upon new orders, which Dimaggio comes to embody. As Sachs explains to Aaron during their final encounter, his exchanging his role of angel of Lillian's household for the Phantom of Liberty owes itself to the conception of Dimaggio as his active alter ego, whereby the coincidences that brought Sachs and Dimaggio violently together symbolize a conspiracy of reintegration, or at least a transference of directed political energies. Once he determines to carry out Dimaggio's work, "All of a sudden, my life seemed to make sense to me. . . . It was a miraculous confluence, a startling conjunction of motives and ambitions." It is a reprieve from randomness, as well as a fitting ransom for having killed the man. "I had found the unifying principle, and this one idea would bring all the broken pieces of myself together. For the first time in my life, I would be whole" (256). Being the Phantom of Liberty requires elaborate designs and impostures; it combines dimension with articulate fixation. Whereas Sachs proclaims that the decision has become a source of bracing liberation—significantly, only during his hitch in prison, when life was so completely mapped out for him, had he enjoyed freedom at all comparable to this (22)—he is less a crusader for liberty than its shadow negative. Destroying replicas of the Statue of Liberty is a terrorist assault *on* liberty through its idiosyncratically focused exercise.

It would be convenient, surely, to embroider this interpretation with references to Sachs's childhood scare at the Statue of Liberty and to connect this last effort at self-mythologization with clues from his published fiction, and thereby guide future readings with the orthodox *Leviathan*. Instead, Aaron closes his account by reconciling himself to his limited capacity for executing his friend's will. (We recall Melville's muttering Ahab, heaped and tasked in ambiguous pursuit of his own leviathan: "Swim away from me, do ye?" [203], he thinks, thwarted once again by his elusive prey.) As to the consolations of an open text, Annie Dillard offers the following in *Living by Fiction:*

> If art objects quit the bounds of the known and make blurry feints at the unknown, can they truly add to knowledge or understanding? I think they can; for although we may never exhaust or locate precisely the phenomena they signify, we may nevertheless approximate them—

and this, of course, is our position in relation to all knowledge and understanding. (166–167)

Aaron adds to the burden of Sachs's confidence the burden of his own confession. Yet he, too, lives by fiction — stands by fiction — as a method of tempering judgment with compassion, and vanquishment of mystery with the inviolability of some of its remotest precincts. We learn from a particularly diligent FBI agent who has been scouring used bookstores that Sachs had been surreptitiously signing copies of Aaron's books, which means that just as Aaron's intentions cloud his rendition of Sachs's life, the dead man's fingerprints are all over our narrator's work. We likewise recall Aaron's suspicion (again, *City of Glass* provides the model for this) of whatever findings may have arisen from watching a man who may have known he had been tailed . . . much less the dictated details of an authorized biography. ("Bio-hazards" have been clearly posted in *The Locked Room*, which ends with Fanshawe dying from poison behind a locked door and dictating the terms of his reception to the narrator, who subsequently destroys each page of Fanshawe's notebook after reading it.) Our three novelists, Auster, Aaron, and Sachs, seemingly bent upon triangulation so as to converge upon the truth, instead play out as concentric perspectives. We find ourselves addressed by an oddly corporate author in *Leviathan* who pitches intent at the frayed edge of belief.

Works Cited

Auster, Paul. *City of Glass*. Los Angeles: Sun & Moon Press, 1985.
——. *Disappearances: Selected Poems*. Woodstock, N.Y.: The Overlook Press, 1988.
——. "Interview with Larry McCaffery and Sinda Gregory." In *The Art of Hunger: Essays, Prefaces, Interviews*. Los Angeles: Sun & Moon Press, 1992. Pp. 269–312.
——. *Leviathan*. New York: Viking, 1992.
——. *The Locked Room*. Los Angeles: Sun & Moon Press, 1986.
——. *The Music of Chance*. New York: Viking, 1990.
Bair, Deirdre. *Samuel Beckett: A Biography*. New York and London: Harcourt Brace Jovanovich, 1978.
Baker, Nicholson. *U and I: A True Story*. New York: Random, 1991.
Dillard, Annie. *Living by Fiction*. New York: Harper and Row, 1982.
Duemer, Joseph. "To Make the Visible World Your Conscience." *New England Review* 14.4 (1992): 268–85.
Melville, Herman. *Moby-Dick*. Ed. Harrison Hayford and Hershel Parker. New York: W. W. Norton, 1967.
Stevens, Wallace. "The Comedian as the Letter C." In *The Collected Poems of Wallace Stevens*. New York: Alfred A. Knopf, 1954. Pp. 27–46.
Thompson, Michael. *Rubbish Theory: The Creation and Destruction of Value*. New York: Oxford University Press, 1979.
Thoreau, Henry David. *Walden*. Ed. J. Lyndon Shanley. Princeton, N.J.: Princeton University Press, 1971.

A Look Back from the Horizon

Eric Wirth

Between the completed overrunning of the earth by humankind and the future spread of the species or its successors to other planets, it may be that the slough Paul Auster and the rest in the hiatus explore had to open. That we have filled up the world eliminates the world or (this amounts to the same thing) itself becomes the world (the new world of *Moon Palace*). The equation that leaves us solitary cancels us out.

The cataclysm I'm getting at is the loss of the nonhuman, of a contrast to the human. This event can be related to a worldly development: conquest of the globe by consciousness, domestication of all terrestrial sectors, as every inch of the planet became not only occupied by our houses and litter but also potentially known back and forth by human inhabitants everywhere, who were linked in the common languages of rationalism, commercialism, scientism. The suggestion in Auster's *Ghosts* that Blue would find *Walden* a key out of confusion strengthens the interpretive role of ecology, not because of the face value of this seeming recommendation of a panacea but because it takes the Thoreauvian philosophy to prompt the crucial demonstration that even the purported antidote to irony does not escape ironization. (By imagining Blue's "entire life" changing under the influence of Thoreau, the narrator negates the story under narration — the story of Blue's life — making *Walden* an anti-*Ghosts*. This textual self-abnegation cannot contain a straightforward alternative for Blue, since the paradox is congruent with the ironism, or skepticism, or nihilism, controlling his present story. There is no backing out of, no returning from, ironism: "a story cannot dwell on what might have been" finishes the Thoreau episode [194]. The ironic is defined by its infinite dissatisfaction, by the irrevocability of its rupture with every position, including its own.)

The precursor of American ecologism has a similarly perverse place in *Leviathan*. In the novel by Sachs, destroyer of replica icons through prudent explosions, Thoreau is the vehicle for the message Sachs's own life proves: "we have no hope of finding ourselves again" (43). Thoreau's useless compass here effects the same ironization as Blue's encounter with *Walden:* in a self-reflexive text about writers and writing, the author who most must be read is unreadable. Appropriately, the two pathetic heirs of Thoreau in *Leviathan*—the murderous ecoterrorist Dimaggio and Sachs, whose "model" was the transcendentalist (29)—are missing men.

When all things on earth became fingerable, then all images available to imagination thenceforth were images of ourselves. No longer determined by the opposing category of the nonfinite (primordially the category of unmastered geography, I claim), the ontology of the mortal vanished. The foundation, of being, gave way to unconditioned, total self-consciousness, whose attitudes, questioning, languages now circumscribe all the evidence in the world (but go not a hair farther). Every configuration of the world is anticipated in thought. There is nothing outside human acts, no recourse beyond considerations of our use.

Wittgenstein describes the implications this state has for the individual: "I can know what someone else is thinking, not what I am thinking" (222). You do not speak of knowing your thoughts, since your having them is the precondition of anything you can call your knowing. Thought must live some form of public life to be conceivable. So I is never complete, and the "kind of certainty is the kind of language-game." "[N]ow it does appear that 'what went on within me' is not the point at all" (224, 222). With the collapse of the dualism human/nonhuman, accompanied by every lesser binary, like within/without, naturally also fails the coherence of polarity itself. It is at this limit of all previous possibilities of the human that Wittgenstein slyly dismisses common sense: if "I" "know" only others, what is left to I, to knowing? Interiority yields to that which is formed contingently and which therefore has no opposite or depth. Out of the interim condition—the oscillation between nothingness (the void self) and the plenitude of the just attestable (Wittgenstein's "don't think, but look!" [sec. 66] or Auster's ostensible surrender to chance)—the writers of the hiatus people their books with threshold figures.

(None of the above should be taken as backing a linear or developmental history of consciousness. What I call the threshold insight and connect to a particular moment was also the earliest insight.[1] The human is always ending—or it *is* not. So far. Technology, the domain of quantity, has only proposed to change our nature qualitatively. [But wouldn't such a self-transformation be merely another instance of consciousness reaching farther and finding itself?] I should also interject that if my sweeping talk of "our nature" is deemed imperial, I might respond that the presumption of the talk is not to impose any essence [or to reverse such an imposition] but rather to consider how presentations said to be of the human, in ceasing to cohere, according to the record of some artworks, thereby promise, always for the first time, what they can never accomplish. In short, what flows from the impossibility and evident possibility of positing "our nature"?)

Specifically, Auster documents the reduction of the mundane subject.

By the term "reduction" I try to bring usefully to light the phenomenological pilings of the Austerian outlook. Edmund Husserl conceives the phenomenological reduction as a liberating movement made of three inseparable moments: the natural standpoint, the reduction of that standpoint, and the constitution of the world by consciousness. In the natural standpoint I "liv[e] naïvely in experience" and see "nothing . . . except the natural world," which I believe " 'given' to me in advance" (secs. 50, 33; p. 11). But I can be overcome by the suspicion (called skepticism) that objects do not in every sense exist. This perturbation leads me to the tactical decision to suspend my primitive thesis (or positing) of the world. I perform the suspension by setting aside every judgment about the being of objects (including cultural artifacts, like values), *reducing* them to their appearing. In so doing, I do not despise or deny the world; I regard it descriptively. But to understand objects as appearance is to make them dependent on something: on that before which they appear. Thus the reduction, in exposing consciousness, determines it as absolute consciousness. To be available to awareness, an object must be (and can be known as nothing more than) a "unity of meaning" — a form of presentation that presupposes "*a sense-giving consciousness,* which, on its side, is [therefore] absolute and not dependent in its turn on sense bestowed on it from another source" (Husserl, sec. 55). As Husserl says right out, "[T]he whole *spatio-temporal world* . . . has the merely secondary, relative sense of a Being *for* a consciousness" (sec. 49). Auster's roots in phenomenology are visible in his essay on Charles Reznikoff, for example, which covers the basic doctrine: "we do not find ourselves in the midst of an already established world. . . . Each moment, each thing, must be earned [Husserl would say "constituted"] . . . by a steadiness of gaze, a purity of perception . . ." ("Decisive Moment" 35–36). The peripatetics in Auster's novels make a practice of the theory (e.g., *City of Glass* 8–9).

But the consensus of the modern movements is that consciousness, in graduating to absoluteness through the phenomenological reduction of the world, or whatever you want to call the perpetual discovery of the earth's limit, is itself identically reduced. By coming to constitute the world, consciousness loses for itself every world and persists as an abolished self-creation in either exaltation or misery, depending on the interpreter.

Reduced, the individual subject, retaining in force feeling that is nonetheless suspended, becomes the automaton.[2] The automaton is the last person. Peter Stillman's speech in *City of Glass* summons Nietzsche's versions of this horizon figure.[3] Husserl describes the phenomenologist, originarily free, as the "letzte Subjekt" (Ricoeur 69), or last subject. The apocalyptic rhetoric falls from Auster as critic, who calls the poet of the eye the first to be born and also the last ("Decisive Moment" 35). The procedures of the reduction leave in Auster's novels the analogue of what Maurice Blanchot, in *Le dernier homme (The Last Man)*, calls "le plus pauvre des hommes" 'the poorest of individuals' (47).

The catalogue of these procedures would include Auster's characters' asceticisms, deprivations affecting every level of experience — routine materiality, knowledge, personal identity. The formulas of disconnection stand out from Auster's prose and cast a certain cool:

> He had nothing, he knew nothing, he knew that he knew nothing. (*City of Glass* 159)
>
> He had come to the end of himself. (191)
>
> Alone, his supplies dwindling . . . (*Locked Room* 91)
>
> By wanting less, you are content with less, and the less you need, the better off you are. (*In the Country* 2)
>
> Let everything fall away . . . to see what happens when there is nothing. . . . (29)
>
> I saw my money dwindle to zero. . . . (*Moon Palace* 1)
>
> My life had become a gathering zero. . . . Piece by piece, I could watch myself disappear. (24)
>
> [T]he food supplies were going to run out. . . . (168)
>
> [H]e waited for the money to run out. (*Music of Chance* 1)
>
> I actually saw myself disappear. (*Leviathan* 131)

The deteriorative surveillances of *City of Glass* and *Ghosts;* the *Locked Room* narrator's absorption into the Fanshawe biography; the slide of the urban society in *In the Country of Last Things;* Fogg's starvations and eviction and the parallel trajectories of wandering and loss in the lineage Effing-Barber-Fogg in *Moon Palace;* the wall-building sentence in *The Music of Chance;* Sachs's abandonment of wife, lovers, and career in his drive toward literal fragmentation in *Leviathan* — all are variants of getting "back to zero" (*Music of Chance* 204). The stripping impulse traverses the productions of modernity, but the atmosphere of masochism and adolescent yearning in which Auster's mostly male agents often undertake their ordeals bespeaks a nostalgia or unreadiness that coordinates with the agents' heroic (I leave this adjective undefined) stature in the narratives.

Having become, through the severing, "no longer . . . human Ego[s] *in* the universal, existentially posited world" (Husserl 8), Auster's figures are prone to vanishing. They may be superseded by the notebook, the description. But, made contingent like every other object by the enclosure of absolute consciousness, even the notebook is not necessary: the automaton may disappear by so-called chance (like Nashe at the close of *The Music of Chance* or like Sachs, whose fatal bomb detonates "accidentally" [*Leviathan* 1]). "Chance" is recognizable by its air of the inevitable (these opposites too mingle in this milieu, where, in the absence of the notion of determination, that of chance is meaningless). Irony, "chance" — the indifferent possibility of every conjunction, the disqualifying of all dualisms that construct cause and judgment — defines this phenomenological condition. Hence the automaton's unending surrender: "He decided to postpone thinking about it" (*City of Glass* 187); "for the time being he decides to suspend judgment" (*Ghosts* 11; there is humor in the deluded provisionality of these resolves by Quinn and Blue); "he had already given up . . . there was nothing to lose anymore. . . . It was almost a relief to have the decision taken out of his hands. . . . Just take it as it comes, he told himself" (*Music of Chance* 1, 110, 118). The interior registers, such as will, memory, or continuous desire, do not persuade in exile. From the stranding of the vestigial subject in exteriority derive Austerian motifs like the two modes of this poorest person's relation to wealth: the unexpected inheritance (the award from the outside that sets a life on a new course over the world) and scavenging ("hover[ing] stupidly on the surface of things" [*City of Glass* 95]). (The notebook that Fanshawe recommends be saved for his son is a permutation of inheritance [*Locked Room* 175], as are Flower and Stone's lottery winnings, in *The Music of Chance,* and the money that, in *Leviathan,* Sachs takes from Dimaggio.)

Radical passivity, the prior giving way to every pressure, would be a method properly succedent to thought based on binary opposition. Fogg: "I decided that the thing I should do was nothing: my action would consist of a militant refusal to take any action at all" (*Moon Palace* 20–21). Husserl: phenomenologists "allow no judgment that makes any use of the affirmation that posits a 'real' thing or 'transcendent' nature as a whole, or *'cooperates' in setting up these positions"* (sec. 90; my italics). Husserl's subsequent argument that the withdrawal of cooperation does not do away with the "positions" of thing and nature (which remain "there still, and belong essentially to the phenomenon" [sec. 90]) may give perspective to Auster's almost neutral prose style and his preference for traditional novelistic practices over the chimera of what is called experimentation.

Style is an important consideration for a reading that aims to disperse interiority. Materialist sensitivity to craft can be rescued from critical banishment to meet the need to reencounter living partialness. Auster's prose appears nearly colorless because it adheres to conventions for relating events and communicating ideas. Thus one of its most remarkable aspects is the problem posed by his mistakes. Auster relies lazily on absolute modifiers beginning with "given" or "given that" (e.g., *Moon Palace* 6, 10, 15, 185, 232, 238, 278, 300; *Leviathan* 44, 58, 62, 97, 119, 141, 165, 175, 262). He admits clichéd formulas of melodrama:

> It was part of a life that had ended for me, and here was my chance to set out on a fresh course, to take my life in my own hands and do something about it. (*In the Country* 83)

> No one could have known what would happen; no one could have guessed the dark and terrible things that lay in store for us. (*Moon Palace* 237–238)

> At bottom, he knew that she was right, but that did not make it any easier to absorb the blow. (*Music of Chance* 18)

> They exchanged addresses and telephone numbers, promising to stay in touch with each other, but Nashe knew that it would never happen, that this was the last time he would ever see Pozzi. (168–169)

Auster's predilection for artless language reaches to hackneyed and redundant figures of speech (the italics in the following examples are mine):

> [T]here was no *earthly* reason. . . . (*Locked Room* 18)

> . . . a thing *totally* out of character . . . (132)

> Without even pausing *in my tracks* . . . (*In the Country* 83)

> . . . brandishing his stick and hooting *as if there was no tomorrow*. (*Moon Palace* 203)

> [H]e began to *show his true colors*, and it wasn't long before he was *talking his head off*. (*Music of Chance* 25)

> If he ever bared his soul to the kid, *all hell would break loose*. It would be like *opening a can of worms*. . . . (127)

> [I]t was probably a wash. *Six of one, half a dozen of another.* (130)

I introduce at length matters of taste because they are matters of taste. An enterprise of this essay is to suggest that the notion of evidence as something external to assertion does not survive, in the circumstances I sketch. Instead, assertion envelops evidence and offers itself bare for acceptance or rejection, and publicness is formed in the sequel. Taste is the entire critical field.

Some might hold that the "postmodern" artist's language cannot help being borrowed or empty, that triteness in Auster is a deliberate, or at least natural, product of his insight. In support of this contention is Auster's regeneration of Flaubert's Bouvard and Pécuchet as Flower and Stone. Accepting this view would not, however, nullify the point of saying whether Auster carries out its program well or poorly. From *City of Glass* to *Leviathan* his only novel in which banality, if it is to be considered a tool, is used with skill is *Ghosts* (in the paraphrases of Blue's hapless ratiocinations: e.g., "The real problem boils down to identifying the nature of the problem itself" [56]), a text whose sarcasm seems to me learned from Samuel Beckett's *Watt*. Nevertheless, I'd reject this argument. It implies that the nihilistic forces forming the world known in the West for at least two centuries (since Sade, at the latest) — that is, coengendered rationalism and irrationalism — are limited in their effect on artworks to obliging mimicry. But the more subtle and interesting effect of these forces is to encourage the training that makes the individual exercise of taste possible, for the abyss that nihilism uncovers, in destroying all footings, is the infinitely variable human historical record. In the modern arena, where claims compete without the referee of truth, assertion is modulated by the criterion of quality. You ceaselessly draw comparisons with what you have experienced and, solely through this personal-historical resort, decide on some ground (or perhaps, as Wittgenstein might add, on no particular ground) whether to damn or bless. Such a decision — defensible by no more than the assertion of it — founds the notion of quality itself. Choosing in the absence of absolute recourse for defending the choice makes the discrimination everything. Auster's stylistic conventionality (which is different from his tritenesses) is like a result of the pragmatism and historicism for which the idea of false speech is as meaningless as that of true speech. Speech can be neither true nor false; it is simply at work, engaging response. This conclusion makes convention potentially justifiable and platitude, which deadens response, inexcusable.

Along with asceticism, another outcome of the subject's reduction, under absolute consciousness, to the automaton is the emergence of the doppelgänger, of the substitute. This appearance might be reexpressed as the emergent synonymy of zero and two, when the poles of expiring dualisms alternately merge into indistinction and diverge in exaggerated, artificial contrariety. Writing on Blanchot, Michel Foucault summarizes this algebra in a sentence that could replace my entire commentary:

The instant interiority is lured out of itself, an outside empties the place into which interiority customarily retreats and deprives it of the possibility of retreat: a form arises — less than a form, a kind of stub-born, amorphous anonymity — that divests interiority of its identity, hollows it out, divides it into non-coincident twin figures, divests it of its unmediated right to say *I,* and pits against its discourse a speech that is indissociably echo and denial. (47–48)

The reciprocal motion of zero-two determines that the sighting of the surrogate coincides with the perfecting of solipsism. To be removed from that which most concerns you is to observe it continuing to be performed as everything that you are not. "No one can cross the boundary into another — for the simple reason that no one can gain access to himself" (Auster, *The Locked Room* 80–81), a self that is consequently perpetually outside itself. (Not in a locked room, though. Out in the open.) In a continual amoebism across Auster's novels, characters share names, re-peat one another's actions and speech, follow parallel careers, find strangers familiar, form twin pairs charged by repulsion and attraction. *Leviathan,* while repeating the Ishmael-Ahab setup of *The Locked Room,* augments the exponent, producing the triplet Aaron-Sachs-Dimaggio: Aaron substitutes in Sachs's bed and Sachs in Dimaggio's; Sachs, who "had stood for the same things" as Dimaggio (191), adopts Dimaggio's mission and, while carrying out a form of it, forges in Aaron's books the signature of the author, who himself will borrow the name of Sachs's own unfinished project to title the account of Sachs's life, a life without which Aaron says he "can hardly imagine" his own (21). That it is senseless to say whether the three names correspond to three characters enacting a single life or to one character living three lives is the point — don't say either, and certainly don't say three characters live three lives that are intricately enmeshed by coincidence. For Hobbes the leviathan is the commonwealth, the multitude voluntarily united under the absolute sov-ereign so that the interest of each individual is not absolute. For Auster, a counter-Hobbes surveying anarchy, the leviathan is the aggregation of missing male adults, which any one man and all men compose equally well — an anticommunal totality of zero, the whiteness of the whale, non-individuated consciousness itself: "He had to make sure that the missing man could have been anyone. Once he did that, he would be home free" (173). Black's valediction mourns the all-and-nothing status of the repre-sentation under total self-consciousness: "You were the whole world to me, Blue, and I turned you into my death" (*Ghosts* 93). If there is to be the whole world (publicness itself, the ground of thought), there must be nothing (in any absolute sense). Thought must entirely enclose (be satis-fied by ["accept" is Wittgenstein's verb (226)]), but may not exceed, *some* form of life.

Despite the scientific pretensions Husserl absorbed from his age, he

recognized the extrarational terminus of the reduction: "We have literally lost nothing, but have won the whole Absolute Being, which, properly
understood, conceals in itself all transcendences [i.e., roughly, everything that is over against consciousness], 'constituting' them within itself" (sec. 50). Let it not be ignored that this statement may as well
propose the fusion of the areas formerly known as the human and the
divine. Auster continually approaches the same transvaluation. It is implied by all in his books and is often explicit in endings: the leave-taking
of purgatory in *In the Country of Last Things* ("I cannot even begin to think
of what will happen to us out there. Anything is possible, and that is
almost the same as nothing, almost the same as being born into a world
that has never existed before" [187–188]); Fogg moon gazing on the rim
of the American continent, looking at one new world from the edge of
another (*Moon Palace* 306–307); Nashe's own final, transfiguring encounter with "a cyclops star," concluding when "the light was upon him"
(*Music of Chance* 216–217). Auster's documents of loss, disintegration,
and exile characteristically cut off at the transition for which they are
groundwork, at the point when the backward-looking anxieties marking
his work as modern would be outstripped. Is his arrest at the threshold a
reflection of the historically most salient of the American characters —
the contradictory, youthful combination of flexibility and stubborn rationalism, in which relativism coexists with the expectation that just foundations for all things should be found with businesslike dispatch? I mean
the mistrust, among both the complacent and the discontent, of the
constructs and arts of civilization for being no more than constructs and
arts — that is, no more justifiable — as if methods of justification existed
outside constructs and arts (a mistrust that differs from constructive
challenges to particular constructs and arts on local grounds). Auster's
glumness has, perhaps, a root in the American earnestness that can de-
clare, out of its birthright of philosophical pragmatism, the contingency
of self and society only to undertake, inexplicably because of that declaration, a search for the genuine and underlying — for example, by embrac-
ing myths of personal liberation. Auster shows that the testaments of such
a search should be received with a smile (Nashe on his Sisyphean sentence: "The wall would not be a punishment so much as a cure, a one-way
journey back to earth" [*Music of Chance* 110]; Sachs, who will later blow
himself to bits: "I had found the unifying principle, and this one idea
would bring all the broken pieces of myself together" [*Leviathan* 256]),
but he is not therefore less preoccupied with it.

Insofar as Auster's works derive from the American odyssey to perfection, both questioning and extending it, they presume the same utopianism, if only to memorialize its failure. Always an iconoclast, the ironist is
tethered to a toppled statue. The automaton's further fate, however, is to

know nothing of irony and so of sincerity and to find the threat of disintegration as uninteresting as the fantasy of wholeness.[4]

Notes

1. "Be cheerful while you are alive," from an Egyptian maxim of the third millennium BC (Simpson 171), exhibits this insight — by not beginning "Be happy. . . ." The maxim in literal translation starts, "Be bright-faced . . . ," and it has also been rendered, "Be generous as long as you live" (Lichtheim 79 n.56, 72). In any of the three translations the phrase appeals to what is public (acts, external appearance) rather than to what is private (emotion) in trying to understand the highest human aspiration. And to reinforce this appeal the author alludes to the life span, the sum of public activity. The philosophical work of this homily is to face finitude. Yet the effort leads not to mechanism or nihilism but to the discovery that outward gestures, undertaken for pragmatic reasons, are what determine individual ethical endurance, beyond the life span: the maxim concludes, "[G]raciousness is a man's memorial . . ." (Simpson 172). Such obliviousness to the phantasms of metaphysics, whether inner (psychology) or outer (utopianism), is typical of ancient wisdom literature and, unless I'm mistaken, is largely what Wittgenstein teaches.

2. The automaton is a commonplace of the modern period, exemplarily in the cinema, where Robert Bresson, for instance, created a "vigilambulist" that is "as bereft of ideas as of feelings, reduced to the automatism of segmented daily gestures, but endowed with autonomy. . . . [I]t is precisely the automaton, petrified in this way, that thought seizes from the outside, as the unthinkable in thought" (Deleuze 178). Auster's Nashe likewise feels "as if he were no more than an actor performing on the stage of some imaginary theater, repeating lines that had been written for him in advance." On another occasion Nashe falls into a "trance": "his head seemed curiously emptied out. . . . [A]n abrupt and radical shift of his inner bearings, as if the world around him had suddenly lost its reality . . . made him feel like a shadow, like someone who had fallen asleep with his eyes open" (*Music of Chance* 36, 65).

3. Stillman says, "The last thing I will be is a high-wire walker. . . . That is what I would like. To dance on the wire until I die. . . . I am the last one. There are no others. I am the end of everyone, the last man" (32). I take this declaration to echo, and perhaps to mock (in the spirit in which Auster mocks Céline, with Ferdinand in *In the Country of Last Things*), the parable of the tightrope walker who is killed in the prologue of *Thus Spoke Zarathustra*. The crisis of the human subject in Auster's narratives resembles a development of both the optimistic and the pessimistic Nietzschean outlooks for the "letzten Menschen" 'last people': Auster faces the untenability of the highest values, but the result is paralyzing obsession with loss, not joy and self-overcoming.

4. The Greek Stoics, for instance, contemplated this further fate. In their view there is no real contrast between reason and the emotions. Someone in the ideal state of *apatheia*, "so far from being emotionless, is possessed of the three basic and stable emotional — and at the same time rational — dispositions of joy, wishfulness and a sense of precaution . . ." (Rist 25). In contrast with the ultimatums of perfectionism, these dispositions are attitudes of cooperation toward the everyday. *Apatheia*, combining the neutral phenomenological gaze with a Wittgensteinian discovery of use, offers no support for exclusive judgment. Epictetus says,

"Materials are indifferent, but the use which we make of them is not a matter of indifference.... [I]n that which is another's [i.e., in all areas except your assimilation of external impressions] never employ the words 'good' or 'evil,' or 'benefit' or 'injury,' or anything of the sort" (2.5.1, 2.5.5). A key test is the Stoics' response to those who dismiss the Stoic ideal. It is of the essence of this school to hold that dissenters should "be just as they are" (Epictetus 1.12.21). Blanchot provides modern testimony of the same waking noctambulism, in which one is never adrift because one was never anchored. The effect of Blanchot's Christian overtones is to erase from his vision any hint of what the irreligionist understands as religion. The following is from a text named in part for the pre-Socratic Heraclitus:

> S'il existait encore, c'était pour reconnaître, dans cette chambre pleine de fleurs funèbres, de lumière spectrale, l'impossibilité de revivre. Il retrouvait le souffle dans l'asphyxie.... [I]l apparaissait sur la porte étroite de son sépulcre, non pas ressuscité, mais mort et ayant la certitude d'être arraché en même temps à la mort et à la vie. Il marchait, momie peinte.... Assurément, [dit-il,] je pouvais mourir, mais la mort perfidement brillait pour moi comme la mort de la mort, de sorte que, devenant l'homme éternel qui prend la place du moribond, cet homme sans crime, sans raison de mourir qu'est tout homme qui meurt, je mourais, mort si étranger à la mort, que je passais mon instant suprême dans un temps où il n'était déjà plus possible de mourir et que je vivais cependant toutes les heures de ma vie à l'heure où je ne pouvais plus les vivre. (*Thomas l'obscur* 41–42, 103)

> If he still existed, it was to recognize, in this room full of funereal flowers, of spectral light, the impossibility of returning to life. He regained breath in asphyxiation. . . . He appeared in the narrow doorway of his sepulcher, not resurrected but dead and certain of being torn at once from death and from life. He walked, a painted mummy. . . . Assuredly, [he said,] I could die, but death shone treacherously for me as the death of death, so that, becoming the eternal man who replaces one who is dying, that man without crime, without reason to die, which is everyone who dies, I died, a dead man so foreign to death that I passed my supreme moment in a time when it was already no longer possible to die and that I nevertheless lived all the hours of my life at the hour when I could no longer live them. (My translation)

Works Cited

Auster, Paul. *City of Glass*. Los Angeles: Sun & Moon Press, 1985.
———. "The Decisive Moment." In *The Art of Hunger: Essays, Prefaces, Interviews*. Los Angeles: Sun & Moon Press, 1992. Pp. 35–53.
———. *Ghosts*. Los Angeles: Sun & Moon Press, 1986.
———. *In the Country of Last Things*. New York: Penguin, 1987.
———. *Leviathan*. New York: Viking, 1992.
———. *The Locked Room*. Los Angeles: Sun & Moon Press, 1986.
———. *Moon Palace*. New York: Penguin, 1989.
———. *The Music of Chance*. New York: Penguin, 1990.
Blanchot, Maurice. *Le dernier homme [The Last Man]*. Paris: Gallimard, 1957.
———. *Thomas l'obscur [Thomas the Obscure]*. Paris: Gallimard, 1950.
Deleuze, Gilles. *Cinema 2: The Time-Image*. Trans. Hugh Tomlinson and Robert Galeta. Minneapolis: University of Minnesota Press, 1989.

Epictetus. *Arrian's Discourses of Epictetus*. In *The* Discourses *as Reported by Arrian, the Manual, and Fragments*. Trans. W. A. Oldfather. 2 vols. Cambridge, Mass.: Harvard University Press, 1925–28. Pp. 1–435 (vol. 1); 2–437 (vol. 2).

Foucault, Michel. "Maurice Blanchot: The Thought from the Outside." Trans. Brian Massumi. In *Foucault/Blanchot*, by Michel Foucault and Maurice Blanchot. New York: Zone, 1987. Pp. 7–58.

Husserl, Edmund. *Ideas: General Introduction to Pure Phenomenology*. Trans. W. R. Boyce Gibson. New York: Collier, 1962.

Lichtheim, Miriam, ed. and trans. "The Instruction of Ptahhotep." In *The Old and Middle Kingdoms*. Berkeley: University of California Press, 1973. Pp. 61–80. Vol. 1 of *Ancient Egyptian Literature: A Book of Readings* (3 vols., 1973–80).

Nietzsche, Friedrich. *Also sprach Zarathustra: Ein Buch für Alle und Keinen [Thus Spoke Zarathustra: A Book for Everyone and No One]*. Berlin: Gruyter, 1968.

Ricoeur, Paul. *Husserl: An Analysis of His Phenomenology*. Trans. Edward G. Ballard and Lester E. Embree. Evanston, Ill.: Northwestern University Press, 1967.

Rist, J. M. *Stoic Philosophy*. Cambridge: Cambridge University Press, 1969.

Simpson, William Kelly, ed. "The Maxims of Ptahhotpe." Trans. R. O. Faulkner. In *The Literature of Ancient Egypt: An Anthology of Stories, Instructions, and Poetry*. Trans. R. O. Faulkner, Edward F. Wente, Jr., and William Kelly Simpson. New Haven, Conn.: Yale University Press, 1972. Pp. 159–176.

Wittgenstein, Ludwig. *Philosophical Investigations*. Trans. G. E. M. Anscombe. Oxford: Blackwell, 1958.

Being Paul Auster's Ghost

Motoyuki Shibata

The attempt to discuss the experience of translating Paul Auster is a slightly discouraging task, since one cannot help feeling that such experience has already been given a perfect expression by Auster himself. I am referring to a memorable passage in *The Invention of Solitude:*

> He sits at his desk reading the book in French and then picks up his pen and writes the same book in English. It is both the same book and not the same book, and the strangeness of this activity has never failed to impress him. Every book is an image of solitude. . . . A man sits alone in a room and writes. Whether the book speaks of loneliness or companionship, it is necessarily a product of solitude. A. sits down in his own room to translate another man's book, and it is as though he were entering that man's solitude and making it his own. But surely that is impossible. For once a solitude has been breached, once a solitude has been taken on by another, it is no longer solitude but a kind of companionship. Even though there is only one man in the room, there are two. A. imagines himself as a kind of ghost of that other man, who is both there and not there, and whose book is both the same and not the same as the one he is translating. Therefore, he tells himself, it is possible to be alone and not alone at the same moment. (136)

Having quoted the passage that marvelously illustrates my own fascination in translating Auster into Japanese, there still remains one question that seems to be worth pursuing. Is translating Auster in any significant sense different from translating other authors? In other words, does this passage apply more aptly to the experience of translating Auster than to that of translating others? In my case, the answer seems to be yes.

I have translated four of Mr. Auster's books: *Ghosts, The Locked Room, The Invention of Solitude,* and *Moon Palace,* in the order of publication, and am currently working on *In the Country of Last Things.*[1] Among other contemporary American writers I have translated are Steven Millhauser, Ethan Canin, Steve Erickson, and Stuart Dybek. These authors have all given me both the translator's usual bliss (the grand illusion that you yourself are writing the great book) and the usual despair (the ever-lingering frustration that you can never do justice to the original no matter how hard you rack your brain), and on this point Auster has been no exception.

Something is different, though. Without belittling the joy and honor of translating other writers, I can say that translating Paul Auster has been a singular experience. This essay is an attempt to explain why it feels different to be the ghost of the author of *Ghosts*.

I am well aware that my position may not be so unique. It can be argued that every reading is an act of translation; translation, the theory goes, is only a more deliberate, more self-conscious kind of reading. Granting that, I would still claim that translation is a moderately special kind of experience in that it involves the effort at transparency. There is an element of self-effacement. Walter Benjamin said that the task of the translator consists in "finding that intended effect upon the language into which he is translating which produces in it the echo of the original" (76). One tries to play the role of Echo, to Narcissus that is the author. It is not the author alone that is "both there and not there"; the translator, too, tries not to be there while still being there. An Echo never completely successful, the translator is forever trying to disappear.

And disappearing, needless to say, is a quintessential Austerian act. Daniel Quinn, Blue, Fanshawe, Benjamin Sachs: so many of Auster's central characters go through various stages of disappearance — social, existential, literal — as the plot unravels, or rather ravels even more. The female protagonist in *In the Country of Last Things* searches for her brother who has disappeared in a country where things are disappearing one after another. *The Music of Chance* begins at a point where the protagonist thinks he has made his social disappearance complete. It is not for nothing that Auster's book of selected poems is entitled *Disappearances*.

These disappearances are often preceded by the state of destitution. In American literature, destitution in most cases simply means social victimization: an oblique comment on the betrayal of the American dream. Think of the stories by Raymond Carver and Richard Ford, or for more classic examples, Hurstwood's downfall in Theodore Dreiser's *Sister Carrie* or Maggie's tragedy in Stephen Crane's first novel, *Maggie: A Girl of the Streets*. In Auster, however, destitution is a process, often self-imposed, through which the character elaborates his disappearing act.

For Quinn learned that eating did not necessarily solve the problem of food. A meal was no more than a fragile defense against the inevitability of the next meal. Food itself could never answer the question of food; it only delayed the moment when the question would have to be asked in earnest. The great danger, therefore, was in eating too much. If he took in more than he should, his appetite for the next meal increased, and thus more food was needed to satisfy him. By keeping a close and constant watch on himself, Quinn was gradually able to reverse the process. His ambition was to eat as little as possible, and in this way to stave off his hunger. In the best of all worlds, he might have been able to approach absolute zero, but he did not want to be overly ambitious in his present circumstances. Rather, he kept the total fast in his mind as an ideal, a state of perfection he could aspire to but never achieve. He did not want to starve himself to death — and he reminded himself of this every day — he simply wanted to leave himself free to think of the things that truly concerned him. For now, that meant keeping the case uppermost in his thoughts. Fortunately, this coincided with his other major ambition: to make the three hundred dollars last as long as he could. (*City of Glass* 174–175)

This kind of self-imposed destitution is encountered so often in Auster's work that it could be argued that it points to one of the writer's central themes: the possibility of confronting, by shedding the social strata of the identity, the nothingness hidden at the core. But what I sense here most is the *delight* the author takes in delineating the process of self-eradication. "Two eggs a day, soft-boiled to perfection in two and a half minutes," Marco Fogg, the narrator-protagonist in *Moon Palace* not unhappily reports: "two slices of bread, three cups of coffee, and as much water as I could drink. If not inspiring, the plan at least had a certain geometrical elegance" (29). I can in no way prove this, but I suspect the character's satisfaction in minimizing his physical existence is fully shared by the author. And this delight in the game of getting as close as possible to absolute zero without actually becoming zero is, to me, analogous to the translator's delight in self-effacement. Through the endless revisions that he imposes on himself, with the rigidity comparable to Marco Fogg's regimen, the translator tries to eliminate himself, to erase his own footsteps. When things are going well it is as if my own linguistic idiosyncrasies have disappeared, and I begin to hear *what the author would write if Japanese were his language,* though of course I am fully aware that it is only an illusion. The complete self-effacement is, like turning oneself into a perfect hunger artist, a "state of perfection" I can "aspire to but never achieve."

*   *   *

But it is not only when a character "disappears" that I find an analogy between the text and translating it. Indeed, being there and not there seems to be the essential attitude of Auster's narrators. Thus Marco Fogg observes in *Moon Palace:*

> There is a particular glaze that comes over the eyes of New Yorkers when they walk through the streets, a natural and perhaps necessary form of indifference to others. It doesn't matter how you look, for example. Outrageous costumes, bizarre hairdos, T-shirts with obscene slogans printed across them — no one pays attention to such things. On the other hand, the way you act inside your clothes is of the utmost importance. Odd gestures of any kind are automatically taken as a threat. Talking out loud to yourself, scratching your body, looking someone directly in the eye: these deviations can trigger off hostile and sometimes violent reactions from those around you. You must not stagger or swoon, you must not clutch the walls, you must not sing, for all forms of spontaneous or involuntary behavior are sure to elicit stares, caustic remarks, and even an occasional shove or kick in the shins. (56–57)

This is a statement by a person who obviously knows New York well, who knows what it feels like being there, but at the same time his tone is that of a man who stands completely outside the experience of being there: the lucid effect of the prose here in no way depends on any previous knowledge of New York on the reader's part. The meaning is fully articulated, as if Marco were translating the city for visitors from another planet.

And this attitude is not only confined to descriptive passages. The basic approach to the problem of the self — Auster's most constant theme — often adopts such a stance. In *The Invention of Solitude,* the book in which the problem of the self comes foremost, Auster seeks to reach himself through writing about his father in the first half of the book, and in the second half examines himself by exploring the inner life of a person called "A." He tries, in other words, to probe himself first through the other, then as the other. Either way, just as Marco Fogg is both in and outside New York, he is both in and outside himself:

> Christmas Eve, 1979. His life no longer seemed to dwell in the present. Whenever he turned on his radio and listened to the news of the world, he would find himself imagining the words to be describing things that had happened long ago. Even as he stood in the present, he felt himself to be looking at it from the future, and this present-as-past was so antiquated that even the horrors of the day, which ordinarily would have filled him with outrage, seemed remote to him, as if the voice in

the radio were reading from a chronicle of some lost civilization. Later, in a time of greater clarity, he would refer to this sensation as "nostalgia for the present." (76)

It is not just that Auster the protagonist sees the outer world as if from a remote future; Auster the author also sees Auster the protagonist in exactly the same way. To Auster, who obviously feels more affinity with the doubting Pascal than with the ultimately confident Descartes, to think does not lead to the conviction "I am." Part of himself is always standing outside, observing himself as if observing a stranger. Auster remarks in an interview: "I was looking at myself in the same way a scientist studies a laboratory animal. I was no more than a little gray rat, a guinea pig stuck in the cage of my own consciousness. The book . . . was an attempt to turn myself inside-out and examine what I was made of. Myself, yes — but myself as anyone, myself as everyone" (*Art of Hunger* 292). The impulse is anything but confessional; the point is not to expose secrets of the private self to the world but to translate that private realm into general terms. A self is translated into the Self. This tendency to universalize the self and to turn the particular into the general also can be found in narrators in Auster's other works. They are, to a certain degree, all translators of themselves.

Perhaps this is one of the reasons why Auster "travels well." It is well known that Mr. Auster has been highly successful in Europe, especially in France where inspection of the self has always been a central philosophical concern. The reception in Japan has been no less warm.[2] At a time when Japanese readers had begun to believe that all new fiction imported from America was pseudo-sociological reports of the mostly sordid aspects of contemporary American life, Auster is seen as a welcome alternative. *The Invention of Solitude,* incidentally, is also a refreshing change from the Japanese tradition of *shi-shosetsu* (I-novel), a strongly autobiographical, and highly confessional type of novel: something that resembles but is entirely different from Mr. Auster's book.[3]

Finally, translating Auster *feels* different from translating other contemporary American writers because his text itself is analogous in various aspects — the way characters make themselves disappear, the way narrators tell their tale, the way protagonists look at themselves — to the act of translation. The commonplace observation that the original text is already a translation of the world rings especially true in Auster's case. I cannot, however, chase off the doubt that this is all too neat, that this all may be a roundabout, futile excuse for justifying my life as Paul Auster's ghost. Emerson said, "The ghosts are tormented with the fear of death, and cannot remember that they have died" (678). Perhaps it is high time that I remembered being dead and shut up.

Notes

1. In addition to my four translations, *City of Glass* and *Disappearances: Selected Poems* have been translated into Japanese by other translators.

2. *Ghosts*, which was published in 1989, has sold 24,500 copies so far; *The Locked Room*, also published in 1989, has sold 16,000; *The Invention of Solitude*, published in 1991, has sold 16,000; and *Moon Palace*, published in 1994, has sold 12,000 copies. Rather extraordinary figures for the translation of serious fiction, though some feel that they should be even higher, considering the high critical acclaim accorded to the author in Japan.

3. Perhaps influenced by this tradition of *shi-shosetsu*, most reviewers in Japan identified, I think rightly, *The Invention of Solitude* as a novel; almost no one called it a memoir or an autobiography.

Works Cited

Auster, Paul. *City of Glass*. Los Angeles: Sun & Moon Press, 1985.
——. "Interview with Larry McCaffery and Sinda Gregory." In *The Art of Hunger: Essays, Prefaces, Interviews*. Los Angeles: Sun & Moon Press, 1992. Pp. 269–312.
——. *The Invention of Solitude*. New York: Penguin, 1988.
——. *Moon Palace*. New York: Viking, 1989.
Benjamin, Walter. "The Task of the Translator." In Hannah Arendt, ed., *Illuminations*. Trans. Harry Zohn. New York: Schocken Books, 1969. Pp. 69–82.
Emerson, Ralph Waldo. "Swedenborg; or, the Mystic." In *Essays and Lectures*. New York: The Library of America, 1983. Pp. 661–689.

Paul Auster: A Selected Bibliography

William Drenttel

This bibliography is a selected chronological checklist of the primary and secondary works of Paul Auster, edited to highlight fiction and prose. While Auster has published a significant amount of poetry and translation in literary journals, catalogues, and anthologies, this list includes only separate publications and major translations. Contributions to periodicals are limited to first appearances of prose works, including stories, fiction excerpts, memoirs, critical essays, and reviews. Selected secondary works in English are included to provide a critical perspective.

Many limited editions and special printings have been made of works by Auster; these are included only where they are the first separate edition. Also, subsequent paperback editions of separate publications are noted in parentheses. This checklist does not include works set to music, broadsides and other ephemera, recorded readings, works dedicated to Auster, plays, or screenplays by Auster or based on Auster's work.

SEPARATE PUBLICATIONS

POETRY

Unearth. Weston, Conn.: *Living Hand* 3 (Spring 1974).
Wall Writing. Berkeley: The Figures, 1976.
Effigies. Paris: Orange Export Ltd., 1977.
Fragments from Cold. Brewster, N.Y.: Parenthèse, 1977.
Facing the Music. Barrytown, N.Y.: Station Hill, 1980.
Disappearances: Selected Poems. Woodstock, N.Y.: The Overlook Press, 1988. (Woodstock, N.Y.: The Overlook Press, 1988.)
Ground Work: Selected Poems and Essays, 1970–79. London: Faber and Faber, 1990. (London, Faber and Faber, 1991.)
Autobiography of the Eye. Portland, Ore.: The Beaverdam Press, 1993.

NOVELS AND PROSE

White Spaces. Barrytown, N.Y.: Station Hill, 1980.

The Art of Hunger and Other Essays. London: The Menard Press, 1982.

The Invention of Solitude. New York: Sun Press, 1982. (New York: Avon Books, 1985; New York: Penguin Books, 1988; London: Faber and Faber, 1988.)

City of Glass. Los Angeles: Sun & Moon Press, 1985. (New York: Penguin Books, 1987.)

Ghosts. Los Angeles: Sun & Moon Press, 1986. (New York: Penguin Books, 1987.)

The Locked Room. Los Angeles: Sun & Moon Press, 1986. (New York: Penguin Books, 1988.)

The New York Trilogy. London: Faber and Faber, 1987. (London: Faber and Faber, 1988; New York: Penguin Books, 1990.)

In the Country of Last Things. New York: Viking, 1987. London: Faber and Faber, 1988. (New York: Penguin Books, 1988; London: Faber and Faber, 1989.)

Moon Palace. New York: Viking, 1989. London: Faber and Faber, 1989. (New York: Penguin Books, 1990; London: Faber and Faber, 1990.)

The Music of Chance. New York: Viking, 1990; London: Faber and Faber, 1991. (New York: Penguin Books, 1991; London: Faber and Faber, 1991.)

Leviathan. New York: Viking, 1992; London: Faber and Faber, 1992. (New York: Penguin Books, 1993; London: Faber and Faber, 1993.)

The Art of Hunger: Essays, Prefaces, Interviews. Los Angeles: Sun & Moon Press, 1992. (New York: Penguin Books, 1993.)

Auggie Wren's Christmas Story. Birmingham, U.K.: The Delos Press, 1992; New York: William Drenttel New York, 1992.

Mr. Vertigo. New York: Viking, 1994; London: Faber and Faber, 1994.

TRANSLATIONS

A Little Anthology of Surrealist Poems. New York: Siamese Banana Press, 1972. (Translations of Breton, Éluard, Char, Péret, Tzara, Artaud, Soupault, Desnos, Aragon, Arp.)

Fits and Starts: Selected Poems of Jacques Dupin. Weston, Conn.: *Living Hand* 2 (June 1974).

The Uninhabited: Selected Poems of André du Bouchet. New York: *Living Hand* 7 (1976).

Jean-Paul Sartre. *Life/Situations: Essays: Written and Spoken.* Trans. Paul Auster and Lydia Davis. New York: Pantheon Books, 1977; London: Andre Deutsch, 1978. (New York: Pantheon Books, 1977.)

Georges Simenon. *African Trio: Talatala, Tropic Moon, Aboard the Aquitaine.* Trans. Stuart Gilbert, Paul Auster, and Lydia Davis. New York: Harcourt Brace Jovanovich, 1979.

The Random House Book of Twentieth Century French Poetry. New York: Random House, 1982. Ed. Paul Auster. Trans. Auster (of 42 poems by various poets). (New York: Random House/Vintage Books, 1984.)

The Notebooks of Joseph Joubert: A Selection. Ed., trans., and preface Paul Auster. Afterword Maurice Blanchot. San Francisco: North Point Press, 1983.

Stéphane Mallarmé. *A Tomb for Anatole.* Bilingual edition. Trans. and introduction Paul Auster. San Francisco: North Point Press, 1983.

Philippe Petit. *On the High Wire.* Trans. Paul Auster. Preface Marcel Marceau. New York: Random House, 1985.

Maurice Blanchot. *Vicious Circles: Two Fictions & ⟨⟨After the Fact⟩⟩.* Trans. Paul Auster. Barrytown, N.Y.: Station Hill Press, 1985. (Barrytown, N.Y.: Station Hill Press, 1985.)

Joan Miró: Selected Writings and Interviews. Ed. Margit Rowell. Trans. (French) Paul Auster. Trans. (Spanish and Catalan) Patricia Mathews. Boston: G.K. Hall and Co., 1986.

Selected Poems of René Char. Ed. Mary Ann Caws and Tina Jolas. Includes translations by Paul Auster of five early Char poems. New York: New Directions, 1992. (New York: New Directions, 1992.)

Selected Poems of Jacques Dupin. Selected by Paul Auster. Trans. Paul Auster, Stephen Romer, and David Shapiro. Preface by Mary Ann Caws. Winston-Salem, N.C.: Wake Forest University Press, 1992. New Castle-upon-Tyne, U.K.: Bloodaxe Books, 1992.

PROSE CONTRIBUTIONS TO PERIODICALS

" 'Truth' Perseveres." *Columbia Daily Spectator* 113:15 (October 11, 1968): 4. Review of *Mingus,* a film about Charlie Mingus.

"Harried Leisure in a Monstrous World: Notes on Godard's *Weekend.*" *Columbia Daily Spectator* 113:21 (October 21, 1968): C2, 4.

"*Fireman's Ball.*" *Columbia Daily Spectator,* 113:35 (November 15, 1968): 4. Review of *Fireman's Ball,* a film by Milos Foreman.

"The Hollywood Mentality." *Columbia Daily Spectator* 113:49 (December 10, 1968): 4. Review of *The Fixer,* a film of the Bernard Malamud novel by John Frankenheimer.

"Was Christopher Smart?" *Columbia Daily Spectator* 113:50 (December 11, 1968): C6. Review of *The Collected Poems of Christopher Smart.*

"Letter from the City." *Columbia Review Magazine* (Fall 1969): 27–33.

"The Cruel Geography of Jacques Dupin's Poetry." *Books Abroad* 47:1 (Winter 1973): 76–78.

"Pages for Kafka." *European Judaism* 16, 8:2 (Summer 1974): 36–37.

"Itinerary." *Chelsea* 33 (September 1974): 169–170. Essay on Laura Riding.

"Some Notes on Charles Reznikoff's Poetry." *European Judaism* 17, 9:1 (Winter 1974/5): 13, 34–35.

"The Death of Sir Walter Raleigh." *Parenthèse* 4 (1975): 223–227.

"One-Man Language." *New York Review of Books* 22:1 (February 6, 1975): 30–31. Review of Louis Wolfson's *Le Schizo et Les Langues.*

"From Cakes to Stones." *Commentary* 60:1 (July 1975): 93–95. Review of Samuel Beckett's *Mercier and Camier.*

"The Return of Laura Riding." *New York Review of Books* 22:13 (August 7, 1975): 36–38. Review of Laura Riding's *Selected Poems* and *The Telling.*

"Ideas and Things." *Harper's* 25:1506 (November 1975): 106–110. Review of John Ashbery and John Hollander poetry collections.

"Poet of Exile." *Commentary* 61:2 (February 1976): 83–86. Review of Paul Celan poetry collections.

"Man of Pain." *New York Review of Books* 23:7 (April 29, 1976): 35–37. Review of Guiseppe Ungaretti's *Selected Poems.*

"Flight Out of Time." *Mulch* 8/9, 3:4/4:1 (Spring–Summer 1976): 186–191. Review of Hugo Ball's *A Dada Diary.*

"The Rebirth of a Poet." *Harper's Bookletter* 2:21 (June 21, 1976): 15. Review of Carl Rakosi's *Ex Cranium.*

"In Memoriam: Charles Reznikoff (1894–1976)." *Harper's Bookletter* 3:1 (August 16, 1976): 14, 16.

"Contemporary French Poetry: An Introduction against Introductions." *Tri-Quarterly* 35 (Winter 1976): 99–116.

"Private I, Public Eye." *Harper's Bookletter* 3:11 (January 31, 1977): 12–13. Review of George Oppen's *Collected Poems.*

"Story of a Scream." *New York Review of Books* 24:7 (April 28, 1977): 38–40. Review of Edmond Jabès' *The Book of Questions.*

"Chaos and Beauty." *Saturday Review* 4:24 (September 17, 1977): 34–37. Essay on John Ashbery.

"Northern Lights: The Paintings of Jean-Paul Riopelle." *The Merri Creek, Or Nero* 3 (September/October 1977): 9.

"*Letters to Friends, Family and Editors.*" *San Francisco Review of Books* 3:10 (February 1978): 8–9. Review of collection of letters by Franz Kafka.

"The Poetry of William Bronk." *Saturday Review* 5:20 (July 8, 1978): 30–31.

"Happiness, or a Journey through Space: Words for One Voice and One Dancer." *Grosseteste Review* 12 (1979): 67–75.

"The Decisive Moment: Charles Reznikoff." *Parnassus* 7:2 (Spring/Summer 1979): 105–118.

"From *The Notebooks of Joseph Joubert.*" *Montemora* 7 (1980): 147–162.

"Stéphane Mallarmé's *A Tomb for Anatole.*" *Paris Review* 22:78 (Summer 1980): 134–148.

"The Art of Hunger." *Shearsman* 3 (1981): 62–68. Essay on Knut Hamsun.

"Apollinaire's *Le Pont Mirabeau:* Wilbur/Auster Exchange on Translation." *Modern Poetry in Translation* 41–42 (March 1981): 28–32.

"A Few Words in Praise of George Oppen." *Paideuma* 10:1 (Spring 1981): 49–52.

"*The Notebooks of Joseph Joubert.*" *The New Criterion* 1:4 (December 1982): 17–31.

"The Poetry of Exile: Paul Celan." *Studies in Twentieth Century Literature* 8:1 (Fall 1983): 101–110.

"From *The Book of Memory.*" *Action/Image: A Journal of Memory and History* 1:1 (Autumn 1984): 31–36.

"*In the Country of Last Things.*" *Paris Review* 27:96 (Summer 1985): 204–225.

"Across the River and Into the Twilight Zone." *New York Times Book Review* 91 (September 21, 1986): 14. Review of Steve Erickson's *Rubicon Beach.*

"From *The Locked Room.*" *Pequod* 23/24 (1987): 148–156.

"Moonlight in the Brooklyn Museum." *Art News* 86:7 (September 1987): 104–105.

"The Bartlebooth Follies." *New York Times Book Review* 92 (November 15, 1987): 7. Review of George Perec's *Life, A User's Manual.*

"A Conversation with William Bronk." *Sagetrieb* 7:3 (Winter 1988): 17–44.

"From *The Invention of Solitude.*" *Aperture* 114 (Spring 1989) 24–26.

"Auggie Wren's Christmas Story." *New York Times* 140 (December 25, 1990): A31.

"The Red Notebook." *Granta* 44 (Summer 1993): 232–253.

"Black on White: Paintings by David Reed." *Denver Quarterly* 28:1 (Summer 1993): 63–64.

"A Prayer for Salman Rushdie." *New York Times* 142 (July 1, 1993): A31.

"From *Mr. Vertigo*." *The Review of Contemporary Fiction* 14:1 (Spring 1994): 13–25.
"True Stories: Coincidence." *Harper's* 28:1726 (March 1994): 31–33.
"Dizzy." *Granta* 46 (Winter 1994): 215–234.
"*Mr. Vertigo*." *Grand Street* 49 13:1 (Summer 1994): 37–48.

SECONDARY SOURCES

Barone, Dennis. Review of *Leviathan*. *The Review of Contemporary Fiction* 11:2 (Fall 1992): 193–194.
———. "Paul Auster/Danilo Kis Issue." *The Review of Contemporary Fiction* 14:1 (Spring 1994): 7–96. Includes essays by Dennis Barone, Charles Baxter, Sven Birkerts, Paul Bray, Mary Ann Caws, Robert Creeley, Alan Gurganus, Gerald Howard, Mark Irwin, Barry Lewis, Mark Osteen, Mark Rudman, Chris Tysh, Katherine Washburn, Steven Weisenburger, and Curtis White.
Bawer, Bruce. "Fiction Chronicle: Literature & Revolution." *The New Criterion* 11:4 (December 1992): 51–58. Review of *Leviathan*.
———. "Family Ties with an Athenian Twist." *Wall Street Journal* (September 21, 1990): A12. Review of *The Music of Chance*.
———. "Fiction Chronicle: Doubles and More Doubles." *The New Criterion* 7:8 (April 1989): 67–74. Review of *Moon Palace*.
Begley, Adam. "Case of the Brooklyn Symbolist." *New York Times Magazine* 141 (August 30, 1992): 41.
Bell, Madison Smartt. "Poker and Nothingness." *New York Times Book Review* (November 4, 1990): 15–16. Review of *The Music of Chance*.
Benedetti, David. "An Interview with Paul Auster." *American Poetry* 8 (Fall 1990): 188–192.
Birkerts, Sven. *American Energies: Essays on Fiction*. New York: William Morrow, 1992. Includes chapter on *Moon Palace*.
Bradbury, Malcolm. *The Modern American Novel: New Edition*. New York: Viking, 1993. Includes chapter on *The New York Trilogy*.
Brooks, Peter. "Re-imagined in English." *New York Times Book Review* (January 23, 1983): 9. Review of *Random House Book of Twentieth Century French Poetry*.
Drenttel, William, ed. *Paul Auster: A Comprehensive Bibliographic Checklist of Published Works 1968–1994*. New York: William Drenttel New York, 1994. Includes over 800 citations of primary and secondary works by and about Auster; with an introduction by Robert Hughes.
Duperray, Annick, ed. *L'Oeuvre de Paul Auster: Approaches et Lectures Plurielles*. Aix-en-Provence, France: L'Université de Provence, 1995. Forthcoming collection of essays and lectures from an international conference of 28 participant speakers held in Aix-en-Provence in June 1994.
Edwards, Thomas R. "Sad Young Men." *New York Review of Books* 36:13 (August 17, 1989): 52–53. Review of *Moon Palace*.
Ford, Mark. "Citizens of A Sinister City." *Times Literary Supplement* (March 15, 1991): 11. Review of *The Music of Chance*.
Frank, Joan. "The Art of Austerity." *San Francisco Review of Books* 17:3 (Winter 1992): 20–22. Interview.
Greenland, Colin. "The Novelist Vanishes." *Times Literary Supplement* (December 11, 1987): 1375. Review of *The New York Trilogy*.
Horne, Philip. "Making Faces." *London Review of Books* 13:9 (May 9, 1991): 26. Review of *The Music of Chance*.

———. "It's Just a Book." *London Review of Books* 14:24 (December 17, 1992): 20–22. Review of *Leviathan*.

Howe, Fanny. "A Thriller Well-Crafted and Philosophical." *Boston Globe* (December 13, 1985): 79. Review of *City of Glass*.

Irwin, Mark. "Memory's Escape: Inventing *The Music of Chance*—A Conversation with Paul Auster." *Denver Quarterly* 28:3 (Winter 1994): 111–122.

Lavender, William. "The Novel of Critical Engagement: Paul Auster's City of Glass." *Contemporary Literature* 34:2 (1993): 210–239.

Lewis, Roger. "In the Country of Literary Things." *Punch* 295 (July 15, 1988): 49. Review of *In the Country of Last Things*.

Locke, Richard. "Bookshelf: A Man Transformed." *Wall Street Journal* (September 15, 1992): A14. Review of *Leviathan*.

Malin, Irving. *The Review of Contemporary Fiction* 11:1 (Spring 1991): 315–317. Review of *The Music of Chance*.

Mallia, Joseph. "Paul Auster Interview." *Bomb* 23 (Spring 1988): 24.

Mannes-Abbott, Guy. "The Music of Chance." *New Statesman & Society* 4:143 (March 22, 1991): 45. Review.

McCaffery, Larry, and Sinda Gregory. "An Interview with Paul Auster." *Mississippi Review* 20:1–2 (1991): 49–62.

———. "An Interview with Paul Auster." *Contemporary Literature* 33:1 (Spring 1992): 1–12.

McPheron, William. "Remaking Narrative." *Poetics Journal* 7 (1987): 140–149. Essay on *The New York Trilogy* and fiction by Kathy Acker and Steve McCaffery.

Merwin, W. S. "*The Invention of Solitude*." *New York Times Book Review* (February 27, 1983): 10–11. Review.

Michel, Deborah. "Interview with Paul Auster." *Turnstile* 2:1 (1990): 85–95.

Motte, Jr., Warren F. *Questioning Edmond Jabès*. Lincoln: University of Nebraska Press, 1990. Citations of Auster's work on Jabès.

Olson, Toby. "Metaphysical Mystery Tour." *New York Times Book Review* (November 3, 1985): 31. Review of *City of Glass*.

Parrinder, Patrick. "Austward Ho." *London Review of Books* 11:10 (May 18, 1989): 12. Review of *Moon Palace*.

Powell, Padgett. "The End Is Only Imaginary." *New York Times Book Review* (May 17, 1987): 11–12. Review of *In the Country of Last Things*.

Powers, Katherine A. "Grand Attempt Succeeds in Truth Telling Before Official Version Appears." *Boston Globe* (September 13, 1992): 106. Review of *Leviathan*.

Ramalho de Sousa Santos, Maria Irene. "Plagiarism in Praise: Paul Auster and Herman Melville." *Dedalus: Revista Portuguesa de Literatura Comparada* 1 (December 1991): 105–114.

Rowen, Norma. "The Detective in Search of the Lost Tongue of Adam: Paul Auster's *City of Glass*." *Critique: Studies in Contemporary Fiction* 32:4 (Summer 1991): 224–235.

Russell, Alison. "Deconstructing *The New York Trilogy:* Paul Auster's Anti-Detective Fiction." *Critique: Studies in Contemporary Fiction* 31:2 (Winter 1990): 71–84.

Saltzman, Arthur. *Designs of Darkness*. Philadelphia: University of Pennsylvania Press, 1990. Includes commentary on *The New York Trilogy*.

———. *The Novel in the Balance*. Columbia, S.C.: University of South Carolina Press, 1993. Includes commentary on *The Music of Chance*.

Schiff, Stephen. "Inward Gaze of a Private Eye." *New York Times Book Review* 92 (January 4, 1987): 14. Review of *The Locked Room*.

Sorapure, Madeleine. *Assuming Authority: Self-Conscious Authorship in Contemporary*

Fiction. State University of New York at Binghamton, 1990. Dissertation. Examines authorship in Barth, Calvino, Auster, Didion, and Coetzee.

Sorrentino, Gilbert. "Language: Lying and Treacherous." *New York Times Book Review* (May 25, 1986): 23. Review of translation of Blanchot's *Vicious Circles.*

Thiébaux, Marcelle. "PW Interviews Paul Auster." *Publishers Weekly* 235:9 (March 3, 1989): 80–81.

Towers, Robert. "Fiction: *The Music of Chance.*" *New York Review of Books* 38:1–2 (January 17, 1991): 31–33. Review of *The Music of Chance.*

Walters, Michael. "Life's Punning Plots." *Times Literary Supplement* (February 17, 1989): 158. Review of *The Invention of Solitude.*

Weinstein, Norman. "*The Invention of Solitude.*" *Sulfur* 8, 3:2 (1983): 195–197. Review of *The Invention of Solitude.*

FOREIGN LANGUAGE EDITIONS

BRAZIL

A Trilogia de Nova York. Trans. Marcelo Dias Almada. Editora Best Seller, 1989.
No País das Últimas Coisas. Trans. Luiz Araújo. Editora Best Seller, 1990.
Palacio de Lua. Trans. Marcelo Dias Almada. Editora Best Seller, 1991.
A Música do Acaso. Trans. Marcelo Dias Almada. Editora Best Seller, 1992.
Leviatá. Trans. Thelma Médice Nóbrega. Editora Best Seller, 1993.

CATALAN

Trilogia de Nova York. Trans. Joan Sellent Arús. Edicions Proa, 1991.
La Música de L'Atzar. Trans. Jordi Civís I Pol. Edicions 62, 1992.

DENMARK

By af glas. Trans. Jan Bredsdorff. Per Kofod, 1987.
Genfærd. Trans. Jan Bredsdorff. Per Kofod, 1987.
Det Aflaste Vaerelse. Trans. Jan Bredsdorff. Per Kofod, 1989.
I det sidstes land. Trans. Jan Bredsdorff. Per Kofod, 1990. (Per Kofod, 1993.)
Tilfaeldets Musik. Trans. Jan Bredsdorff. Per Kofod, 1991. (Per Kofod, 1993.)
Moon Palace. Trans. Jan Bredsdorff. Per Kofod, 1992.
Auggie Wrens Julefortaelling. Trans. Jan Bredsdorff. Per Kofod, 1993.
Leviathan. Trans. Jan Bredsdorff. Per Kofod, 1993.
New York-Trilogien. Trans. Jan Bredsdorff. Per Kofod, 1993.
Opfindelsen Af Ensomhed. Trans. Jan Bredsdorff. Per Kofod, 1993.

FINLAND

Lasikaupunki. Trans. Jukka Jääskeläinen. Tammi, 1988.
Aaveita. Trans. Jukka Jääskeläinen. Tammi, 1988.
Lukittu huone. Trans. Jukka Jääskeläinen. Tammi, 1989.
Kuun maisemissa. Trans. Jukka Jääskeläinen and Jukka Sirola. Tammi, 1990.
Sattuman Soittoa. Trans. Erkki Jukarainen. Tammi, 1992.

FRANCE

Espaces blancs. Trans. Françoise de Laroque. Editions Unes, 1985.
Cité de verre. Trans. Pierre Furlan. Actes Sud, 1987. (Livre de Poche, 1994.)
Effigies. Trans. Emmanuel Hocquard. Editions Unes, 1987.
Murales. Trans. Daniele Robert. Editions Unes, 1987.
La Chambre dérobée. Trans. Pierre Furlan. Actes Sud, 1988. (Livre de Poche, 1994.)
Dans la Tourmente. Trans. Danièle Robert. Editions Unes, 1988.
Fragments du Froid. Trans. Danièle Robert. Editions Unes, 1988.
L'Invention de la Solitude. Trans. Christine Le Bœuf. Actes Sud, 1988. (Babel, 1992;
    Livre de Poche, 1994.)
Revenants. Trans. Pierre Furlan. Actes Sud, 1988. (Livre de Poche, 1994.)
Le Voyage d'Anna Blume. Trans. Patrick Ferragut. Actes Sud, 1989. (Babel, 1993.)
Moon Palace. Trans. Christine Le Bœuf. Actes Sud, 1990. (Babel, 1993.)
Trilogie New Yorkaise. Trans. Pierre Furlan. Babel, 1991.
La Musique du Hasard. Trans. Christine Le Bœuf. Actes Sud, 1991. (Editions Corps
    16, 1992; Babel, 1993.)
Le Conte de Noël d'Auggie Wren. Trans. Christine Le Bœuf. Actes Sud, 1991.
L'Art de la Faim. Trans. Christine Le Bœuf. Actes Sud, 1992.
Fausse Balle. Trans. Lili Sztajn. Gallimard, 1992.
Le Carnet rouge. Christine Le Bœuf. Actes Sud, 1993.
Leviathan. Trans. Christine Le Bœuf. Actes Sud, 1993.
Disparitions. Trans. Danièle Robert. Editions Unes, 1994.
Mr. Vertigo. Trans. Christine Le Bœuf. Actes Sud, 1994.

GERMANY

Stadt aus Glas. Trans. Joachim A. Frank. Hoffmann und Campe, 1987.
Die New York-Trilogie. Trans. Joachim A. Frank. Rowohlt, 1989.
Im Land der Letzten Dinge. Trans. Werner Schmitz. Rowohlt, 1989. (Rowohlt,
    1989.)
Mond über Manhattan. Trans. Werner Schmitz. Rowohlt, 1990. (Rowohlt, 1992.)
Auggie Wrens Weihnachtsgeschichte. Trans. Werner Schmitz. (Rowohlt, 1991.)
Die Musik des Zufalls. Trans. Werner Schmitz. Rowohlt, 1992.
Die Erfindung der Einsamkeit. Trans. Werner Schmitz. Rowohlt, 1993.

GREECE

City of Glass. Editors Zacharopoulos, 1991.
Ghosts. Editors Zacharopoulos, 1991.
The Locked Room. Editors Zacharopoulos, 1991.
In the Country of Last Things. Editors Zacharopoulos, 1991.
Moon Palace. Editors Zacharopoulos, 1992.

HUNGARY

New York trilógia. Trans. László Vághy. Európa, 1991.
Holdpalota. Trans. László Vághy. Európa, 1991.

ISRAEL

The New York Trilogy. Trans. Moshe Singer. Keter, 1990.
The Music of Chance. Trans. Moshe Ron. Am Oved, 1992.
Leviathan. Trans. Moshe Ron. Am Oved, 1992.

ITALY

La Trilogia di New York. Trans. Giuseppe Settanni. Rizzoli, 1987.
Il Palazzo della Luna. Trans. Mario Biondi. Rizzoli, 1990.
La Musica del Caso. Trans. Massimo Birattari. Guanda, 1991.
L'Invenzione della Solitudine. Trans. Massimo Bocchiola. Anabasi, 1993.

JAPAN

City of Glass. Trans. Yumiko Yamamoto and Hiroshi Gouhara. Kadokawa Shoten, 1989. Kadokawa Shoten, 1993.
Ghosts. Trans. Motoyuki Shibata. Shincho Sha, 1989.
The Locked Room. Trans. Motoyuki Shibata. Hakusui Sha, 1990. (Hakusui Sha, 1993.)
The Invention of Solitude. Trans. Motoyuki Shibata. Shinchosha, 1991.
Disappearances. Trans. Tomoyuki Iino. Shinchosha, 1992.
Moon Palace. Trans. Motoyuki Shibata. Shinchosha, 1994.

THE NETHERLANDS

Het spinsel van de eenzaamheid. Trans. Annelies Eulen. Arbeiderspers, 1988.
Broze stad. Trans. Bartho Kriek. Arbeiderspers, 1988.
Schimmen. Trans. Bartho Kriek. Arbeiderspers, 1988.
De gesloten kamer. Trans. Bartho Kriek. Arbeiderspers, 1989.
In het land der laatste dingen. Trans. Annelies Eulen. Arbeiderspers, 1990.
Maanpaleis. Trans. Annelies Eulen. Arbeiderspers, 1990.
De Muziek van het Toeval. Trans. Annelies Eulen. Arbeiderspers, 1991.
Leviathan. Trans. Ton Heuuelmans. Arbeiderspers, 1993.

NORWAY

New York Trilogien. Trans. Asgjerd Taksdal. Norsk Samlaget, 1988.
Moon Palace. Trans. Knut Ofstad. Aschehoug, 1991.
Sjansespill. Trans. Knut Ofstad. Aschehoug, 1992.
Leviathan. Trans. Knut Ofstad. Aschehoug, 1993.

PORTUGAL

No País das Últimas Coisas. Trans. Ana Patrão. Editorial Presença, 1990.
Palácio da Lua. Trans. Rui Wahnon. Editorial Presença, 1990.

A Trilogia de Nova Iorque. Trans. Luzia Maria Martins. Difusão Cultural, 1990.
A Música do Acaso. Trans. Ana Patrão. Editorial Presença, 1992.
Leviathan. Trans. Ana Patrão. Editorial Presença, 1993.

SPAIN

La Ciudad de Cristal. Trans. Ramón de España. Jucar, 1988.
Fantasmas. Trans. Jorge de Lorbar. Jucar, 1988.
La Habitacion Cerrada. Trans. Jorge de Lorbar. Jucar, 1989.
El País de las Últimas Cosas. Trans. Maria Eugenia Ciocchini. Edhasa, 1989. (Editorial Anagrama, 1994.)
El Palacio de la Luna. Trans. Maribel de Juan. Editorial Anagrama, 1990. (Círculo de Lectores, 1991.)
La Invención de la Soledad. Trans. Maria Eugenia Ciocchini. Edhasa, 1990. (Editorial Anagrama, 1994.)
La Música del Azar. Trans. Maribel De Juan. Editorial Anagrama, 1991.
El Art del Hambre: Ensayos. Trans. María Eugenia Ciocchini. Edhasa, 1992.
El Cauderno Rojo. Trans. Justo Navarro. Editorial Anagrama, 1994.

SWEDEN

Stad av glas. Trans. Ulla Roseen. Hammarström & Åberg, 1988.
Vålnader. Trans. Ulla Roseen. Hammarström & Åberg, 1989.
Det låsta rummet. Trans. Ulla Roseen. Hammarström & Åberg, 1989.
Månpalatset. Trans. Love Kellberg. Hammarström & Åberg, 1990. (Tidens Förlag, 1992.)
New York-trilogin. Trans. Ulla Roseen. Hammarström & Åberg, 1991. (Tiden Förlag, 1992.)
Slumpens Musik. Trans. Love Kellberg. Hammarström & Åberg / Tiden, 1991.
Att Uppfinna Ensamheten. Trans. Aris Fioretos. Tidens Förlag, 1992. (Tidens Förlag, 1993.)
Auggie Wrens Julberättelse. Trans. Ulla Roseen. Tiden Förlag, 1993.
I De Sista Tingens. Trans. Ulla Roseen. Tiden Förlag, 1993.
Den Röda Anteckningsboken. Trans. Aris Fioretos. Umbra Solis, 1993.

TURKEY

Ay Sarayi. Trans. Seçkin Selui. Can Yayinlari, 1991.
Yalnizligin Kesfi. Trans. Ilknur Özdemir. Can Yayinlari, 1991.
Son Seyler Ulkesinde. Trans. Seçkin Selui. Can Yayinlari, 1991.
Kam Kent. Trans. Yusuf Eradam. Metis Edebiyat Dizisi, 1991.
Hayaletler. Trans. Fatih Özgüven. Metis Edebiyat Dizisi, 1991.
Kilitli Oda. Trans. Yusuf Eradam. Metis Edebiyat Dizisi, 1991.
Kirmizi Defter. Trans. Münir H. Göle. Can Yayinlari, 1993.
Sana Müzi'gi. Trans. Seçkin Selui. Can Yayinlari, 1993.

OTHER LANGUAGES

Translations into Bulgarian, Icelandic, Polish, and Romanian.

Contributors

DENNIS BARONE is Professor of American Studies and English at Saint Joseph College (Connecticut). He is the author of many articles on early American and contemporary American literature. A fiction writer and poet, his most recent works are *The Returns* (Sun & Moon Press, 1995) and *Waves of Ice, Waves of Rumor* (Zasterle Press, 1993). He is co-editor of *The Art of Practice: Forty-Five Contemporary Poets* (Potes & Poets Press, 1994).

STEPHEN BERNSTEIN is an Assistant Professor of English at the University of Michigan–Flint. He has published essays on Charles Dickens, Wilkie Collins, Samuel Beckett, and gothic fiction. He is currently at work on a book about gothicism and intertextuality, and is co-editing a collection of essays on Don DeLillo.

PASCAL BRUCKNER, an essayist and novelist, lives in Paris. His novel *Lunes de fiel* (*Evil Angles*) was published in translation by Grove Press in 1987, and his book on "third worldism," *Le sanglot de l'homme blanc,* was published in English as *The Tears of the White Man: Compassion as Contempt* (The Free Press, 1986).

MARC CHÉNETIER is Professor of American Literature at the Ecole Normale Superieure (Fontenay/Saint Cloud) in Paris and author of numerous books and articles on contemporary American fiction. His book on fiction since 1960, *Beyond Suspicion,* is forthcoming from the University of Pennsylvania Press.

WILLIAM DRENTTEL is president of the design firm Drenttel Doyle Partners in New York City. He also publishes fine press literary editions and is on the board of the Poetry Society of America.

NORMAN FINKELSTEIN is the author of a book of poems, *Restless Messengers* (University of Georgia Press, 1992), and two books of criticism, *The Utopian Moment in Contemporary American Poetry* (Bucknell University Press, revised edition, 1993), and *The Ritual of New Creation: Jewish Tradition and Contemporary Literature* (SUNY Press, 1992). He is a Professor of English at Xavier University.

KAREN PALMUNEN holds a Ph.D. from Brown University and teaches French language, literature, and civilization at Saint Joseph College (Connecticut). Her areas of interest include the teaching of culture and the adult language-learner.

DEREK RUBIN teaches American literature at the Vrije Universiteit in Amsterdam and at the Universiteit van Amsterdam. He has published articles on Saul Bellow and Philip Roth and is at work on a study of marginality in Bellow's early fiction.

ARTHUR SALTZMAN is Professor of English at Missouri Southern State College, where he was named Outstanding Teacher in 1992. His books include *The Fiction of William Gass: The Consolation of Language* (Southern Illinois University Press, 1986), *Understanding Raymond Carver* (University of South Carolina Press, 1988), *Designs of Darkness in Contemporary American Fiction* (University of Pennsylvania Press, 1990), and *The Novel in the Balance* (University of South Carolina Press, 1993).

MOTOYUKI SHIBATA teaches at the University of Tokyo, College of Arts and Sciences. He has translated many works of contemporary American fiction into Japanese, including Paul Auster's *Ghosts,* Steven Millhauser's *In the Penny Arcade,* Steve Erickson's *Tours of the Black Clock,* and Stuart Dybek's *The Coast of Chicago.*

MADELEINE SORAPURE teaches in the Writing Program at the University of California at Santa Barbara. She has published essays on contemporary fiction in *Modern Fiction Studies* and *Studies in Short Fiction.* She is currently working on a study of friendship in contemporary feminist fiction.

STEVEN WEISENBURGER is an Associate Professor of English at the University of Kentucky and author of *The* Gravity's Rainbow *Companion* (University of Georgia Press, 1988) and *Fables of Subversion: Satire and the American Novel, 1930–1980* (University of Georgia Press, 1994), as well as numerous articles on contemporary American fiction and narrative theory.

ERIC WIRTH, a poet and essayist, lives in New York City. His writing has appeared in *O.ARS, Aerial,* and other literary journals.

TIM WOODS teaches at the University of Wales, Aberystwyth. He wrote his dissertation on the politics and poetics of Louis Zukofsky, Charles Olson, and the "Language" Poets, specifically in relation to the theories of Theodor Adorno and the ethical phenomenology of Emmanuel Levinas.

Index

Grateful acknowledgment is made for permission to reprint material from the following sources:

Paul Auster. Personal correspondence: letter to Dennis Barone, 19 January 1994; letter to Norman Finkelstein, 15 October 1988. By permission of Paul Auster.

Paul Auster. *Disappearances: Selected Poems.* Copyright © 1987 by Paul Auster; first published 1988 by The Overlook Press. By permission of the Carol Mann Agency and The Overlook Press.

Paul Auster. *In the Country of Last Things.* Copyright © 1987 by Paul Auster. By permission of the Carol Mann Agency and Viking Penguin, a division of Penguin Books USA.

Paul Auster. *The Invention of Solitude.* Copyright © 1982 by Paul Auster. By permission of the Carol Mann Agency.

Paul Auster. *Leviathan* (copyright © 1992 by Paul Auster), *Moon Palace* (copyright © 1989 by Paul Auster), *The Music of Chance* (copyright © 1990 by Paul Auster). By permission of Viking Penguin, a division of Penguin Books USA.

Paul Auster. *The Art of Hunger* (Los Angeles: Sun & Moon Press, 1992; copyright © 1992 by Paul Auster), *City of Glass* (Los Angeles: Sun & Moon Press, 1985; copyright © 1985 by Paul Auster), *Ghosts* (Los Angeles: Sun & Moon Press; copyright © 1986 by Paul Auster), *The Locked Room* (Los Angeles: Sun & Moon Press, 1986; copyright © 1986 by Paul Auster). By permission of Sun & Moon Press.

Pascal Bruckner. "Paul Auster, or The Heir Intestate." Originally published as the afterword to *L'Invention de la Solitude,* pp. 283–294. Copyright © 1992 by Actes Sud. By permission of Actes Sud.

Marc Chénetier. "Paul Auster's Pseudonymous World." Originally published as the afterword to *Trilogie New Yorkaise,* pp. 431–445. Copyright © 1991 by Actes Sud. By permission of Actes Sud.

Norman Finkelstein. "In the Realm of the Naked Eye: The Poetry of Paul Auster." Originally published in *American Poetry* vol. 8 (1990): 175–188. Copyright © 1990 by American Poetry. By permission of American Poetry.

George Oppen. "Of Being Numerous." From *Collected Poems* by George Oppen. Copyright © 1968 by George Oppen. By permission of New Directions Publishing Corporation.

Wallace Stevens. "The Comedian as the Letter C" (copyright © 1923; renewed 1951 by Wallace Stevens) and "Of Modern Poetry" (copyright © 1942 by Wallace Stevens; renewed 1970 by Holly Stevens). From *Collected Poems* by Wallace Stevens. By permission of Alfred A. Knopf, Inc.

Steven Weisenburger. "Inside *Moon Palace.*" Originally published in *Review of Contemporary Fiction* vol. 14, no. 1 (1994): 70–79. Copyright © 1994 by The Review of Contemporary Fiction. By permission of The Review of Contemporary Fiction.

Penn Studies in Contemporary American Fiction
A Series Edited by Emory Elliott, University of California at Riverside

This book was set in Baskerville and Eras typefaces. Baskerville was designed by John Baskerville at his private press in Birmingham, England, in the eighteenth century. The first typeface to depart from oldstyle typeface design, Baskerville has more variation between thick and thin strokes. In an effort to insure that the thick and thin strokes of his typeface reproduced well on paper, John Baskerville developed the first wove paper, the surface of which was much smoother than the laid paper of the time. The development of wove paper was partly responsible for the introduction of typefaces classified as modern, which have even more contrast between thick and thin strokes.

Eras was designed in 1969 by Studio Hollenstein in Paris for the Wagner Typefoundry. A contemporary script-like version of a sans-serif typeface, the letters of Eras have a monotone stroke and are slightly inclined.

Printed on acid-free paper.